BINGE DRINKING RESEARCH PROGRESS

BINGE DRINKING RESEARCH PROGRESS

KEVIN I. DIGUARDE
EDITOR

Nova Science Publishers, Inc.
New York

NOTICE TO THE READER

The Publisher has taken reasonable care in the preparation of this book, but makes no expressed or implied warranty of any kind and assumes no responsibility for any errors or omissions. No liability is assumed for incidental or consequential damages in connection with or arising out of information contained in this book. The Publisher shall not be liable for any special, consequential, or exemplary damages resulting, in whole or in part, from the readers' use of, or reliance upon, this material. Any parts of this book based on government reports are so indicated and copyright is claimed for those parts to the extent applicable to compilations of such works.

Independent verification should be sought for any data, advice or recommendations contained in this book. In addition, no responsibility is assumed by the publisher for any injury and/or damage to persons or property arising from any methods, products, instructions, ideas or otherwise contained in this publication.

This publication is designed to provide accurate and authoritative information with regard to the subject matter covered herein. It is sold with the clear understanding that the Publisher is not engaged in rendering legal or any other professional services. If legal or any other expert assistance is required, the services of a competent person should be sought. FROM A DECLARATION OF PARTICIPANTS JOINTLY ADOPTED BY A COMMITTEE OF THE AMERICAN BAR ASSOCIATION AND A COMMITTEE OF PUBLISHERS.

LIBRARY OF CONGRESS CATALOGING-IN-PUBLICATION DATA

Binge drinking research progress / Kevin I. DiGuarde (editor).
    p. cm.
 ISBN 978-1-60692-065-7 (hardcover)
 1. Binge drinking. I. DiGuarde, Kevin I.
 HV5035.B56 2008
 362.292'20941--dc22
                          2008032527

Published by Nova Science Publishers, Inc. ✛ New York

CONTENTS

PREFACE

Binge drinking is now usually used to refer to heavy drinking over an evening or similar time span - sometimes also referred to as heavy episodic drinking. Binge drinking is often associated with drinking with the intention of becoming intoxicated and, sometimes, with drinking in large groups. It is sometimes associated with physical or social harm.

Chapter 1 - As with elsewhere in the world, the United Kingdom has witnessed an increase in public and academic interest in heavy episodic alcohol consumption - or 'binge drinking' as it is often referred. In the British context, binge drinking is frequently cited as a target for intervention in government policy documents, such as the Alcohol Harm Reduction Strategy for England, and the Plan for Action on Alcohol Problems. Part of the reason for this concern stems from the apparent rise in alcohol consumption and alcohol related deaths. Indeed, per capita alcohol consumption in the UK has risen steadily since the 1940s. Furthermore, Scotland's liver cirrhosis mortality rate doubled between 1987 and 2001, while the rate in England rose by two thirds.

At the same time, however, it is important to note that discussing this style of alcohol consumption is not quite so straightforward. One of the main reasons for this is that there is growing controversy as to what the term 'binge drinking' should actually be used to refer to. As highlighted by Gmel et al., 2003, there are in fact two different versions of the meaning of the phrase 'binge drinking' currently in use. The first is the traditional, clinically based definition, which refers to patterns of planned, sustained heavy drinking involving an aspect of alcohol dependence. In this instance, drinking is typically portrayed as occurring over several days or weeks, matching the term of a 'bender' as referred to by Jellinek 1952. It is this pattern of drinking which, until recently, 'binge drinking' was predominately associated with, and featured in the WHO Lexicon of Alcohol and Drug Terms. On the other hand, the second version of the phrase 'binge drinking' refers to excessive drinking in a shorter time period (i.e. in one night) and does not require the individual to have a dependence on alcohol. It is claimed that this latter conceptualization was introduced by the Harvard School of Public Health in the early 1990s, in order to describe the heavy episodic drinking style of college students (Perkins et al. 2001; Goodhart et al. 2003). As Gmel et al. 2003 note, when used in this respect the term 'binge drinking' has often been used as a byword for drinking to intoxication in a heavy episodic style At the moment, this more recent conceptualization of 'binge drinking' has largely replaced its previous meaning, although both versions do remain in circulation amongst professionals at least. However, there is little known about the extent to which these professional viewpoints concerning 'binge drinking' are shared by the wider public. It is this gap in knowledge that the current research project aims to address. Before reporting the results of this study, it is important to provide an account of what is already known in relation to both the professional and public conceptualisations of binge drinking.

Chapter 2 - Alcohol use disorders, with their numerous adverse health and economic effects, are a worldwide public health concern. Problem drinking is associated with both increased mortality rates and premature mortality. Estimates indicate that 9-22 years of potential life are lost for an individual death from alcoholic liver disease, compared to two years for cancer and four years for heart disease. Fetal alcohol effects occur in one in 1,000 live births. The economic costs of alcohol abuse in the U.S. alone are estimated to have been $184.6 billion in 1998.

Poland has one of the highest rates of per-capita alcohol consumption in the world, estimated at 8 ltr/100 persons in 1999. In Poland's population of almost 40 million, nearly 800,000 persons are dependent on alcohol and an additional 1-1.2 million abuse alcohol. In 1998, alcohol abuse resulted in economic losses of PLN 25 billion, compared to PLN 6.5 billion in revenue generated by alcohol sales. The testing and implementation of effective alcohol abuse prevention strategies has become an important national priority.

Researchers in other countries have been testing the use of brief intervention techniques in clinical settings to reduce alcohol use and alcohol-related harm. These clinically-based interventions include assessment and direct feedback, contracting and goal setting, behavioral modification techniques, and the use of written materials such as self-help manuals. Meta analyses performed by Bien, Kahan, and Wilk, found that most brief intervention trials showed a positive effect on reducing consumption levels and suggest that clinicians can expect 10-30% of their patients to change their drinking behaviors as a result of brief intervention.

This report presents the results of the first clinical trial conducted in Polish community-based primary care practices to test the efficacy of brief physician advice for reducing alcohol use by problem drinkers. The research procedures are similar to those utilized in previous trials.

Chapter 3 - Even though the majority of students drink alcohol, and many drink excessively [Wechsler, Davenport, Dowdall, Moeykins, & Castillo, 1994], little research has focused on the romantic context of college drinking and binge drinking. Heavy drinking (including binge drinking) is associated with many individual (e.g., legal) problems, but it could also be associated with romantic problems. Relationship quality might not simply be affected by individual drinking, but rather by the compatibility of partners' drinking habits. The present study examined congruent/discrepant patterns (as perceived by one partner) in unmarried romantic couples. Respondents (50 female, 42 male undergraduates) completed daily diary records on self and partners' drinking behaviors for 10 days. In addition, respondents completed a questionnaire to assess relationship satisfaction, commitment, alcohol-related problems, and alcohol abuse. Three methods were used to examine discrepancy and congruence in drinking: (1) a cluster analysis of drinking frequency and quantity, (2) absolute difference scores on frequency and quantity, and (3) absolute difference scores on number of binge drinking episodes. Consistent with Roberts and Leonard [1998], this chapter identified five different drinking clusters. Greater differences in binge drinking episodes were related to lower relationship quality (e.g., less commitment). In addition, greater differences in binge drinking were associated with more alcohol-related problems.

Given the severity of potential drinking consequences for both individuals and relationships, differences in partner drinking patterns merit more empirical attention.

Chapter 4 – Alcohol use is associated with the leading causes of death and injury in adolescents (i.e. motor vehicle accidents, homicides and suicides). The purpose of the current study is to examine gender and ethnic differences in the risk and protective factors for binge drinking among Hispanic Florida youth utilizing the Florida Youth Substance Abuse Survey 2002. We used a subset of 10,690 Hispanic youth from the original sample of 62,934 students surveyed. Risk and protective factors were first examined in each of five domains, then altogether using logistic regression. Sixteen percent of these students admitted to having binged on one or more occasions in the two weeks prior to the survey and the frequency increased with grade level. Males were more likely to have binged (17% vs. 15%, p<.000). Mexican students were the most likely, Dominicans and Puerto Ricans were the least likely, while Central American and Cubans were intermediate in their frequency of binge drinking. Risk and protective factor analyses suggest that Hispanic youth who grow up in families with poor discipline and have parents with a favorable attitude towards ATOD use are likely to form favorable attitudes towards ATOD use themselves. Males who are sensation seekers and those with low resistance skills are at greater risk of initiating drug use early on, associating with and/or being influenced by friends who use drugs and being binge drinkers. The presence of risk factors in multiple domains endorses the need for a multi-pronged approach to prevention and intervention. Tailoring programs and activities to address risk and protective factors in sub-groups may be an important consideration when participants are homogenous in terms of gender and/or ethnicities.

Chapter 5 - Alcohol use often co-occurs with one or more other behavioral health risk factors that can place women and their offspring at heightened risk for morbidity and mortality. Women with co-occurring alcohol use and behavioral health risk factors, such as tobacco use, illicit drug use, and mental illness are especially vulnerable. These women are not only at increased risk for hazardous reproductive outcomes, but also physical and psychological illness, disability and premature death, interpersonal conflicts, violence and legal problems, unemployment, and poverty. Despite evidence that co-occurring multiple behavioral health risk factors are prevalent and often associated with more severe adverse health outcomes and higher social economic costs, a majority of health promotion and intervention programs are designed to target only one risk factor of concern. Given that many of these behavioral health risk factors are interrelated and amenable to interventions, and that many patients frequently present for treatment with two or more behavioral risk factors in various health care settings, establishing paradigms of assessment and intervention for multiple behavioral health risk factors could be more successful in preventing initiation of high-risk behavior, improving targeted health conditions, decreasing the likelihood of co-morbidity, enhancing treatment adherence, preventing relapse, and subsequently maintaining long-term behavioral changes. Prevention of alcohol-related morbidity and mortality among women of childbearing age needs to incorporate the success of evidence-based strategies that address interrelated risk factors across more than one domain.

Chapter 6 - The association between prenatal alcohol exposure and its teratogenic effect on the developing fetus was first observed in Nantes, France by paediatrician Paul Lemoine in 1968. He described similar dysmorphic facial features and growth delays in 127 infants of mothers who had drank alcohol during their pregnancies. The clear central nervous system sequelae and associated physical manifestations from prenatal alcohol were elaborated upon and named the Fetal Alcohol Syndrome in two classic papers from Seattle by David Smith, Ken Jones, Christy Ulleland and Ann Streissguth in 1973.The Seattle group described eight unrelated infants from three different ethnic groups all born to mothers who were chronic alcoholics. Thus, it was established that prenatal alcohol exposure caused facial dysmorphology, growth delays and central nervous system abnormalities The current diagnostic criteria for Fetal Alcohol Syndrome still incorporates this triad of clinical effects, namely, dysmorphic facial features, growth retardation and central nervous system abnormalities.

Chapter 7 - The term binge drinking is in common usage. Having gained some degree of international credibility, it is employed frequently in reports emerging from research and national agencies, but also within the media and popular press. Implicitly it is linked with the negative consequences of the excesses of alcohol consumption, particularly within the younger members of the population.

This chapter will consider the evolution of the term in the recent past, how it is interpreted and will discuss its value as society in general seeks to curb the excesses of alcohol consumption and address the short and longer term harm that ensues.

Chapter 8 - The study involving four case studies is a clinical exploration of the styles (among chemical dependent clients) of significant others using personal construct methodology. In this sense attempts were made to analyse the pattern of social networks which may characterise male and female alcohol or drug addicts, and identify the underlying personal characteristics they use in their description of family and non-family members. For this purpose, a series of multivariate techniques were implemented, including cluster analyses and linear discriminant analyses, as well as principal component analyses. The implication of the findings are discussed within the framework of providing an insight into the value of social relationships and social skill training among adolescents as a prophylactic method towards drug prevention.

Chapter 9 - Ethyl alcohol is a simple chemical substance produced by yeast as it ferments a readily available naturally occurring sugar compound. It is a psychoactive drug widely consumed and promoted for recreational or relaxational purposes. Like other such agents it is often abused, some individuals being prone to develop a dependency or addiction after chronic drinking. With long term use alcoholics may suffer serious complications, such as liver disease or brain disorders. The hereditary nature of alcoholism tendency has been fully established through investigations of twins and foster reared individuals. Pedigree studies as well as precise determinations of comparative risks in close relatives of alcoholic patients have been found to be consistent with a dominant form of inheritance, showing incomplete penetrance that is lower in females than in males. Personality information on families of alcoholics reveals attitudes of self assurance, verbal fluency, and preference for certain types of occupations. They appear to seek fields requiring socialization and communication skills. Leadership tendencies and desire for power are predominant. Performance is sought in the political arena or entertainment industries as well as in business. High activity level and motivation for prominence are characteristic of families prone to alcohol use. The high frequency of the alcoholism gene is presumably maintained by these favorable traits.

In: Binge Drinking Research Progress
Editor: Kevin I. DiGuarde

ISBN 978-1-60692-065
© 2009 Nova Science Publishers, Inc.

Chapter 1

PUBLIC AND PROFESSIONAL CONCEPTUALISATIONS OF BINGE DRINKING: ARE WE ALL TALKING THE SAME LANGUAGE?

John McMahon[1], John McAlaney[2] and Fiona Edgar[3]

1) School of Social Sciences
University of the West of Scotland
High Street, Paisley PA1 2BE
2) Public and Environmental Health Research Unit
London of School of Hygiene and Tropical Medicine
Keppel Street, London WC1E 7HT
3) School of Social Sciences
University of the West of Scotland
High Street, Paisley PA1 2BE

BACKGROUND

As with elsewhere in the world, the United Kingdom has witnessed an increase in public and academic interest in heavy episodic alcohol consumption - or 'binge drinking' as it is often referred to (Kuntsche et al. 2004). In the British context, binge drinking is frequently cited as a target for intervention in government policy documents, such as the Alcohol Harm Reduction Strategy for England (Cabinet Office 2004) and the Plan for Action on Alcohol Problems (Scottish Executive 2002). Part of the reason for this concern stems from the apparent rise in alcohol consumption and alcohol related deaths. Indeed, per capita alcohol consumption in the UK has risen steadily since the 1940s (Plant and Plant 2006). Furthermore, Scotland's liver cirrhosis mortality rate doubled between 1987 and 2001, while the rate in England rose by two thirds (Leon and McCambridge 2006).

At the same time, however, it is important to note that discussing this style of alcohol consumption is not quite so straightforward. One of the main reasons for this is that there is growing controversy as to what the term 'binge drinking' should actually be used to refer to. As highlighted by Gmel et al. 2003, there are in fact two different versions of the meaning of the phrase 'binge drinking' currently in use. The first is the traditional, clinically based definition, which refers to patterns of planned, sustained heavy drinking involving an aspect of alcohol dependence. In this instance, drinking is typically portrayed as occurring over several days or weeks, matching the term of a 'bender' as referred to by Jellinek 1952. It is this pattern of drinking which, until recently, 'binge drinking' was predominately associated with, and featured in the WHO Lexicon of Alcohol and Drug Terms (World Health Organisation 1994). On the other hand, the second version of the phrase 'binge drinking' refers to excessive drinking in a shorter time period (i.e. in one night) and does not require the individual to have a dependence on alcohol. It is claimed that this latter conceptualization was introduced by the Harvard School of Public Health in the early 1990s, in order to describe the heavy episodic drinking style of college students (Perkins et al. 2001; Goodhart et al. 2003). As Gmel et al. 2003 note, when used in this respect the term 'binge drinking' has often been used as a byword for drinking to intoxication in a heavy episodic style (e.g. International Center for Alcohol Policies 1997; Perkins et al. 2001). At the moment, this more recent conceptualization of 'binge drinking' has largely replaced its previous meaning, although both versions do remain in circulation amongst professionals at least. However, there is little known about the extent to which these professional viewpoints concerning 'binge drinking' are shared by the wider public. It is this gap in knowledge that the current research project aims to address. Before reporting the results of this study, it is important to provide an account of what is already known in relation to both the professional and public conceptualisations of binge drinking.

PROFESSIONAL CONCEPTUALISATIONS OF BINGE DRINKING

Professional Conceptualisations in the USA

In past research the criteria by which alcohol use is categorized as binge drinking has been primarily based on volume and frequency of consumption, with the emphasis on the former. The point of contention, however, is where the cut off points for volume and frequency should be placed. A popular criteria used, particularly in the USA, is what is often referred to as the 5 drinks definition (Midanik 1999; Gmel et al. 2003). Specifically this refers to binge drinking as the act of consuming 5 or more alcoholic drinks in one session. As Midanik 1999 comments the origin of this criteria is unclear, although a 5+ drinks item was first used in a national survey in America in 1969 (Calahan et al. 1969) and was increasingly included as a survey item in the 1970s and 80s. A variation on this approach is the gender specific 5/4 drinks definition, which sets a level of 5 and 4 alcoholic drinks in a session for men and women respectively. This was created in response to research that women require less alcohol in a session to experience the same level of alcohol related problems as men, even when body weight is accounted for (Clark and Midanik 1982). The 5/4 drinks measure has been adopted by governmental bodies, such as the Center for Disease Control and the Substance Abuse and Mental Health Administration (Gfroerer et al. 1996) in the USA. Alternative measures based upon the idea of a certain number of drinks in one session have been suggested, such as the 6 drinks measure cited by Dooley and Prause (1997). Nevertheless, as Gmel et al. (2003) note in their review of binge drinking definitions, the 5/4 measure has become the predominant criteria utilized in American research. This definition appears to have now even been adopted by American college students themselves, who have been found to regard binge drinking in terms of 5 or 6 drinks in one drinking session (Wechsler 2000). However this definition has not been universally adopted worldwide, with marked variance in the binge drinking cut off limits both within and between different countries. Canadian studies have, for example, used the 5+ definition on one occasion (Poulin and Graham 2001), as well as others which include 8+ in a day (Nadeau et al. 1998) or even 10 or more on one occasion (Bondy and Rehm 1998). In Australia a 8+/ 6+ gender specific criteria for men and women has been used (White et al. 1997), as has a 5+/ 3+ measure (Datalounge 1999).

Professional Conceptualisations in the UK

In the UK an altogether different approach has often been taken, particularly in government based research. Rather than using a criteria based on the number of drinks, the overall units of alcohol consumed is measured instead. As such, when an adult man drinks more than 8 alcohol units, or a woman drinks more than 6 alcohol units, they are deemed to be binge drinking. This definition has been applied to many key UK government funded research surveys including the annual General Household Surveys and the Office of National Statistics Omnibus Survey. If this 8/6 unit criteria is applied to data from such studies as the Health Survey for England 2003, (Sproston and Primatesta 2004) then approximately one third of men and one fifth of women in the UK binge drink at least once a week. It should be noted though, as has been discussed elsewhere, that this 8/ 6 unit definition has been applied inconsistently in government publications, which serves to undermine the validity of such figures (McAlaney and McMahon 2006). In addition, whilst this unit based approach provides greater clarity for researchers, it could be argued it does so at the expense of public understanding. To be able to keep track of their own alcohol intake, members of the public would need to know and understand how many units of alcohol each drink and each measure contains. Given that the level of alcohol content differs from one beverage to another, this is far from simple; the study reported here investigates this issue further. As with the number of drinks approach to measuring 'binge drinking', the unit based definition suffer the same main critique: neither has the capacity to take individual factors in to account (such as body weight and age) and, as a result, they cannot reliably predict the level of intoxication.

In addition it is worth noting the discrepancies between the 5/4 drinks and 8/6 units guidelines. A man consuming five pints of Stella Artois – that is 5 drinks – is actually consuming 15 units of alcohol which is nearly twice the recommendation of the 8/6 unit guidelines. Similarly a man drinking four pints of Stella Artois would consume 12 units of alcohol, and as such would be classed as a binge drinker in the UK, but not in the USA. Furthermore, although for research purposes the UK government regards binge drinking in terms of the 8/6 unit definition, it also recommends a maximum daily intake of 3 units for men and 2 units for women. The 3/2 unit average guidelines do not prohibit individuals exceeding these limits on occasion. Thus, a man may infrequently drink 6 units of alcohol (3 pints of Heineken) whilst staying within the overall average recommended consumption and without meeting the 8 unit criteria for binge drinking. Often in the media, however, binge drinking is presented as being functionally the same as exceeding daily drinking guidelines, which by current UK standards it is not. This may be a reflection of the fact that the 3/2 unit daily average drinking guidelines have been widely publicized, whereas the 8/6 unit criteria for binge drinking has not.

Binge Drinking and Blood Alcohol Levels

Overall there is also surprisingly little research confirming the relationship between an individual's binge drinking as defined by the 5/4 drinks criteria and the subsequent blood alcohol count (Lange and Voas 2001). This concept of the blood alcohol count in defining binge drinking is implicitly related to the invention of the 5/ 4 measure. As Midanik (1999) states if the 5+ measure is a valid one then it should be associated with a high blood alcohol count. Lange & Voas explored this assumption using the Widmark (1981) formula for estimating blood alcohol levels. They noted that a 68kg male could indeed reach a relatively high BAC of 0.095 after consuming 5 standard American beers on an empty stomach, but only if these drinks were all consumed within one hour. When it was hypothetically assumed that these 5 drinks were consumed over the course of three hours, it was noted that the individual's BAC would be unlikely to exceed 0.05 – a level at which an individual would legally be able to drive in the UK.

To further test these assumptions Lange & Voas surveyed individuals crossing the Mexican border between San Diego and Tijuana following a drinking session. Participants were measured before and after crossing on a number of questionnaire items and were breathalysed. Focusing on those men who had drank exactly 5 drinks and those women who had drank exactly 4 drinks, they noted an estimated BAC of 0.06 and 0.05 respectively. It was also noted that the mean duration of drinking sessions was approximately 4 hours. Those who stayed longer drank more, although there was evidence that the individual reached a point were they ceased to drink alcoholic beverages and their blood alcohol levels dropped. It was calculated that to reach a BAC of 0.08% - the UK drinking driving limit – men would have had to have consume 8.2 alcoholic drinks, and women 6.7, in a relatively short space of time; figures which are markedly higher than the 5/ 4 drinks criteria allow. Research in the UK would suggest that rapid consumption of alcoholic drinks is not in fact the preferred style of drinking for most people. Hammersley and Ditton (2005), for example, conducted naturalistic research on binge drinking by studying young drinkers in pubs and found that the majority of drinker drank at a moderate rate over many hours.

In further naturalistic research in the UK, Wright (2006) examined the relationship between alcohol consumption and intoxication, in order to assess the appropriateness of the 8/6 units definition of binge drinking. In this instance the group studied were members of the public attending a England versus South Africa cricket test match. A total of 12 men were tested, all of whom were aged 34 – 59 and classed themselves as social drinkers. Although a relatively small sample, this allowed for a more in depth recording of alcohol consumption in a more controlled setting than would perhaps be possible in a bar. Wright used an alcohol breathalyser to confirm that each of the individuals in the study arrived at the cricket ground with a BAC of zero, and took a note of how much they had eaten for breakfast. Additional measures of BAC were taken at each of the scheduled breaks in play and it was noted that the majority of drinks consumed were beer. Wright found that, throughout the course of the day, each participant involved drank a level of alcohol which exceeded the 8/ 6 unit definition, ranging from 8.5 – 21.7 units. However, the blood alcohol concentration of several of the participants at the end of the day had either remained at zero, or was negligible. Interestingly only 4 individuals maintained a BAC of above the legal drink driving limit. As such despite all the participants being 'binge drinkers' under the current UK government criteria, only a third of them were intoxicated to the point of impairment by the end of the day. As Wright comments, the BAC levels found in the study were much lower than would have been predicted by standard medical texts, whose figures are based on laboratory based studies (e.g. Paton and Touquet 2005). Wright argues that such findings emphasis the need for more naturalistic studies of consumption, and that more categories of binge drinking are needed than simple binary opposites of 'binge or no binge'.

The use of the 5/4 drinks definition and other similar criteria has indeed been criticized and is strongly opposed by certain alcohol researchers, such as DeJong 2003. Citing previous co-authored work (Perkins et al. 2001) DeJong notes, for example, that the estimated blood alcohol concentrations of 37% of 'binge drinkers' studied using the 5/4 drinks criteria did not exceed the 0.08%, which is the level used in many states of the USA and the UK as the legal drink driving limit. There is also the fact that some individuals reach a level of blood alcohol concentration from relatively few drinks that the majority of adults would require far more alcohol to reach. This is evidenced in Perkins et al. (2001) study where 80% of binge drinkers and 20% of non binge drinkers reached similar blood alcohol concentrations of over 0.06%, despite the non binge drinkers having consumed markedly less alcohol. This emphasizes the main critique of the 5/4 drinks definition that focusing on the number of drinks consumed alone ignores mediating factors such as weight and metabolism, as has been noted elsewhere (e.g. Midanik 1999; Gmel et al. 2003). As such it cannot reliably predict the level of intoxication in any one individual. The National Institute on Alcohol Abuse and Alcoholism has never endorsed the 5+ definition of binge drinking, using instead a definition of alcohol consumption which results in a blood alcohol level of 0.08% (National Institute of Alcohol Abuse and Alcoholism 2004). Similarly the Journal of Studies on Alcohol and Drugs, one of the leading journals in the field, does not accept articles which use the phrase 'binge drinking' in this way, as publicly stated on their website (accessed March 2007).

Binge Drinking: An Activity of the Young?

In general, the majority of binge drinking research tends to focus on the drinking habits of young adults in the 16–25 year old age range, with little research on the wider adult population. This is perhaps due to the pivotal role that alcohol consumption plays in the lives of young adults. For example, in their longitudinal study of the drinking habits of young people as they progress to early adulthood, Pape and Hammers (1996) concluded that alcohol consumption serves a functional purpose, signifying a progression into the adult world. Similarly, Lyons et al (2006) found that drinking alcohol was represented in young people's magazines as 'normative, cool, adult and professional'; the association with a successful, sophisticated and independent lifestyle poignantly demonstrates its construct as a privilege and reward. In addition, Plant and Plant (2006) highlight that 'getting drunk is a normal part of learning about alcohol', and that the majority of teenagers are drinking quite regularly by the age of 15/16. The current preoccupation with binge drinking has seen young people's drinking habits scrutinised to an even greater degree. It is young adults specifically who are often targeted in binge drinking and alcohol consumption health education, such as in the recent 'Know You Limits' campaign from the UK government (www.knowyourlimits. gov.uk). However it is important to acknowledge that binge drinking is not an activity confined solely to young adults. This is clearly illustrated in the results of the most recently available General Household Survey (Office of National Statistics 2005), which reports that whilst approximately 44% of males aged 16-24 exceed 8 units in one session at least once in the previous week, 38% of older males aged 25–44 did likewise. In addition 18% of males aged 45–64 reported having drank at least once a week over the 8/6 units limit. Thus, although younger age groups do have the highest rates of binge drinking in the population, the level in of binge drinking in adults over 25 is not negligible.

This preoccupation with drinking in young adults has been observed elsewhere by Jeffries et al. (2005), who conducted a longitudinal study into binge drinking in a national birth cohort. They noted that binge drinking was common in older age groups, albeit to a lesser extent than the younger age group. As Weitzman and Nelson (2004) comment in their discussion of the 'prevention paradox', since there are more people in the population in the above 25 group than below it, they may actually be responsible for the bulk of alcohol related harm, regardless of whether their overall level of binge drinking is less than that of their younger counterparts. In addition, the recent study by the Alcohol Education and Research Council (AERC, 2007) further emphasised this point. Based on extensive reviews of the literature and on a workshop with experts, it was highlighted that, rather than constantly increasing, binge drinking among young people has reached a plateau and may even be declining. The study warns of the danger of focusing solely on 'risk' groups, such as young people, at the expense of other groups. Instead it is recommends that the range of different drinking styles among the young be recognised and further explored, as well as the patterns of consumption in the wider population. Whilst the call for more qualitative research to be conducted in to young people's binge drinking has been noted (e.g. Coleman and Cater, 2005), arguably this can also be extended to include the need for more research with members of the general public across the age spectrum.

Therefore the approach by health educators and policy makers in the UK, and many other countries, has thus far centred on young adults and is based on a conceptualisation of 'binge drinking' as defined by the amount of alcohol consumed. In light of this, interventions have been designed accordingly. However the efficacy of these policies, and their associated alcohol education strategies, has come under increasing criticism. The Alcohol Harm Reduction Strategy for England, for example, has been challenged by numerous researchers (e.g. Drummond 2004; Room 2004; Luty 2005) for its lack of any clear, evidence based solutions. Part of the concern about these policies derive from their intended use of alcohol education as a means for reducing binge drinking behaviour, a strategy which has not been established to be effective. Lader and Goddard (2004), for instance, have noted that in spite of various public alcohol education programmes in the UK in recent years, there has not been a rise in the number of adults who can correctly identify what the recommended maximum daily intake of alcohol units actually are. In addition Foxcroft et al. (2003) conducted a systematic review of primary prevention of alcohol misuse in young adults, and concluded that there was no persuasive evidence that alcohol education programmes had any significant effect on long term alcohol consumption behaviour. This sentiment has been echoed by several other researchers in the field (e.g. Babor et al. 2003).

PUBLIC CONCEPTUALISATIONS OF BINGE DRINKING

Whilst increasing attention has been paid to different professional viewpoints concerning binge drinking, there have been comparatively far fewer attempts to explore the viewpoint of the wider public. Arguably, the continued lack of success of alcohol consumption/binge drinking reduction campaigns may be partly due to this fact; there remains surprisingly little research on how binge drinking is perceived by the general public, and how it operates in society. Some of the research which has been conducted in the UK addrersing these points is described below.

Public Knowledge of Alcohol Guidelines in the UK

As discussed whilst the unit based definition of binge drinking may have aided professionals in the field there is a limited understanding about whether such guidelines are internalised by the public. Malam and Angle (2004) used data from the Health Education Population Survey from 1996 to 2003, to provide an overview of Scottish patterns and trends in knowledge of health issues, including alcohol consumption. They report that in each of these years, around 15% of respondents claimed that they did not know what a unit of alcohol was and many of them were unaware of what the recommended maximum alcohol intake guidelines were. In addition the authors suggested that the existance of various daily and weekly recommendations meant that alcohol guidelines are particularly complicated in comparison to the 'give up smoking' and 'eat more fruit and veg' health messages.

Cultural Influences on Binge Drinking

More recently, several authors have stressed the need for a much broader understanding of the cultural and socioeconomic background of binge drinking, in order to enhance our understanding and develop more effective interventions (e.g. Hayward 2004; Measham 2006). This may be indicative of more complex social processes underlying behaviours such as binge drinking than is perhaps generally acknowledged. A better understanding of such processes could allow for the design of more evidence based alcohol education/ harm reduction approaches. The role of culture itself in shaping drinking behaviours has been the subject of relatively little attention. Eckersley (2005) argues that modern western society promotes values that are incompatible with human well-being, and that features such as individualism and materialism have the potential to contribute to drug and alcohol use. In a similar vein, Measham (2006) highlights that 'moderation and restraint are culturally at odds' with the contemporary emphasis on economic deregulation and excessive consumption'. As a result, both call for a greater understanding of the role of culture in contributing to alcohol consumption, both in the UK and elsewhere.

To give an example from Scotland, the Scottish Executive has issued a Plan for Action on Alcohol Problems (2002), which aims to 'reduce alcohol related harm in Scotland'. One of the ways to achieve this is cited as 'culture change', involving a change in 'some harmful' perceptions and attitudes concerning alcohol. However little research has been conducted with the wider Scottish public to ascertain what these perceptions actually are, which could make efforts to change them somewhat problematic. Furthermore it cannot be assumed that alcohol plays the same role in one culture as it does in another, even if those cultures are on the surface broadly similar. Delk and Meilman (1996) for example compared the drinking norms of Scottish students at a university to their American counterparts. They found that the Scottish students reported drinking more frequently and consuming more amounts of alcohol in a session. The authors also found that the Scottish students binge drank more often, experienced more hangovers and missed more classes as a consequence of drinking. On the other hand, a higher percentage of American students were reported to drive whilst intoxicated. To supplement these findings, the authors also conducted qualitative research in order to explore the reasons behind some of these issues. They concluded that student drinking was not perceived to be a particular problem in Scotland because 'alcohol use appears to be part of Scottish culture and is readily accepted'. Similarly, Bromley and Ormston (2005), who used data from the Scottish Social Attitudes Survey (2004), found that 64% of respondents agreed with the statement that 'Drinking is a major part of the Scottish way of life'. At the same time, however, 46% believed that alcohol caused more harm than any other drug to Scotland as a whole; illustrating the complex and ambiguous position that alcohol can have within society.

Thus, there is a growing amount of literature that discusses the differences between various professional conceptualisations of binge drinking. In the UK the public have been tested on how well they know the 'official' alcohol recommendations, and research suggests that their knowledge of the guidelines is relatively poor. However, there is very little known about how the wider public themselves and how they conceptualise binge drinking, and how their definitions compare to those of the professionals. Furthermore there has been an emphasis placed by professionals and policy makers on young adults. If this association is reflected in the public consciousness then it is important it is identified for the purposes of designing more effective binge drinking interventions. These gaps in knowledge was one of the driving forces behind the research upon which this chapter is based.

THE STUDY

The current authors conducted research into the alcohol consumption and the associated perceptions of people living in the Inverclyde area of Scotland, in the UK. This study provided the opportunity to address many of the issues discussed above on the ways in which public alcohol behaviours and conceptualizations differ from those used by academics and policy makers. The Inverclyde area itself is adjacent to the Firth of Clyde and is notable in that it encompasses areas which include both some of the most affluent and the most deprived areas of Scotland. In light of this fact it was felt important to include a measure of socio-economic deprivation in the study. If deprivation does influence how individuals drink and conceptualise alcohol then it is a factor which could potentially widen the gap between lay and professional understanding of alcohol consumption. Although there has been little research exploring this possibility the work which has been done has proved inconclusive. For example, whilst research in Israel has found the most deprived groups to have the highest rates of binge drinking (Neumark et al. 2003), similar work in Brazil found binge drinking in fact to be more common in the most affluent groups (Filho - Almeida et al. 2005). This is a potentially important issue which requires further research.

METHOD

Participants

The participants involved in this study were adults aged 18 or above who reported living within the Inverclyde City Council boundaries. Two sampling methods were used, cluster sampling and quota sampling, to obtain a total sample of 586 respondents (44% male, 56% female) with a mean age of 43.3 (s.d. 17.7).

Measures

Respondents were interviewed using a standardised pro forma which consisted of a mixture of open and closed questions, and covered attitudes to binge drinking, knowledge of alcohol units and personal alcohol consumption.

In the first section respondents were asked to define binge drinking in their own words, and state whether they thought it was a problem in their local area and in British society in general. This was followed by items on what they thought the causes of binge drinking were, what could be done to tackle the behaviour, and in which demographic groups, if any, they thought binge drinking occurred in. The second section included questions on how many units the respondents believed there to be in a range of beverages, and on what the recommended drinking limits are for men and women. The final section, on respondent's personal consumption, was recorded using a 7 day retrospective diary measure, which provided information on both daily consumption levels and total weekly consumption.

Procedure

As mentioned previously, two approaches were used to recruit participants. Half of the sample were recruited through doorstep interviews using cluster sampling of deprivation data zones in Inverclyde. This method was used to ensure that sufficient participants of different levels of socio-economic deprivation were recruited. Information on and selection of the data zones was provided by Inverclyde Council and were based on the Scottish Index of Multiple Deprivation (SIMD) 2004. The SIMD classifies deprivation on five categories, from a score of 1 which indicates the lowest level of deprivation to a score of 5 which indicates the highest level of deprivation. The remainder of the participants were recruited using quota sampling, in order to ensure sufficient numbers of participants in each gender and age range. Potential subjects were approached in the streets surrounding a shopping centre and invited to take part in the survey. This group of participants was asked for the first part of their home post-code to classify their level of deprivation, again using the SIMD categories.

RESULTS

Sample Characteristics

A total of 586 respondents were interviewed, 44% male and 56% female, with a mean age of 43.3 (s.d. 17.7). Deprivation in the sample was notably polarised, with 27.3% of respondents in the lowest category of deprivation and 42.6% in the highest.

Alcohol Consumption

Male respondents had a mean total weekly alcohol consumption which was significantly higher than the mean consumption of females (t = 5.41, df = 584, p < 0.001). Male respondents also had more significantly more drinking days in the last week than female respondents (t = 2.641, df = 584, p < 0.01). In addition, males had significantly higher mean consumption per drinking day than females (t = 5.147, df = 584, p < 0.001). Despite this higher consumption the most common response option with regards to frequency of drunkenness for both males and females was once a month. This reflects past research which has suggested that, due to factors such as lower body weight, women become more easily intoxicated than men. In support of this, male respondents reported that they required twice as many alcohol units as females to feel intoxicated, a difference which was statistically significant (t = 2.837, df = 584, p < 0.05). These alcohol consumption behaviours are broken down by age and gender in Table 1.

Table 1. Alcohol consumption behaviours by age and gender

	Age 18 - 29		Age 30 – 49		Age 50+	
Consumption	*Male*	*Female*	*Male*	*Female*	*Male*	*Female*
Total weekly consumption (units)	22.5	14.3	18.8	8.8	10.5	6.2
Number of drinking days in the last week	1.8	1.6	2.1	1.6	2.2	2.2
Mean consumption per drinking day (units)	10.0	6.5	8.3	4.5	4.0	3.3
Percentage drinking beyond weekly limits	39.5%	37.2%	34.2%	21.6%	11.8%	8.7%
Percentage binge drinking in the past week	57.1%	55.4%	48.1%	42.6%	22.5%	19.2%

In terms of deprivation those in the most deprived group had a significantly higher (t = -2.93, df = 412, p < 0.05) mean total alcohol consumption (14.1 units) than those in the most affluent group (9.4 units). Those in the most affluent group had significantly more (t = 3.206, df = 392, p < 0.01) drinking days in the last week, at 2.2 days, in contrast to the most deprived group who had 1.6 days. However, those in the most deprived group had a marked and significantly higher (t = -6.005, df = 392, p < 0.001) mean number of alcohol units in a drinking day (7.1 units) as compared to those in the most affluent groups (3.1 units). In keeping with this those in the most deprived group had a significantly higher (t = -3.453, df =

388, p <0.001) frequency of drunkenness at once a month as opposed to a couple of times a year, as reported by those in the most affluent group. Overall, therefore, the drinking pattern of those in the most affluent group was more spread out and more moderate than those in the most deprived group, who themselves appeared to have a greater tendency towards a 'binge' style of consumption. A minority of the sample (11%) reported themselves to abstain from alcohol. The reasons that respondents cited as to why they abstained from alcohol included religious reasons, health reasons (including pregnancy), having had a previous alcohol problem, and the cost or family/ work commitments.

Views on Binge Drinking as a Problem in Society

When asked if they considered binge drinking to be a problem, 87.2% of participants responded that they did think that binge drinking was a problem in society in general, with woman (90% vs. 83%) more likely to do so than men ($\chi2=8.187$, $p<0.05$). A significantly lower percentage (70%) of the heaviest drinkers in the sample (those with the highest weekly intake) viewed binge drinking as a problem in society ($\chi2=13.3$, $p<0.01$). When asked whether binge drinking was a problem in their own local area, the overall percentage of people who viewed binge drinking as a problem was considerably lower at 66.9%. There was no significant effect of deprivation or age on these perceptions of binge drinking as a problem locally or in society in general.

When asked who they regarded as the binge drinkers, the majority of respondents, 65.5%, stated that they felt binge drinking was a problem of young adults and teenagers, whereas 31.6% felt that it is a problem in all age groups. There were no significant effects of age, gender, level of deprivation or personal consumption on this item. Therefore the tendency in this population was to perceive binge drinkers as being young adults specifically. As will be discussed in greater depth at a later point this could have severe implications for the delivery of binge drinking public interventions.

Definitions of Binge Drinking

Answers to the question regarding the respondent's definition of binge drinking were coded into six categories. These are portrayed in Table 2. It should be noted that the answers given amass to more than 100% because most respondents gave more than one answer.

Chi-square analysis was conducted to check for any significant differences between groups in terms of gender, age range and level of deprivation. There were no significant age or gender effects evident on the definitions of binge drinking that people gave. There were, however, several significant differences between respondents from the most deprived areas and those from the most affluent. Specifically, those in the most affluent areas were significantly more likely to define binge drinking as drinking to excess than those in the most deprived areas ($x2 = 11.456$, $p < 0.01$). Conversely, those in the most deprived group were significantly more likely to define binge drinking as drinking alcohol with the specific intention to become drunk ($x2 = 13.262$, $p < 0.001$). Respondents from the most deprived areas were also significantly more likely to define binge drinking as drinking constantly and continuously (x2 = 11.667, p < 0.01). There were no significant effects of deprivation of any of the other definitions. Overall, therefore, respondents seemed to primarily define binge drinking in terms of an individual's personal limits, which contrasts the 'one size fits all' approach of the 8/ 6 alcohol unit criteria advocated by the UK government.

Table 2. Definitions of binge drinking

Definition	Percentage	Examples
Drinking beyond personal limits	50%	'People overdoing it, going on a bender and geting smashed' (Male, 20) 'Drinking too much in one go' (Female, 33)
Heavy weekend drinking	21%	'Drinking non-stop on weekends' (Male, 41) 'Getting hammered at weekends' (Male, 19)
Drinking to become drunk	20%	'Going out to get smashed on a night out' (Male, 28) 'Going out in one session to get totally drunk' (Female, 40)
Physically unable to continue drinking	11%	'People drinking till they fall over' (Male, 67) 'People who drink 'til they drop' (Male, 59
Infrequent, episodic drinking	10%	'Going for long periods of time without drinking, and then overindulging' (Female, 37)
Continuous drinking	8%	'Drinking too much all the time' (Female, 20) 'Drinking everyday and getting drunk' (Female, 33)

Point biserial correlations were then conducted to establish if there were any associations between the individual's own personal alcohol consumption and their definition of binge drinking, i.e., if those with heavy consumption were more likely to define it as drinking to excess. The personal consumption measures which were used were: total number of alcohol units in the last week; number of drinking days in the last week; mean number of alcohol units per drinking day and frequency of drunkenness. However no significant relationships were found between any of the consumptions measures and the definitions offered. This is an interesting result which indicates that how people conceptualise the definition of binge drinking is largely independent of their own alcohol consumption.

CAUSES OF BINGE DRINKING

Using the same procedure described above answers to the question regarding the causes of binge drinking were coded into seven categories.

Table 3. Perceived causes of binge drinking behaviour

Perceived causes	Percentage	Examples
Boredom or lack of facilities	35%	'Kids are bored' (Female, 27) 'There's nothing for folk to do' (Male, 79)
Peer pressure and social influences	18%	'Peer pressure and too much bravado' (Male, 53) 'It's ingrained in the culture' (Female, 49)
Availability of alcohol	18%	'Cheap drink' (Female, 28) 'Too many drinks offers and happy hours' (Female, 50)

Table 3. (Continued)

Perceived causes	Percentage	Examples
Socio-economic deprivation	11%	'There's too much unemployment' (Male, 71) 'Poverty – there's not enough jobs' (Male, 34)
Poor parenting/ lack of role models	8%	'Not enough discipline' (Female, 77) 'Adults buying young ones drink and seeing adults getting drunk' (Female, 47)
Relaxation/ socialisation	7%	'It's enjoyment' (Female, 40) 'You work all week you so enjoy a drink' (Male, 45)
Excess disposable income	6%	'Too much money and time' (Female, 85).

Significant differences were again found. Older adults in the 50+ age group were significantly less likely than the younger subjects to cite boredom ($\chi 2$=19.45, p<0.01) or socialisation/fun ($\chi 2$=10.07, p<0.05) as reasons for binge drinking. In addition, those from the most affluent areas were significantly less likely to cite boredom as a reason for binge drinking than those from the most deprived area (x2 = 11.866, p < 0.01). Those in the most affluent group were also significantly more likely to cite having too much disposable income as a cause of binge drinking (x2 = 13.845, p < 0.001). Those from the most deprived group were significantly more likely to cite unemployment and deprivation as a cause than those from the most affluent group (x2 = 9.494, p < 0.01). Those in the most affluent group were significantly more likely to cite poor parental control than those in the most deprived group (x2 = 5.260, p < 0.05). No gender effects were found on any reason given for why people binge drink. Thus, the reasons given were very diverse and demonstrate how the respondent's personal status, in terms of factors such as age and socioecomonic status, influences their conceptualization of why people binge drink.

As with the definitions of binge drinking, analysis was conducted to establish if individual's personal consumption was related to their perception of the causes of binge drinking. The majority of these were non-significant however there were a few associations which are important to acknowledge. Firstly there was a significant correlation between frequency of drunkenness and the belief of boredom as a cause of binge drinking (rpb = 0.103, p < 0.05) with those who were drunk more frequently the most likely to cite this. Secondly there was a significant negative correlation between mean number of alcohol units per drinking session and whether or not peer pressure was cited as a cause of binge drinking (rpb = -0.108, p < 0.01). Specifically the higher mean consumption someone had in a drinking day the less likely they were to see peer pressure as being a cause of binge drinking. This is an interesting result and could suggest that those who drink heavily are less able to acknowledge the fact that their drinking is partly due to social influences.

SOLUTIONS TO PROBLEMS CAUSED BY BINGE DRINKING

The answers respondents gave for possible ways to reduce binge drinking behaviour in society were coded into six categories.

Table 4. Perceived solutions to the problems caused by binge drinking behaviour

Perceived causes	Percentage	Examples
Entertainment facilities	35%	'Provide more sports facilities' (Male, 23) 'If they have things to occupy their minds they won't do it' (Male, 34)
Health education	25%	'More education to show the consequences' (Female, 35) 'More information to change their lifestyles, and more education in schools' (Female, 49)
Cessation of promotional offers	14%	'Put up the prices and stop promos' (Female, 21) 'Restrict the availability of alcohol' (Male, 27)
Law enforcement/ punitive measures	10%	'More police on patrol' (Male, 62) 'Reduce benefits for binge drinkers' (Female, 73)
Economic investment	9%	'Invest more in employment, housing and education' (Male, 24) 'Do more for the community, and put more stuff on for the kids' (Female, 26)
Changes to licensing hours	8%	'Change the drinking culture so that it is more like Europe, with longer opening hours' (Male, 18)

Those in the age group of 30 – 49 were significantly more likely to cite better health education as a possible solution to binge drinking than those in the older or younger age groups ($\chi2$=13.712, p<0.001). Economic investment was significantly more likely to be suggested by respondents in the oldest age group than those in the younger two ($\chi2$=7.001, p<0.01). Those in the youngest age group were significantly more likely to suggest the creation of alternative entertainment facilities ($\chi2$=37.594, p<0.001). In terms of deprivation those in the most affluent group were significantly more likely to cite health education programmes as a solution to binge drinking (x2 = 5.704, p < 0.05). Related to this point those in the most affluent group were also significantly more likely to cite life-skills training for teenagers (x2 = 6.959, p < 0.01). Finally those in the most deprived areas were significantly more likely to cite more employment as a solution to binge drinking (x2 = 8.123, p < 0.01).

Again as with the perceived causes of binge drinking, the perceived solutions were diverse and varied with age and gender. The suggestion that binge drinking rates could be reduced by the provision of alternative entertainment facilities is an interesting one. The fact that binge drinking can be a source of entertainment and that the provision of alternative leisure options may reduce binge drinking rates is not one which has typically acknowledged by the UK government. Instead the approach both in the UK and elsewhere has tended to be a punitive one which focuses on condemning binge drinking behaviour without offering alternative activities. The fact that binge drinking can be a social activity and includes many positive experiences for the individual is a factor which future research should address.

Point biserial correlations were conducted to establish if there were any relationships between personal consumption and perception of the solutions to binge drinking behaviour. There were no significant relationships detected between any of the personal consumption measures and any of the suggested solutions to binge drinking. In conjunction with the aforementioned results then, it would seem that personal consumption is largely unrelated to how people conceptualise binge drinking in terms of its definitions, causes, or indeed solutions.

Knowledge of Alcohol Units and Limits

Individuals were then scored on their knowledge of the number of alcohol units in the following five types of drinks: double whisky, a pint of beer, a can of super strength lager, a bottle of table wine, and a bottle of fortified wine. Each respondent was given a score out of 5, depending on how many of these drinks they correctly identified the alcohol unit content for. This is depicted in Table 5.

Table 5. Knowledge of alcohol units

	Age 18 - 29		Age 30 - 49		Age 50+	
Knowledge of alcohol units	Male	Female	Male	Female	Male	Female
Percentage of sample scoring 0	44.2%	43.0%	31.6%	32.2%	41.2%	60.9%
Percentage of sample scoring 1	14.3%	20.9%	15.2%	21.4%	23.5%	16.5%
Percentage of sample scoring 2	28.6%	22.1%	29.1%	27.0%	16.7%	13.0%
Percentage of sample scoring 3	7.8%	10.5%	10.1%	13.5%	11.8%	5.2%
Percentage of sample scoring 4	2.6%	3.5%	12.7%	4.8%	4.9%	4.3%
Percentage of sample scoring 5	2.6%	0%	1.3%	0.8%	2.0%	0%

Male respondents had a small but significantly higher score than female respondents ($t = 2.193$, $df = 583$, $p < 0.05$). There was a significant age effect in that those in the $30 - 49$ year old age group had a significantly higher score than the other two age groups ($F = 8.417$, $p < 0.001$). Those in the most affluent areas were also found to have a significantly higher knowledge score than those in the most deprived areas ($t = 2.928$, $p < 0.01$). There was a significant negative correlation in that respondent's unit knowledge score rose as did their total weekly alcohol consumption ($r = 0.103$, $p < 0.05$), their number of drinking days in the last month ($r = 0.157$, $p < 0.001$) and frequency of drunkenness ($r = 0.132$, $p < 0.01$). There was, though, no significant correlation between participants' unit knowledge score and their mean number of drinks on a drinking day. There was evidence therefore that men, middle aged adults and heavier drinkers had a better knowledge of alcohol units however these effects were all relatively small.

Participants were then asked what the current UK government guidelines for alcohol consumption are, both for the daily limits (3/2 alcohol units male/ female) and weekly limits (21/14 alcohol units). Participants were given a score of 0, 1 or 2 depending on how many of these they got correct. This is depicted in Table 6. Male respondents again had a significantly higher limit knowledge score than female respondents ($t = 1.620$, $df = 583$, $p < 0.05$). In addition those in the most affluent group had a significantly higher (t = 1.989, df = 583, p < 0.05) limit knowledge score than those in the most deprived group. There were no significant age effects. There was a significant correlation between the limit knowledge score and total weekly consumption (r = 0.093, p < 0.05) and number of drinking days in the last week (r = 0.201, p < 0.001). Again there were therefore differences between groups with regards to their knowledge of drinking guidelines however these were relatively minor. The fact that there was a positive correlation between knowledge of both units and limits and personal consumption could indicate that awareness of these does not actually reduce personal consumption.

Table 6. Knowledge of drinking guidelines

	Age 18 - 29		Age 30 - 49		Age 50+	
Knowledge of drinking guidelines	*Male*	*Female*	*Male*	*Female*	*Male*	*Female*
Percentage of sample scoring 0	62.3%	62.8%	46.8%	54.3%	61.8%	71.9%
Percentage of sample scoring 1	19.5%	20.9%	25.3%	28.3%	13.7%	9.6%
Percentage of sample scoring 2	18.2%	16.3%	27.8%	17.3%	24.5%	18.4%

When asked if they knew what the recommended guidelines were, respondents were not initially prompted on whether or not they were being asked about the daily or weekly limits. As such it was noted if the respondent offered their guess in terms of the weekly limits, the daily limits, or both. If respondents only gave one set of limits then they were asked to provide the other set of limits. The majority of respondents answered in terms of weekly units (62%) whereas only 20% gave an answer in terms of daily units. A minority (6%) replied on both daily and weekly limits and 13% provided no answer. This suggests that the government's attempts to make the public aware of daily drinking guidelines have not been as successful as for weekly limits. This could suggest that individuals who are only aware of the weekly limits assume that it is acceptable to drink a lot of alcohol in one session, as long as they keep inside their 'allowance' for the week.

Respondents were also asked if they felt the current guidelines were too high, too low or at the correct level. The majority of respondents (66%) felt that current guidelines were correct, whilst 12% felt they were too high and 12% felt they were too low. A small number (5%) had no opinion on the matter. There was no significant effect of gender, age or deprivation on this item. Respondents were then asked if they felt the recommended limits helpful. The majority (54%) replied yes, and commented that they felt it acted as a useful guideline to measure one's drinking against. A further 8% stated that the limits were helpful but did not elaborate further. On the other hand, approximately a quarter of respondents (27%) stated that they felt that the limits were ineffective because they had no impact on an individual's drinking, although they did not question the validity of the criteria themselves. A further 5% stated that they did not feel the limits were helpful but did not expand on the point. The remainder did not reply to this item. There were no significant effects of gender, age or deprivation on this item. Overall, therefore, individuals did appear to trust that the advised limits were valid and helpful, although this point must of course be considered in light of the fact that the majority of individuals did not know what the limits actually are.

DISCUSSION

The results of this research present us with an interesting view of the general public's attitudes and beliefs towards alcohol consumption and binge drinking. However it is a view that differs greatly from the 'professional' and/or 'official' view. Since the main policy vehicle to reduce consumption and ameliorate its consequences is education campaigns, it is important that there is a shared understanding of the behaviour, definitions and parameters, that would allow the education to be effective. This research suggests that that shared understanding is absent.

Consumption Levels

The levels of consumption and rates of binge drinking reported in this study are comparable to those found in previous alcohol consumption surveys (e.g. NHS National Services Scotland 2005). The patterns of drinking found in this sample are predominantly light drinking through the week and the bulk of the consumption occurring at the weekend (Friday and Saturday especially). This can be seen clearly in this study in the finding that a greater percentage of the sample met the criteria for binge drinking (40.3%) than exceeded the recommended limits (24.2%). As would be expected there is a significant difference between males and females in terms of amount consumed. However there are no significant differences in terms of bingeing or exceeding the weekly limits is found. Indeed the patterns of male and female drinking look remarkably similar across all age ranges.

As with other surveys, this study demonstrates that binge drinking and drinking to intoxication occur in all ages, albeit to a lesser extent in older age groups. This emphasises the point, that it is important to recognise that binge drinking is an issue for the entire population, and not just the sub group of young adults. However, the popular view that this type of drinking is solely confined to young people was reflected in the current survey; two-thirds of respondents, both young and old, stated that they saw binge drinking to be a problem of young adults specifically. Such a misperception is potentially dangerous for the wider public because it may render older adults, who also drink in this way, less receptive to such campaigns. The older binge drinkers may not identify themselves as belonging to the intended target group, and so may fail to interpret the message in relation to their own drinking. In addition, this misperception also has implications for the younger adult population. The belief that binge drinking is an activity reserved for their age group may also encourage young people to regard this style of drinking as the norm for people of their age. As illustrated in research from the US college system (Bosari and Carey 2003), a belief that binge drinking is the norm for a particular group can result in members of that group adopting this style of drinking; they internalise and reproduce what they believe is the 'norm'. In this sense it becomes a self fulfilling prophecy, even if this perceived norm is in fact incorrect. This idea also applies to the current anti binge drinking campaigns taking place in the UK. As mentioned previously in this chapter, the majority of such campaigns depict young adults engaging in binge drinking. As a result, there is a risk of inadvertently fuelling misperceptions of how common binge drinking among young people actually is.

Definitions of Binge Drinking

The main question underpinning this study was do professionals and lay people have the same definition of binge drinking. This study demonstrates that the general public do not appear to think of binge drinking in terms of a set volume of alcohol; none of the respondents defined binge drinking as consuming 8/ 6 units, or even as a variation of this. Despite the popularity of volume based approaches to a definition, for some time now there has been a move towards defining binge drinking in a way which better incorporates public conceptualisations. The discrepancy between individual's self perception and their actual binge drinker status (as defined by the 5+ criteria in the US) has, for example, been noted elsewhere. In a survey of students, Lederman et al. (2000) found that 92% of respondents did not perceive themselves to be binge drinkers, despite 35% meeting the 5+ binge drinking criteria. Further commenting that 'binge drinking' and the 5/4 definition were concepts that many of their students saw as unrelated to them, Goodhart et al. (2003) proposed a system of definitions intended to have greater personal relevance. Rather than using volume based criteria they suggest that students be encouraged to identify their binge drinking on the basis of their own subjective feelings of drunkenness and subsequent behaviour. By making the conceptualisation of binge drinking more recognisable to them, Goodhart et al hope that more students would in fact acknowledge that they are drinking in a harmful style. Thus by educating students to be more aware of their own individual limits it may be possible that they would learn to stop drinking when they begin to reach unsafe levels of intoxication. However, it could be argued that this is a potentially dangerous approach because it places the responsibility of recognizing an unsafe level of intoxication on individuals who are, after all, intoxicated. It could also be noted that this approach is only useful if it can be demonstrated that an individual's awareness that they are approaching their tolerance limits arises prior to them drinking enough to cause health or social problems.

There are also issues of how subjective measures, such as perception of intoxication, would transfer across different groups and cultures. Green et al,. (2007), for example, investigated how members of the public viewed drinking and drunkenness through a series of surveys and interviews. It was noted that respondents perceive heavy drinking to be very individual and culturally influenced. A number of respondents commented that moderate drinking was not drinking enough to get drunk, and several others also stated that alcohol consumption was moderate if it did not result in alcohol related harm. Furthermore, respondents emphasised the importance of the frequency of heavy drinking in determining whether or not someone was a binge drinker. This is in direct contrast to academic research and government initiatives which tend to focus on the quantity of alcohol consumed per session. Green at al. (2007) also found that certain types of behaviour were associated with alcohol misuse regardless of frequency or quantity, such as woman drinking beer. Interestingly, this suggests, again, that the role of culture is important in transmitting socially constructed norms and values about what 'acceptable' drinking is for different groups.

In further research Midanik (1999) examined how definitions of drunkenness changed over time from the 1979 to 1995 National Alcohol Surveys in the USA. After controlling for demographic variables it was found that there had been a 17% increase in the rate of respondents drinking enough alcohol to feel drunk at least once a week. In contrast, the number of drinks individuals reported requiring to be drunk fell by two drinks, although Midanik acknowledges that this could have been an artefact of slightly different wording in the surveys. It does suggest, however, that public perceptions of drunkenness may vary over time. However, the author also noted that in the survey, frequency of drunkenness was more predictive of social consequences, alcohol dependence symptoms, and alcohol related harm than actual consumption. This concept of subjective intoxication as a measure of binge drinking has been used elsewhere. Davey (1997), for example, defined binge drinking as the intention to get drunk or the intention to drink more than normal. In Finnish studies binge drinking has been measured as the individual's frequency of drunkeness (Lintonen et al. 2000; Makela and Mustonen 2000). Similar items have also been used in Italian studies, in which respondents were asked how often they drank a little too much (Osservatio Permanente sui Giovani e I'Alcool 1998).

There are additional possible biases which may influence whether or not an individual perceives themselves or others to be binge drinkers. Wechsler and Kuo (2000) for example noted in their study that students have gender specific definitions of binge drinking, with woman seen as requiring fewer drinks to be binging. It was also observed, perhaps unsurprisingly, that the more an individual drank the higher their personal threshold for defining binge drinking was. As such it could be dangerous to encourage individuals to base their decision of whether or not they are binge drinkers solely on their own subjective perceptions. In a comparison of objective (6+ alcoholic drinks in one session) and subjective measures in four Nordic countries Makela et al. (2001) noted that there appeared to be little correlation between the two, a factor they attributed to cultural differences in how intoxication is perceived. The ESPAD report on the other hand noted a stronger correlation between objective and subjective measures, which may be due to younger adults becoming more easily intoxicated (Hibell et al. 2004). The subjective measure of drunkenness item of ESPAD recorded that UK teenagers, along with those from Denmark and Finland, drank to intoxication more often than other countries.

Causes of Binge Drinking

In relation to the causes of binge drinking, respondents again gave an array of reasons. These ranged from boredom, the most common, through (in decreasing popularity) peer pressure, availability of alcohol, socioeconomic deprivation, socialisation, poor parenting, to the least popular - excess disposable income. Again there were no gender differences found in relation to the causes of binge drinking, however differences were found with both age and deprivation. The younger respondents and those in the most deprived category were more likely to view boredom as a cause for binge drinking. The most deprived respondents were more likely to offer deprivation as a cause and less likely to cite the availability of alcohol or, unsurprisingly, excess disposable income.

The fact that many respondents, particularly young adults, cited socialising and enjoyment as causes of binge drinking is also interesting. As has been noted elsewhere (e.g.

Wilson 2005) present research tends to focus on alcohol consumption in terms of the problems and adverse affects. However as anthropologists have noted for years drinking alcohol is a culturally significant and celebrated feature for many societies. In a similar vein, Heath (2001) notes his surprise that many researchers fail to recognize that most people drink because they enjoy it and its association with having fun. This is not to belittle some of the consequences of binge drinking, but arguably future research and campaigns would benefit from acknowledging both the positive and negative aspects of binge drinking; doing so might enable a more common ground to be reached which people respect and can identify with.

Solutions to Binge Drinking

This diversity of perceptions of the causes of binge drinking was reflected in the variety of suggested solutions to it. Consistent with their view of the main cause (boredom) the main suggested solution was improved entertainment facilities, in the majority non alcohol-related. Other solutions offered were, in descending order of popularity, health education, ending promotional offers, more visible policing, economic investment in the area (particularly jobs) and changes to the licensing hours (mostly more restrictive). The wide range of solutions offered in this study contrasts with previous research examining the perceptions of solutions to binge drinking in young and underage drinkers. Bromley and Ormston (2005), for example, found that the solutions suggested tended to be more immediate and practical, such as better health education or policing; whilst both of these solutions were mentioned in this study, neither one was the most frequent response. This may reflect the approach taken by the research, which is that no one group (ie. age, gender, deprivation category or other grouping) was specifically targeted, or made the subject of the questions.

Overall the most notable aspect of the respondents' perceptions of binge drinking was how varied they were. This supports the view that, despite the media and government rhetoric on the topic, there is a dearth of understanding as to what binge drinking means to the average adult in the UK. Deprivation in particular appeared to be an important factor in determining one's perceptions of binge drinking, and many of the current subjects suggest that binge drinking behaviour may naturally decrease if wider scale issues of deprivation were addressed. This is something which may need to given greater consideration in the design of future binge drinking interventions.

Knowledge of Alcohol Units and Limits

The respondents' knowledge of units and recommended limits was very poor. Despite the recent focus on binge drinking and expressing the limits in daily rather than weekly terms, most respondents (62%) answered in weekly limits. Only 16% of subjects could correctly answer more than 2 out of 5 questions on how many units were in common drinks and only 20% knew the recommended limits for both males and females, with over 60% knowing neither. Other research has found similar results, eg Ball et al (2007) who concluded 'the sensible drinking message is confused and poorly understood'. It would seem that the same criticism could be made of the binge drinking advice. Despite this finding of poor recall of the limits however more than half of the subjects (54%) reported finding them helpful as a guideline to measure their drinking against.

A CONCEPTUAL GAP?

The current study clearly shows the ambiguity and complexity of the concept of binge drinking, which is a reflection of the wider ambivalence towards alcohol in contemporary society. Whilst the government tends to define binge drinking in terms of the number of units of alcohol consumed, the more individual and subjective perception of the public appears to focus on drinking beyond one's own personal limits. There is a shared view that binge drinking results from deficits. However the official views of the causes and solutions to binge drinking lie in explicitly the knowledge deficits, and implicitly in the moral deficits, of the individual bingers. The public's view is that the deficits are much more systemic and lie in the lack of amenities and opportunities. The absence of a shared understanding of binge drinking renders the design and implementation of effective prevention measures difficult. Therefore, it is essential that further in-depth research be conducted to better understand the public's perception of binge drinking to enable the development of a more coherent and accessible definition, one with which the public could readily identify, and against which they could judge their own drinking behaviours.

In this respect, qualitative research has much to offer to the field of binge drinking. In utilizing such an approach, members of the wider public would be granted the freedom and flexibility to voice, in their own words, own thoughts, feelings and experiences. This would greatly enhance our understanding of binge drinking, and how they themselves regard it. It is acknowledged that such an approach often requires the use of smaller samples, rendering generalizations and claims to representativeness more difficult. However, the richness and detail of the data obtained would make a worthwhile and much needed contribution to the field. As mentioned previously, Delk and Meilman (1996) adopted a mixed methodology approach when comparing the drinking habits of American and Scottish students. In doing so, they were able to locate their initial quantitative findings within the broader social context in which they occurred, resulting in a more holistic account of students' drinking. This demonstrates another advantage of qualitative research, in that it allows for a more detailed insight in to people's perceptions and experiences, with the potential and flexibility to further explore the social context and cultural aspects of their binge drinking.

CONCLUSION

The results of this study suggest a gulf between the laypersons' conceptualisations of binge drinking, its causes and solutions, and that of the 'professionals'. No respondent gave a definition couched in units or even number of drinks; instead emphasis was placed on characteristics such as intoxication and weekend drinking. The perceived causes of binge drinking were diverse, as were the proposed solutions to it. Thus, there lacks a clear messages in relation to drinking per se and binge drinking in particular which seem to have lead to varied, and at times contradictory, understandings. One pervading factor that underlies opinions of bingeing was deprivation. In this sense economic deprivation was expressed as a cause, and more free amenities and entertainment as solutions. It also had the most marked influence on opinions, for although age and gender were factors on several items, levels of deprivation were particularly important in shaping beliefs about binge drinking behaviour and how this may be changed.

In conclusion, there is a need for further, more detailed understandings of how binge drinking is perceived by the public, which can be achieved through the greater use of qualitative research approaches. This would allow for better informed health education messages, which members of the public can more easily relate too. Caution also needs to be taken that media reports and health education campaigns do not indirectly reinforce the stereotype that binge drinking is only a problem of young adults, or only something which happens at weekends. If not then health education campaigns may fail to connect with large sections of the population who, although not the heaviest binge drinkers, still binge drink to an extent which should not be ignored.

REFERENCES

Alcohol Education and Research Council (2007). The normalisation of binge drinking? An historical and cross cultural investigation with implications for action. Alcohol Insight 49. Available online at http://www.aerc.org.uk/documents/pdf/insights/insight_49(ebook) .pdf.

Babor, T. F., Caetano, R., Caswell, S., Edwards, G., Giesbrecht, N. and Graham, K. *et al* (2003). Alcohol: No ordinary commodity. Research and public policy. New York, Oxford University Press.

Ball, D., Williamson, R. and Witton, J. (2007). In celebration of sensible drinking. *Drugs: Education, Prevention and Policy*, 14 (2): 97-102

Bosari, B. and Carey, K. B. (2003). Descriptive and injunctive norms in college drinking: A meta - analytical integration. *Journal of Studies on Alcohol,* 64: 331 - 341.

Bromley, C. and Ormston, R. (2005). Part of the Scottish Way of Life? Attitudes Towards Drinking and Smoking In Scotland - Findings From the 2004 Scottish Social Attitudes Survey. Scottish Executive Social Research Substance Misuse Research Programme. Edinburgh, Scottish Executive.

Cabinet Office (2004). The Alcohol Harm Reduction Strategy for England. Cabinet Office Prime Minister's Strategy Unit. London, Cabinet Office.

Calahan, D., I. Cisin and Crossley, H. (1969). American Drinking Practices: A National Study of Drinking Behavior and Attitudes. New Jersey, Rutgers Center for Alcohol Studies.

Clark, W. B. and Midanik, L. (1982). Alcohol use and alcohol problems among U.S. adults: results of the 1979 survey. *Alcohol and Health Monograph,* No 1, DHHS.

Coleman, L. and Cater, S. (2005). Underage 'binge' drinking: A qualitative study into motivations and outcomes. *Drugs: Education, Prevention and Policy*, 12 (2): 125-136

Datalounge (1999). Australia Releases Study of Gay Teens, Datalounge.

Delk, E. and Meilman, P.W. (1996). Alcohol use among college students in Scotland compared with norms from the United States. *Journal of American College Health*, 44 (6): 274-282.

DeJong, W. (2003). Definitions of binge drinking. *Journal of the American Medical Association*, 289(13): 1635.

Dooley, D. and Prause, J. (1997). Effects of favourable employment change on alcohol abuse: One and five year follow ups in the National Longitudinal study of Youth. *Journal of Community Psychology*, 25(6): 787 - 807.

Drummond, D. C. (2004). An alcohol strategy reduction for England: The good, the bad and the ugly. *Alcohol and Alcoholism*, 39: 377 - 339.

Eckersley, R.M. (2005). 'Cultural Fraud': the role of culture in drug abuse. *Drug and Alcohol Review*, 24: 157-163.

Filho - Almeida, N., Lessa, I., Magalhaes, L., Araujo, M. J., Aquino, E., James, S. A. and Kawachi, I. (2005). Social inequality and alcohol consumption - abuse in Bahia, Brazil: Interactions of gender, ethnicity and class. *Social Psychiatry and Psychiatric Epidemiology*, 40: 214 - 222.

Gfroerer, J., D. Wright and Gustin, J. (1996). Preliminary estimates from the 1995 national household survey on drug abuse. Advance Report No 18. Rockville, Department of Health and Human Services.

Gmel, G., Rehm, J. and Kuntsche, E. (2003). Binge drinking in Europe: Definitions, epidemiology and consequences. *Sucht*, 49(2): 105 - 116.

Goodhart, F. W., Ledermen, L., Stewart, L. P., and Laitman, L. (2003). Binge drinking: Not the word of choice. *Journal of American College Health*, 52(1): 44 - 46.

Hammersley, R. and Ditton, J. (2005). Binge or bout: Quantity and rate of drinking by young people in the evening in the licensed premises. *Drugs: Education, Policy and Prevention*, 12(6): 493 - 500.

Hayward, K. (2004). City Limits: Crime, Consumer Culture and the Urban Experience. London, Glasshouse Press.

Heath, D. (2000). Drinking Occasions: Comparative Perspectives on Alcohol and Culture. International Centre for Alcohol Policies Series on Alcohol in Society. Philadelphia: Brunner/Mazel.

International Center for Alcohol Policies (1997). Limits of Binge Drinking. ICAP Reports 2. Washington DC, International Center for Alcohol Policies.

Jellinek, E. M. (1952). Phases of alcohol addiction. *Quartlerly Journal of Studies on Alcohol*, 13: 673 - 684.

Kuntsche, E., Rehm, J. and Gmel, G. (2004). Characteristics of binge drinkers in Europe. Social Science & Medicine 59: 113 - 127.

Lader, D. and Goddard, E. (2004). Drinking: Adults' Behaviour and Knowledge in 2004. London, Office of National Statistics.

Lange, J. E. and Voas, R. B. (2001). Defining binge drinking quantities through resulting blood alcohol concentrations. *Psychology of Addictive Behaviors*, 15(4): 310 - 316.

Leon, D. A. and McCambridge, J. (2006). Liver cirrhosis mortality rates in Britain from [1950] to 2002: An analysis of routine data. *Lancet,* 367: 52 - 56.

Luty, J. (2005). UK alcohol policy - pure genius. *Psychiatric Bulletin*, 29: 410 - 412.

McAlaney, J. and McMahon, J. (2006). Establishing the rates of binge drinking in the UK: Anomalies in the data. *Alcohol & Alcoholism*, 41(4): 355 - 357.

Measham, F. (2006). The new policy mix: Alcohol, harm minimisation, and determined drunkenness in contemporary society. International Journal of Drug Policy 17: 258 - 268.

Midanik, L. T. (1999). Drunkenness, feeling the effects and 5+ measures. *Addiction,* 94(6): 887 - 897.

Nadeau, L., Guyon, L. and Bourgault, C. (1998). Heavy drinkers in the general population: comparison of two measures. Addiction Research 6(2): 165 - 188.

National Institute of Alcohol Abuse and Alcoholism (2004). NIAAA council approves definition of binge drinking, National Institute of Alcohol Abuse and Alcoholism.

Neumark, Y. D., Rahav, G. and Jaffe, D. H. (2003). Socio - economic status and binge drinking in Israel. *Drug and Alcohol Dependence,* 69: 15 - 21.

NHS National Services Scotland (2005). Alcohol Statistics Scotland. Edinburgh, ISD Scotland Publications.

Office of National Statistics (2005). General Household Survey 2003. London, Office of National Statistics.

Paton, A. and Touquet, R. (2005). ABC on Alcohol. Malden, Mass, Blackwells.

Perkins, H. W., DeJong, W. and Linkenbach, J. (2001). Estimated blood alcohol levels reached by 'Binge' and 'Nonbinge' drinkers: A survey of young adults in Montana. *Psychology of Addictive Behaviors,* 15(4): 317 - 320.

Plant, M. and Plant, M. (2006). Binge Britian: Alcohol and the National Response. Oxford, Oxford University Press.

Poulin, C. C. and Graham, L. (2001). The association between substance use, unplanned sexual intercourse and other sexual behaviours among adolescents. *Addiction,* 96(4): 607 - 621.

Room, R. (2004). Disabling the public interest: Alcohol strategies and policies for England. Addiction 99: 1083 - 9.

Scottish Executive (2002). Plan for Action on Alcohol Problems. Edinburgh, Scottish Executive.

Sproston, K. and Primatesta, P. (2004). Health Survey for England 2003 Volume 2: Risk factors for cardiovascular disease. London, National Statistics.

Wechsler, H., Lee, J, E., Kuo, M. and Lee, H. (2000). College binge drinking in the 1990s: A continuing problem. *Journal of American College Health,* 48: 199 - 210.

Weitzman, E. R. and Nelson, T. F. (2004). College student binge drinking and the 'prevention paradox': Implications for prevention and harm reduction. *Journal of Drug Education,* 34(3): 247 - 265.

White, V. M., Hill, D. J. and Segan, C. J. (1997). Alcohol use among Australian secondary students in 1993. *Drug and Alcohol Review,* 16(2): 113 - 122.

Widmark, E. M. P. (1981). Principles and applications of medicolegal alcohol determination, Biomedical Publications.

Wilson, T. (ed.) (2005). Drinking Cultures. Oxford and New York: Berg

World Health Organisation (1994). Lexicon of Alcohol and Drug Terms. Geneva, Switzerland, World Health Organisation Office of Publications.

Wright, N. R. (2006). A day at the cricket: The breath alcohol consequences of a type of very English binge drinking. *Addiction Research and Theory,* 14(2): 133 - 137.

In: Binge Drinking Research Progress
Editor: Kevin I. DiGuarde

Chapter 2

A TRIAL OF BRIEF PHYSICIAN ADVICE FOR THE TREATMENT OF PROBLEM DRINKING IN POLISH PRIMARY CARE PRACTICES

Linda Baier Manwell[1], Jan Czeslaw Czabala,
Marek Ignaczak and Marlon Mundt
Department of Family Medicine
University of Wisconsin-Madison Medical School
Madison, WI, USA
Institute of Psychiatry and Neurology Warsaw, Poland
Addiction Medicine Institute of Psychiatry and Neurology
Warsaw, Poland
Department of Family Medicine University of Wisconsin-Madison
Medical School Madison, WI, USA

ABSTRACT

Objective

To test the efficacy of brief physician advice in reducing alcohol use.

Design

Randomized, controlled clinical trial with 6-month follow-up.

---

[1]Correspondence to: Linda Baier Manwell, MS,UW Department of Family Medicine 310 N. Midvale Blvd, Suite 205,Madison, WI 53795,FAX 608-263-1076,Phone 608-262-8068,Email lmanwell@wisc.edu

Setting

Twelve community-based primary care practices (20 physicians) located in six cities in Poland.

Participants

Of 4,373 patients screened for problem drinking, 160 males and 59 females met inclusion criteria and were randomized into a control (n=110) or experimental intervention group (n=109). A total of 201 subjects (92%) participated in the 6-month follow-up interview.

Intervention

Two 10-15 minute physician-delivered counseling visits that included advice, education, and contracting using a scripted workbook. Two follow-up phone calls by office nurse.

Main Outcome Measures

Alcohol use, smoking, depression, health care utilization, accidents and injuries.

Results

No significant differences were found between groups at baseline on age, SES, smoking status, rates of depression or anxiety, frequency of conduct disorders, lifetime drug use, or health care utilization. At the time of the 6-month follow-up, the experimental group had reduced alcohol consumption from baseline levels by 44%, compared to a 31% reduction by the control group ($p<0.10$). The experimental group reduced binge drinking by 53%, compared to a 26% reduction by the control group ($p<0.01$). Excessive drinking (>20 drinks/week male, >13 drinks/week female) was exhibited by 16% of both groups at the 6-month follow-up.

Conclusions

This project is the first brief intervention trial conducted in community practices in Eastern Europe. It provides the first evidence that primary care physicians in Poland may be able to reduce alcohol use in at-risk and problem drinkers

INTRODUCTION

Alcohol use disorders, with their numerous adverse health and economic effects, are a worldwide public health concern (Gutjahr et al., 2001; Holder and Blose, 1992). Problem drinking is associated with both increased mortality rates and premature mortality. Estimates indicate that 9-22 years of potential life are lost for an individual death from alcoholic liver disease, compared to two years for cancer and four years for heart disease (Single et al., 2000; Ridolfo and Stevenson, 2001; US DHHS, 1993). Fetal alcohol effects occur in one in 1,000 live births (IOM, 1996). The economic costs of alcohol abuse in the U.S. alone are estimated to have been $184.6 billion in 1998 (Harwood, 2000).

Poland has one of the highest rates of per-capita alcohol consumption in the world, estimated at 8 ltr/100 persons in 1999 (Mellibruda, 1999). In Poland's population of almost 40 million, nearly 800,000 persons are dependent on alcohol and an additional 1-1.2 million abuse alcohol (Mellibruda, 1999). In 1998, alcohol abuse resulted in economic losses of PLN 25 billion, compared to PLN 6.5 billion in revenue generated by alcohol sales (State Agency for the Prevention of Alcohol Problems, 2000). The testing and implementation of effective alcohol abuse prevention strategies has become an important national priority.

Researchers in other countries have been testing the use of brief intervention techniques in clinical settings to reduce alcohol use and alcohol-related harm. These clinically-based interventions include assessment and direct feedback, contracting and goal setting, behavioral modification techniques, and the use of written materials such as self-help manuals (Heather, 1987; Miller, 1987; Wallace, 1988; Babor, 1990; Nilssen, 1991; Anderson and Scott, 1992; Richmond, 1995; Fleming, 1997,1999, 1999; Gentilello, 1999; Manwell, 2000). Meta analyses performed by Bien (1993), Kahan (1995), and Wilk (1997) found that most brief intervention trials showed a positive effect on reducing consumption levels and suggest that clinicians can expect 10-30% of their patients to change their drinking behaviors as a result of brief intervention.

This report presents the results of the first clinical trial conducted in Polish community-based primary care practices to test the efficacy of brief physician advice for reducing alcohol use by problem drinkers. The research procedures are similar to those utilized in previous trials (Wallace, 1988; Fleming, 1997, 1999; Ockene, 1999)

METHODS

Two research teams were formed: the principal investigator and a project director in the United States and the co-principal investigator and a site manager in Poland. Physician participants were recruited by mail and telephone by the Polish research team during the Spring of 1998. About half of these physicians had been participants in a previous faculty development course on substance abuse conducted by the principal investigator (Murray and Fleming, 1996; Ostaszewski, 2000). Physician participation criteria included: 1) trained in family medicine; 2) practicing medicine at least 50% time; 3) based in a community primary care clinic; 4) amenable to participating in a brief intervention training program; and 5) amenable to following the research protocol. The physicians received $400 for their participation.

The physicians learned to administer the brief intervention through a 4-hour role-playing and skills training program conducted at a conference facility in Warsaw. The US research team conducted the training in English with simultaneous translation by members of the Polish research team. Each physician received additional training in a booster session at his or her clinic prior to patient randomization into the trial.

Patient data were collected in 1998-2000 over a twenty-one-month period of time. All adult patients visiting participating physicians for routine care were approached by the clinic receptionist or nurse and asked if they would like to participate in a research study. Patients who were willing to participate completed a five-minute Health Screening Survey (HSS) containing parallel quantity/frequency and CAGE-style questions (Ewing, 1984) on exercise, smoking, weight, and alcohol. The HSS was designed as a general health questionnaire to minimize the intervention effect of the alcohol questions. More details about this survey have been published elsewhere (Manwell, 2002).

Men drinking more than 20 drinks per week, or women drinking more than 13 drinks per week, or subjects consuming more than 4 drinks five or more times in the previous 30 days, or subjects giving 2 or more positive answers to the CAGE questions were invited to participate in a face-to-face assessment interview. This interview, administered by a clinic nurse, gathered detailed alcohol consumption data using the timeline follow-back method (Sobell and Sobell, 1992). Information was also collected on licit and illicit drug use, injuries, emergency department visits, hospitalizations, health status, family function, and mental health. Those subjects who remained eligible were randomized into either a brief intervention experimental group or a "usual care" control group. Patients were excluded if they were pregnant, under age 18 or over 80, had attended an alcohol treatment program in the previous year, reported symptoms of alcohol withdrawal in the last 12 months, received advice from their physician to change their alcohol use in the previous three months, drank more than 56 drinks per week, or reported symptoms of suicide.

The unit of randomization was the individual patient. Randomization of the subjects was carried out separately for men and women in each physician's practice. Each physician had both control and experimental patients in his or her practice. Subjects assigned to the control group received a general health booklet and were instructed to address any health concerns in their usual manner. Patients in the experimental group were given the same booklet and scheduled to see their personal physician for the brief intervention treatment. Clinic nurses, blinded to randomization status, administered a six-month follow-up interview to all participating patients. Subjects were paid a total of $14 if they completed the required procedures.

The intervention was based on protocols developed for the MRC trial (Wallace, et al., 1988) and Project TrEAT (Fleming, et al., 1997). Two 15-minute visits with the physician were scheduled one-month apart (brief intervention and reinforcement session). The brief intervention protocol consisted of a 2-part workbook. Part 1 contained a page to record feedback on each patient's current health behaviors, a review of the prevalence of problem drinking, a list of the adverse effects of alcohol, a drinking agreement in the form of a prescription, and drinking diary cards. Part 2 contained a form to review the drinking diary cards, a worksheet on drinking cues, and an exercise to identify coping methods. The patients received a supportive follow-up phone call from the clinic nurse two weeks after each physician visit.

Outcome variables included previous seven-day use, binge drinking, excessive drinking, hospital days and emergency department visits, smoking status, accidents, and injuries. Statistical analyses of the data examined changes in alcohol consumption over time by comparing outcome measures at the baseline survey with the six-month follow-up report. Paired t-tests of means and chi-square tests of independence provided estimates of significant differences in outcome measures between the experimental and control groups. A logistic regression model was developed to examine the independent effect of treatment status on alcohol use after controlling for other variables. Analyses were conducted separately for men and women and by group status (experimental and control).

The research protocol and consent forms were reviewed and approved by the University of Wisconsin Committee for the Protection of Human Subjects and the Local Ethics Committee at the Institute of Psychiatry and Neurology in Warsaw. Physician consent was obtained prior to the brief intervention training session. Patient consent was obtained twice; prior to the initial screening and prior to the face-to-face assessment interview.

RESULTS

A total of 4,373 subjects from 12 clinics completed the Health Screening Survey (see Figure 1). Approximately 50% completed the instrument as a self-administered questionnaire. The remainder completed the HSS as a nurse-administered interview due to illiteracy, language barriers, or vision problems. The patient refusal rate was not tracked, however research staff reported that refusals were very rare. Of the 4,373 subjects who completed the HSS, 663 (15%) screened positive for problem drinking and were invited to participate in a face-to-face assessment interview at their physician's office.

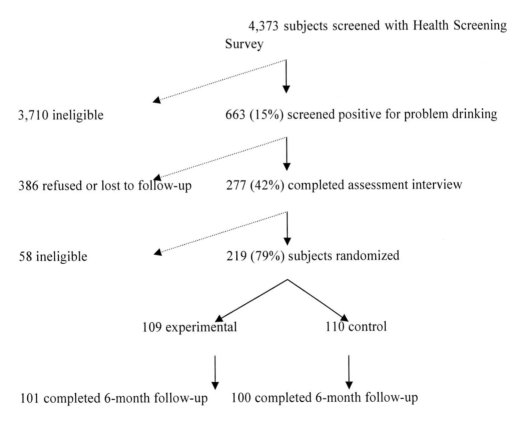

Figure 1. Subject sample.

Only 277 (42%) of the 663 subjects completed the assessment interview. Of the 386 subjects who did not complete the interview, about half were working at seasonal jobs in other areas of the country. For those who refused to complete the interview, the most common excuse was inadequate time to complete the survey. Approximately 8% of the subjects refused after reading the second consent form, administered prior to the face-to-face assessment. Most were uncomfortable being asked about drug use. Unfamiliarity with research procedures and a past history of living under a repressive government generated fears regarding breach of confidentiality.

Of the 277 subjects who completed the assessment interview, 219 (79%) met all inclusion criteria and were randomized into an experimental (n=109) and a control group (n=110). A total of 201 (92%) subjects completed the 6-month follow-up interview. Of those who did not, one refused, 15 were lost to follow-up mostly due to taking a job abroad, and two had died.

The sample consisted of 160 males and 59 females. Minimal differences were found between the experimental and control groups in terms of baseline sociodemographic characteristics (Table 1). Most of the study sample were married or living with a partner (56%), had a high school education or less (74%), and worked in a technical, mechanical, or general labor position (45%). Forty-four percent of the subjects smoked tobacco in the three months prior to interview and 64% reported alcohol consumption within the previous three months. Mental health disorders were common, with 35% of the sample meeting DSM-III-R (American Psychiatric Association, 1987) criteria for depression in the last 30 days, and 51% reporting depression in their lifetime. A small percentage self-reported marijuana (5%) or cocaine use (5%) in the 6 months prior to the assessment interview.

At 6 months post-intervention, the experimental subjects showed a 44% reduction in weekly alcohol use, from a baseline average of 17.1 drinks to 9.6 drinks per week (p<0.10). The control subjects reduced their weekly alcohol consumption as well, by an average of 31% (p<0.10).

The experimental group showed a 53% reduction in binge drinking episodes in the previous 30 days (p<0.01), compared to a 26% reduction by the control group (p<0.01). Men in the experimental group reduced their binge consumption by 55% from an average of 8.0 episodes in the 30 days prior to the study, to 3.6 episodes post-intervention (p<0.01). Women reduced their number of binge drinking episodes by 48% from 6.4 to 3.3 (p<0.05).

The numbers of subjects who binge drank in the past 30 days remained essentially unchanged except for women in the experimental group where a 25% reduction was noted. The numbers of subjects drinking excessively in the week prior to the interviews (21 or more standard drinks for men, 14 or more drinks for women) declined substantially for all groups.

A total of 106 (53%) of the 201 subjects who completed the 6-month follow-up interview cut their alcohol consumption by at least 20%. The results of a logistic regression model show that experimental group status (odds ratio 1.68; 95% confidence interval 0.93-3.06; p<0.10) was the variable most strongly associated with a 20% reduction in consumption, but only to a marginal level of statistical significance. Ninety-eight (49%) of the subjects reduced binge consumption by 30% or more. Logistic regression analyses showed that the associated variables included younger age group of 18-30 years (OR 2.66; CI 1.60-4.41; p<0.01) and experimental group status (OR 2.78; CI 1.51-5.13; p<0.01). Analysis results also indicated that subjects in the 31-50 year old age group were less likely to reduce binge consumption.

Table 1. Subject Sociodemographic Characteristics of the Sample

	Control		Experimental	
	M (n=78)	F (n=32)	M (n=82)	F (n=27)
Age:				
18-30	25 (32%)	14 (44%)	30 (37%)	11 (41%)
31-40	19 (24%)	8 (25%)	24 (29%)	9 (33%)
41-50	22 (28%)	9 (28%)	17 (21%)	7 (26%)
51-65	11 (14%)	1 (32%)	10 (12%)	0
66-80	1 (1%)	0	1 (1%)	0
Marital status:				
Never married	22 (28%)	12 (37%)	29 (35%)	10 (37%)
Widow, divorced, separated	5 (6%)	7 (22%)	5 (6%)	6 (22%)
Married, living w/partner	50 (64%)	13 (41%)	48 (59%)	11 (41%)
Education:				
High school or less	61 (78%)	21 (66%)	63 (77%)	16 (59%)
Some college	8 (10%)	5 (16%)	10 (12%)	5 (19%)
College degree or more	7 (9%)	5 (16%)	9 (11%)	6 (22%)
Occupation:				
Professional	16 (21%)	12 (38%)	15 (18%)	8 (30%)
Technical/mechanical	16 (21%)	4 (13%)	26 (32%)	6 (22%)
Student	9 (12%)	3 (9%)	9 (11%)	5 (19%)
Labor/machine	24 (31%)	1 (3%)	20 (24%)	2 (7%)
Retired	7 (9%)	2 (6%)	6 (7%)	0
Homemaker	0	4 (13%)	0	3 (11%)
Unemployed	5 (6%)	5 (16%)	4 (5%)	3 (11%)
Mental Health:				
Depression in lifetime	38 (49%)	15 (47%)	43 (52%)	5 (56%)
Depression in last 30 days	25 (32%)	13 (41%)	33 (40%)	10 (37%)
Childhood conduct disorder	26 (33%)	7 (22%)	26 (32%)	3 (11%)
Antisocial disorder	28 (36%)	8 (25%)	26 (32%)	5 (19%)
Health Behaviors:				
Exercised in last 6 months	44 (56%)	20 (63%)	46 (56%)	15 (56%)
Smoked in last 6 months	54 (69%)	19 (59%)	51 (62%)	16 (59%)
Marijuana use last 6 months	1 (1%)	2 (6%)	3 (4%)	4 (15%)
Cocaine use last 6 months	0	0	0	1 (4%)

ALCOHOL USE OUTCOMES

As illustrated in Table 2, differences were found for baseline alcohol consumption, with experimental subjects averaging 4 more drinks per week than control subjects.

Table 2. Subject Alcohol Consumption at Baseline and 6-Month Follow-up by Treatment Status

	All subjects		Males		Females	
	Experimental	Control	Experimental	Control	Experimental	Control
Number of drinks in past 7 days (mean, SD)						
Baseline	17.1 (12.0)	12.9 (12.1)	17.2 (13.0)	14.2 (12.4)	17.0 (8.4)	9.8 (10.8)
6 month follow-up	9.6 (10.0)	8.9 (9.9)	10.2 (9.9)	10.3 (10.9)	7.6 (10.4)	5.8 (6.6)
% reduction from baseline	44%*	31%*	41%	27%	55%	41%
Number of binge drinking episodes in past 30 days (mean, SD)						
Baseline	7.6 (7.1)	3.8 (4.2)	8.0 (7.6)	4.4 (4.6)	6.4 (5.3)	2.4 (2.8)
6 month follow-up	3.5 (3.9)	2.8 (3.1)	3.6 (4.0)	3.3 (3.3)	3.3 (3.6)	1.7 (2.3)
% reduction from baseline	53%***	26%***	55%***	25%***	48%**	29%**
Number of subjects binge drinking in past 30 days (≥6 drinks on one occasion) (N, %)						
Baseline	89 (82%)	72 (65%)	66 (80%)	54 (69%)	23 (85%)	18 (56%)
6 month follow-up	73 (72%)	70 (70%)	57 (75%)	52 (75%)	16 (64%)	18 (58%)
% reduction from baseline	12%	8%	6%	9%	25%	4%
Number of subjects drinking excessively in past 7 days (≥21 drinks men, ≥14 drinks women) (N, %)						
Baseline	52 (48%)	31 (38%)	31 (38%)	29 (37%)	20 (74%)	12 (38%)
6 month follow-up	16 (16%)	16 (16%)	10 (13%)	12 (17%)	6 (24%)	4 (13%)
% reduction from baseline	67%	57%	66%	54%	68%	66%

*p<0.10, **p<0.05, ***p<0.01

HEALTH CARE UTILIZATION, ACCIDENTS, AND INJURIES

Health care utilization and numbers of accidents or injuries did not differ significantly between members of the experimental and control groups in the 6 months following the intervention. Twelve control subjects (12%) and nine experimental subjects (9%) reported suffering from an accident or injury. Eleven control subjects reported going to the emergency room, compared to eight experimental subjects. Three experimental and three control subjects reported being hospitalized overnight.

HEALTH STATUS OUTCOMES

Patient self-rating of overall health was little changed between baseline and 6 months post-intervention for members from both the experimental and control groups. Twenty-eight experimental subjects and 26 control subjects reported improved health at 6 months compared to baseline. The experimental group reported no significant changes in smoking status (60% smoked at baseline vs. 59% at 6 months post-intervention), while the control subjects reported a slight decrease (65% at baseline vs. 54% post-intervention). Fifty-one percent of the smokers reported that their physicians had recommended that they stop or cut down in the past 6 months.

DISCUSSION

This is the first brief intervention trial to be conducted in community-based practices in Eastern Europe. It provides the first evidence that Polish primary care physicians may be able to reduce alcohol use in at-risk drinkers. At the 6-month follow-up, participants reported reductions in both 7-day alcohol use and the number of binge drinking episodes in the past month. In addition, significantly fewer numbers of subjects reported drinking excessively in the past week. Reductions were noted for both men and women, with a slightly larger reduction seen in the female sample. These findings are consistent with both the MRC (Wallace et al., 1988) and Project TrEAT (Fleming et al., 1997) trials. The changes in health care utilization and accidents and injuries were not significant, however the 6-month follow-up period may have been too short for differences in these variables to appear.

This trial has a number of strengths. It was conducted in a diverse sample of community-based, primary care practices in rural and urban settings. As a result of using community-based physicians who provide a large amount of medical care, the findings may be applicable to primary care practices throughout Poland. The patient sample represents a population of adults in a country with a growing economy, a stable government, and a high rate of alcohol use. We had a 100% physician retention rate and no turn-over among data collection staff. Even though a disproportionate number of heavier drinkers were randomized to the experimental intervention group, this group still showed greater reductions in 7-day drinking, binge consumption, and excessive drinking than the control group. In the regression model, the experimental status variable is significant in side-by-side t-tests for both males and females.

A number of issues should be considered when interpreting the study results. With only 201 subjects, the study did not have the power to detect subtle treatment effects and a significant effect was demonstrated only for binge consumption. The small sample size also inhibits the generalizability of the results. The reliance on self-report of alcohol use is an important consideration. Even though self-report has been shown to be a valid method of collecting consumption data (Del Boca and Darkes, 2003; Del Boca and Noll, 2000), the physicians and nurses in Poland felt that the subjects enrolled in this study may have underreported their levels of consumption. However, several subjects reported consuming similar amounts of alcohol when they spontaneously visited their doctors requesting help for their drinking after completing the Health Screening Survey. Methods used in this trial to minimize self-report bias included: 1) reassuring subjects that the information provided to the researchers was confidential; 2) using questionnaires containing parallel questions on weight, exercise, sleeping patterns, alcohol use, and smoking to lessen the impact of the alcohol questions; and 3) using multiple measures of alcohol use.

The reduction in alcohol use among subjects in the control group is a finding consistent with results seen in other alcohol trials (Bien et al., 1993; Kahan et al., 1995; Wilk et al., 1997; Fleming et al., 1997 and 1999). The reason for this change is unknown, but may be related to regression to the mean, historical changes in alcohol use, and the intervention effect of the research procedures. Because each control group subject was asked about his or her alcohol use three times over the 6-month period, the latter reason is likely.

This trial indicates that brief physician advice may be a successful strategy for changing drinking behavior for at-risk and problem drinkers in primary care settings. Since many people visit their physician at least once every two years, brief advice may prove advantageous for the Polish health care system. Future trials with larger numbers of subjects are warranted to assess the benefit-costs of providing screening, assessment, and brief intervention activities for all patients who seek health care services in primary care community-based settings.

Table 3. Logistic Regression Models

Reduction in 7-day Drinking: 106 out of 201 subjects cut 20% or more

Adjusted odds ratio	95% confidence interval		
Female	1.33		(0.67, 2.65)
Smoked in last 6 months	0.89		(0.48, 1.65)
Age: 18-30	**1.63**		**(0.89, 3.00)**
31-50	0.77		(0.41, 1.46)
51-80	0.82		(0.53, 1.26)
Depressed in last 30 days	1.14		(0.60, 2.14)
Experimental status	1.68	p< 0.10	(0.93, 3.06)
Child conduct disorder	0.36		(0.09, 1.46)
Adult antisocial personality	0.89		(0.29, 4.63)

Reduction in Binge Drinking: 98 out of 201 subjects cut 30% or more

Table 3. (Continued)

Adjusted odds ratio95% confidence interval

Female	0.81		(0.40, 1.62)
Smoked in last 6 months	1.30		(0.68, 2.46)
Age: 18-30	**2.66**	**p< 0.01**	**(1.60, 4.41)**
31-50	0.48	p< 0.05	(0.24, 0.96)
51-80	0.78		(0.49, 1.24)
Depressed in last 30 days	1.55		(0.81, 2.98)
Experimental status	2.78	p< 0.01	(1.51, 5.13)
Child conduct disorder	0.37		(0.08, 1.66)
Adult antisocial personality	1.52		(0.36, 6.47)

ACKNOWLEDGMENTS

This work was supported by grant R21 AA11450 from the National Institutes of Health, National Institute on Alcohol Abuse and Alcoholism.

The authors would like to thank Margaret Murray, MSW, from the National Institute on Alcohol Abuse and Alcoholism, and the 20 primary care physicians who participated in the trial.

REFERENCES

American Psychiatric Association. Diagnostic and statistical manual of mental disorders, third edition, revised. Washington, DC: American Psychiatric Association, 1987..

Anderson P, Scott E. The effect of general practitioners' advice to heavy drinking men. Br J Addiction. 1992;87:891-900, 1992.

Babor TF. Brief intervention strategies for harmful drinkers: new directions for medical education. *Can Med Assoc J.* 1990;143(10):1070-6.

Bien TH, Miller WR, Tonigan JS. Brief interventions for alcohol problems: a review. *Addiction.* 1993;88:315-35.

Del Boca FK and Darkes J. The validity of self-reports of alcohol consumption: state of the science and challenges for research. Addiction. 2003;98 Suppl 2:1-12.

Del Boca FK and Noll JA. Truth or consequences: the validity of self-report data in health services research on addictions. Addiction. 2000;95 Suppl 3:S347-60.

Ewing JA. Detecting alcoholism: the CAGE questionnaire. *JAMA.* 1984; 252:1905-7.

Fleming MF, Barry KL, Manwell LB, Johnson K, London R. Brief physician advice for problem alcohol drinkers: a randomized controlled trial in community-based primary care practices. JAMA. 1997;277(13):1039-1045.

Fleming MF, Manwell LB, Barry KL, Adams W, Stauffacher EA. Brief physician advice for alcohol problems in older adults: a randomized community-based trial. J Fam Pract. 1999;48(5):378-384.

Fleming MF, Manwell LB. Brief intervention in primary care settings: a primary treatment method for at-risk, problem, and dependent drinkers. Alcohol Res Health. 1999;23(2):129-137.

Gentilello LM, Rivara FP, Donovan DM, Jurkovich DJ, Daranciang E, Dunn CW, Villaveces A, Copass M, Ries RR. Alcohol interventions in a trauma center as a means of reducing the risk of injury recurrence. *Ann Surg.* 230(4):473-80, 1999.

Gutjahr E, Gmel G, Rehm J. Relation between average alcohol consumption and disease: an overview. *Eur Addict Res.* 7(3):117-27, 2001.

Harwood, H. *Updating Estimates of the Economic Costs of Alcohol Abuse in the United States: Estimates, Update Methods, and Data.* Report prepared by The Lewin Group for the National Institute on Alcohol Abuse and Alcoholism, 2000. Based on estimates, analyses, and data reported in Harwood, H.; Fountain, D.; and Livermore, G. *The Economic Costs of Alcohol and Drug Abuse in the United States 1992.* Report prepared for the National Institute on Drug Abuse and the National Institute on Alcohol Abuse and Alcoholism, National Institutes of Health, Department of Health and Human Services. NIH Publication No. 98-4327. Rockville, MD: National Institutes of Health, 1998.

Heather N, Campion PD, Neville RG, MacCabe D. Evaluation of a controlled drinking minimal intervention for problem drinkers in general practice (the DRAMS scheme). *J R Coll Gen Pract.* 1987;37(301):358-63.

Holder HD, Blose JO. The reduction of health care costs associated with alcoholism treatment: a 14-year longitudinal study. *J Stud Alcohol.* 1992;53(4):293-302.

Institute of Medicine, Committee to Study Fetal Alcohol Syndrome. *Fetal Alcohol Syndrome: Diagnosis, Epidemiology, Prevention, and Treatment*, K Stratton, C Howe, F Battaglia (eds.). Washington, DC: National Academy Press, 1996.

Kahan M, Wilson L. Becker L. Effectiveness of physician-based interventions with problem drinkers: a review. *Can Med Assoc J.* 1995;152(6):851-859.

Manwell LB, Fleming MF, Mundt MP, Stauffacher EA, Barry KL. Treatment of problem alcohol use in women of childbearing age: results of a brief intervention trial. *Alcohol Clin Exp Res.* 2000;24:1517-1524.

Manwell LB, Ignaczak M, Czabala, JC. Prevalence of tobacco and alcohol use disorders in Polish primary care settings. *Euro J Public Health.* 2002:12:139-144.

Mellibruda J. Alcohol related problems in Poland. The Globe Magazine, 1999.

Miller WR. Techniques to modify hazardous drinking patterns. *Recent Dev Alcohol.* 1987;5:425-38.

Murray M, Fleming MF. Prevention and treatment of alcohol-related problems: an international medical education model. *Acad Med.* 1996;71:1204-1210.

Nilssen O. The Tromso Study: identification of and a controlled intervention on a population of early-stage risk drinkers. Prevent Med, 1991;20:518-28.

Ockene JK, Adams A, Hurley TG, Wheeler EV, Hebert JR. Brief physician- and nurse practitioner-delivered counseling for high risk drinkers: does it work? *Arch Int Med.* 1999;159:2198-205.

Ostaszewski K, Fleming M, Murray M, Modrzejewska G. Evalution of training courses for family physicians in prevention and treatment of alcohol-related problems. *Alkoholizm i Narkomania.* 2000;13(2):269-287.

Richmond R, Heather N, Wodak A, Kehoe L, Webster I. Controlled evaluation of a general practice-based brief intervention for excessive drinking. Addiction. 1995;90:119-32.

Ridolfo B, Stevenson C. *The Quantification of Drug-caused Mortality and Morbidity in Australia, 1998.* Canberra: Australian Institute of Health and Welfare, 2001. AIHW cat no PHE 29.

Single E, Rehm J, Robson L, Van Truong M. The relative risks and etiologic fractions of different causes of death and disease attributable to alcohol, tobacco and illicit drug use in Canada. *CMAJ.* 162(12): 1669-1675, 2000.

Sobell LC, Sobell MB. Timeline follow-back: a technique for assessing self-reported alcohol consumption. In: Litten R and Allen J, eds. *Measuring Alcohol Consumption.* Totowa, NJ: Humana Press, 1992: pp. 41-72.

State Agency for the Prevention of Alcohol-Related Problems. *The National Program for Prevention of Alcohol-Related Problems: Goals and Action Plan for the Years 2000-2005.* http://www.parpa.pl/parpaeng/?action=boxandid=2

US Department of Health and Human Services. *Eighth Special Report to the US Congress on Alcohol and Health from the Secretary of Health and Human Services, September 1993.* Washington, DC: DHHS, Public Health Service, National Institutes of Health, National Institute on Alcohol Abuse and Alcoholism, 1993: ADM-281-91-0003.

Wallace P, Cutler S, Haines A. Randomized controlled trial of general practitioner intervention in patients with excessive alcohol consumption. *BMJ.* 1988;297(6649):663-8.

Wilk AI, Jensen NM, Havighurst TC. Meta-analysis of randomized control trials addressing brief interventions in heavy alcohol drinkers. *J Gen Intern Med.* 1997;12:274-283.

In: Binge Drinking Research Progress
Editor: Kevin I. DiGuarde

ISBN 978-1-60692-065
© 2009 Nova Science Publishers, Inc.

Chapter 3

THE ROLE OF UNDERGRADUATE ROMANTIC PARTNERS' DRINKING AND BINGE DRINKING IN RELATIONSHIP QUALITY AND ALCOHOL-RELATED PROBLEMS*

Jacquelyn D. Wiersma, Judith L. Fischer and Jacki Fitzpatrick
Texas Tech University
Department of Human Development and Family Studies

ABSTRACT

Even though the majority of students drink alcohol, and many drink excessively [Wechsler, Davenport, Dowdall, Moeykins, & Castillo, 1994], little research has focused on the romantic context of college drinking and binge drinking. Heavy drinking (including binge drinking) is associated with many individual (e.g., legal) problems, but it could also be associated with romantic problems. Relationship quality might not simply be affected by individual drinking, but rather by the compatibility of partners' drinking habits. The present study examined congruent/discrepant patterns (as perceived by one partner) in unmarried romantic couples. Respondents (50 female, 42 male undergraduates) completed daily diary records on self and partners' drinking behaviors for 10 days. In addition, respondents completed a questionnaire to assess relationship satisfaction, commitment, alcohol-related problems, and alcohol abuse. Three methods were used to examine discrepancy and congruence in drinking: (1) a cluster analysis of drinking frequency and quantity, (2) absolute difference scores on frequency and quantity, and (3) absolute difference scores on number of binge drinking episodes. Consistent with Roberts and Leonard [1998], this chapter identified five different drinking clusters. Greater differences in binge drinking episodes were related to lower relationship quality (e.g., less commitment). In addition, greater differences in binge drinking were associated with more alcohol-related problems. Given the severity of potential drinking consequences for both

* This research was supported, in part, by Texas Tech University's Multidisciplinary Seed Grant Program awarded to Judith Fischer, Jacki Fitzpatrick and John Morrow. Correspondence regarding this paper should be sent to: Jacquelyn D. Wiersma, Texas Tech University, Dept. of Human Development and Family Studies, P.O. Box 41162, Lubbock, TX 79409-1162, email: jackie.wiersma@ttu.edu. A poster version of this paper was presented at the National Council on Family Relations' Annual Conference in November, 2006.

individuals and relationships, differences in partner drinking patterns merit more empirical attention.

Keywords: alcohol; binge drinking; compatibility theory; relationship quality; romantic partners

INTRODUCTION

Late adolescent and young adult individuals have considerable freedom to choose their relationship partners and engage in risky behaviors, such as excessive alcohol consumption [Bingham & Shope, 2004]. Despite the many studies conducted on adolescent alcohol use [Mason & Windle, 2002] and young adult alcohol use, there is still insufficient attention given to some aspects of drinking behaviors and attitudes. One aspect that requires more attention is the social context of drinking behaviors. For example, adolescent drinking behaviors vary in the presence of nuclear family members, extended family members or peers [Stewart & Power, 2003], such that specific relationships differentially affect drinking choices. During late adolescence and young adulthood, an important social context is the romantic relationship [e.g., Gilmartin, 2005]. The quality of the romantic relationship is affected by drinking behaviors [Fischer, Fitzpatrick, & Cleveland, 2007] and the congruence (or discrepancy) of couple drinking patterns [Roberts & Leonard, 1998]. In the present chapter, we describe how discrepant and congruent drinking patterns (as perceived by one partner in a romantic relationship) are associated with romantic quality and alcohol-related issues.

College Drinking Behaviors

There has been much research on drinking behaviors among college students, which has revealed that the majority of college students drink alcohol [Wechsler, Davenport, Dowdall, Moeykens, & Castillo, 1994; Wechsler, Lee, Kuo, & Lee, 2000]. It is true that some undergraduates drink in moderation, however many students engage in heavy drinking or binge drinking. Whether it is called heavy episodic drinking [c.f., Dawson, Grant, Stinson, 2004] or binge drinking, the behavior described includes high levels of alcohol intake in a single drinking episode. Binge drinking is defined as four or more consecutive drinks for women, and five or more consecutive drinks for men [Wechsler, Dowdall, Maener, Gledhill-Hoyt, & Lee, 1998; Wechsler & Nelson, 2001]. Approximately half of college students report binge drinking at least once in a 10-14 day period [Fischer, Fitzpatrick, Cleveland, Lee, McKnight, & Miller, 2005; Wechsler & Nelson, 2001; Wechsler et al., 2000]. According to Wechsler et al. [1994], binge drinking is connected to alcohol-related problems, such as trouble with the police, academic difficulties, driving under the influence of alcohol, injuries and even death [Wechsler & Austin, 1998; Wechsler & Isaac, 1992; Wechsler et al., 2000]. As well, repeated binge drinking may constitute levels of misuse that can be described as abuse. Misuse is not limited to binge drinking, but can include other drinking patterns. According to Fischer and Lyness [2005], alcohol abuse is evidenced by a great deal of time dedicated to alcohol intake, serious problems tied to intake, and unsuccessful efforts to cease or control intake. Alcohol abuse is reflected in work, legal and family problems, as well as others' perceptions of a drinking problem. In addition to alcohol-related problems and alcohol abuse, individual binge drinking behaviors and couple drinking patterns can impact romantic relationships. However, few studies have focused on the romantic context of college drinking.

Romantic Relationships

Romance is a central relationship in young adults' lives [Arnett, 2004; Gilmartin, 2005]. Given this centrality, it is important to examine behaviors that impact romantic interactions and quality. Repeated behaviors, such as binge drinking, are common to college students and likely to impact romance. For example, binges were associated with more romantic disagreements [Fischer et al., 2005] and excessive drinking was linked to lower romantic quality [Fischer et al., 2007]. These studies indicate that alcohol misuse is related to romantic interactions and outcomes. However, research has not considered differences in drinking patterns between dating romantic partners. Thus, it is unknown how partner's drinking compatibility (or lack of compatibility) affects romance.

Compatibility Theory and Drinking Partnerships

Compatibility theory provides a useful framework for understanding how couples match on key characteristics. According to compatibility theory, matching on similar interests increases the likelihood that couples will establish a mutually satisfying partnership. Similarity is the tendency for two individuals to be alike at one moment in time [Gonzaga, Compos, & Bradbury, 2007]. Similarity predicts initial attraction [Klohnen & Luo, 2003], and perceived similarity is related to increased feelings of being understood [Murray, Holmes, Bellavia, Griffin, & Dolderman, 2002]. Individuals who are more similar to their partners in personality traits and values are more satisfied than dissimilar individuals [Acitelli, Kenny, & Weiner, 2001; Gaunt, 2006; Gonzaga et al., 2007; Wilson & Cousins, 2003]. Couple similarity also provides reward value to the partners, in the form of validation and approval [Houts, Robins, & Huston, 1996]. Compatible, or similar, couples who share mutual interests may experience more love, positivity, commitment [Houts et al., 1996], satisfaction, intimacy, and relationship longevity [Acitelli et al., 2001]. Thus, compatibility between romantic partners predicts relationship quality.

Given the frequency and breadth of partner interactions, it makes sense that romantic quality is affected by more than personality or values. Research has indicated that the nature of partner behaviors and the compatibility (or incompatibility) of such behaviors impact relationship dynamics [e.g., Noller & White, 1990]. Similar couples, for example, experience less conflict and more commitment to one another. In contrast, dissimilar couples experience more conflict, negativity and ambivalence about the relationship [Houts et al., 1996]. Partners who are compatible engage more frequently in leisure activities together [Houts et al., 1996], which may include drinking. This premise supports Leadley, Clark and Caetano [2000]'s study of cohabiting and married couples, in which they found that discrepant couple drinking was positively related to partnership distress. The impact of congruency/discrepancy should be evident as well in dating couple drinking patterns (e.g., partnerships).

Roberts and Leonard [1998] defined a "drinking partnership" as the drinking levels and contexts that are patterned within couples. They identified five types of clusters for marital couples' drinking partnerships based on (a) the quantity and frequency of alcohol intake, (b) the drinking context (location), and (c) the match between husbands and wives' drinking levels. Two clusters consisted of congruent drinking couples with compatible, light, and infrequent drinking styles; the clusters differed by drinking location. The most discrepant levels of drinking, in which husbands drank heavily and separately from their wives, characterized a third cluster. A fourth cluster was identified by couples who had higher levels of alcohol intake. The fifth cluster was characterized by very frequent alcohol intake.

The cluster approach can be applied to unmarried romantic relationships among college students. Similar to married couples, college couples may be compatible or incompatible in the quantity, location and frequency of alcohol consumption. Given that drinking compatibility was related to qualities (e.g., satisfaction, commitment) of marital relationships [Roberts & Leonard, 1998], it is expected that drinking compatibility will be an important issue for unmarried romantic partners as well.

Although research on drinking often focuses on negative aspects, both positive and negative consequences accrue to individuals and relationship partners who consume alcohol [e.g., Bingham & Shope, 2004]. If there is a primacy to compatibility, then couples who drink congruently (in frequency and quantity) should have higher relationship quality than couples who drink discrepantly. Spouses report higher marital satisfaction when both partners drink alcohol in the same frequency and quantity [Homish & Leonard, 2007; Leonard & Roberts, 1996].

In contrast, discrepant drinking patterns have been associated with less satisfaction and more conflict [Homish & Leonard, 2007; Mudar, Leonard, & Soltysinski, 2001]. In a study of first-year marriages, couples with discrepant drinking patterns were less satisfied than congruent couples, even if those in congruent patterns indicated heavy consumption [Mudar et al., 2001]. It may be that discrepancies in drinking consumption and frequency form the basis for greater conflicts that contribute to decreased relationship satisfaction and commitment. Indeed, differences in partner alcohol consumption should constitute a risk for greater partner dissatisfaction [Kurdek, 1993]. Similar to married couples [Roberts & Leonard, 1998], compatibility or discrepancy in alcohol consumption is expected to be associated with dating couples' romantic quality. In addition to romantic problems, discrepant drinking patterns could be associated with more alcohol-related problems [Birch, Stewart, & Brown, 2007; Cooper, Frone, Russell, & Mudar, 1995]. Compared to congruent light drinking couples, more alcohol-related problems should be seen in discrepantly drinking couples and congruent heavy drinking couples. Alcohol-related issues include alcohol abuse and a range of difficulties that stem from excessive alcohol use (e.g., legal problems).

THE PRESENT STUDY AND HYPOTHESES

Drinking partnerships have been examined in married couples [Roberts & Leonard, 1998], but have received less attention among dating individuals. Given that college romantic and alcohol-use experiences are formative life choices, the intersection of such experiences is consequential. This study extends Roberts and Leonard's [1998] research on married couples by examining the patterns of association among relationship quality, alcohol-related problems and romantic drinking partnerships. In addition to employing Roberts and Leonard's cluster approach, this chapter also introduces absolute difference scores to measure drinking partnerships. Three methods were used to examine discrepancy and congruence in drinking: (1) a cluster analysis of drinking frequency and quantity, (2) absolute difference scores on frequency and quantity, and (3) absolute difference scores on number of binge drinking episodes.

The conceptualization and measurement of congruency/discrepancy are important issues. In order to enhance clarity in our chapter, this study uses the term "discrepancy" or "discrepant" with respect to clusters of drinking partnerships. The term "difference" is used to identify magnitude of difference between partners on frequency, quantity, and binge drinking. One approach to identifying drinking discrepancies is the use of a difference score between the participant and the partner on drinking quantity and frequency. This approach has the advantage of simplicity because it captures the magnitude of differences. However, it does not take into account the joint effects of quantity and frequency.

In contrast, a measure of difference in the number of binge episodes in a particular time frame has the advantage of combining quantity and frequency into one item. However, it does not capture the range of congruence and discrepancy seen in the cluster approach of Roberts and Leonard [1998]. A possible disadvantage of the cluster approach is small group membership (if participants are distributed unequally across clusters). By contrast, an advantage of the other two approaches (magnitude of difference scores) is that the full sample, rather than comparison of subgroups, is used for each statistical test. This chapter employs all three approaches to investigate the role of compatibility in dating couples' alcohol consumption. As such, this research generates clusters in the same manner as Roberts and Leonard to determine if similar clusters are found among dating couples. As data were gathered from only one respondent in each romantic couple, we also assess whether such an approach provides results comparable to Roberts and Leonard's two-respondent method.

The following hypotheses were tested, which focus on romantic quality factors:

(1) Participants in discrepant drinking clusters will report less romantic satisfaction and commitment than participants in congruent drinking clusters.
(2) The magnitude of participant-partner differences in drinking frequency and quantity will be negatively related to relationship quality.
(3) The magnitude of participant-partner difference in number of binge drinking episodes will be negatively related to relationship quality.

Of concern are the alcohol issues associated with discrepant couple drinking patterns. There is empirical support that individual heavy drinking is associated with consequences, such as alcohol problems and abuse [e.g., Wechsler & Austin, 1998]. Yet, potential associations between alcohol consequences and cluster memberships or differences in partner drinking remain unexplored. Such associations matter because they would reveal that the impact of couples' drinking patterns extends beyond the romantic (e.g., relationship satisfaction) domain. Rather, the associations would suggest that the nature of drinking and binge drinking among romantic partners has more pervasive life consequences (e.g., legal, medical, academic, social network). Thus, the present study addresses the gap in prior research by exploring these issues. More specifically, this study addressed the following research questions:

(1) Do participants in compatible (low frequency/quantity) drinking clusters experience fewer alcohol-related problems and alcohol abuse than participants in other (discrepant, heavy, and/or frequent) clusters?

(2) Are the magnitudes of participant-partner differences in drinking frequency and quantity associated with alcohol-related problems and alcohol abuse?

(3) Is the magnitude of participant-partner difference in number of binge drinking episodes associated with alcohol problems and alcohol abuse?

(4) To what extent do the drinking partnership clusters differ in the rate of binge drinking?

METHOD

Participants and Procedures

This IRB-approved study included 92 undergraduates (50 females, 42 males) from a large southwestern university. In order to participate in the study, the participants had to (a) be involved currently in unmarried romantic relationships and (b) have consumed at least one alcoholic beverage during the 10-day period of the study. The majority of respondents were Anglo/Caucasian American (78%) and Christian (76%). Mean participant age was 20 years (SD=1.36; Range: 18-23). Seventy-two percent were in a steady dating relationship and 68% had been with the partner for seven or more months.

The respondents completed a questionnaire packet and were taught how to complete the daily diary records. Throughout the school year, participants began diaries on a Friday and completed the records for a 10-day period. The participants were instructed to record all of their own drinking behaviors each day (with or without their romantic partners). When they drank with their romantic partners, individuals reported the partners' total number of drinks. Thus, only one individual within the romantic partnership reported the couple's drinking behaviors in this study. Diaries were returned every three days and small incentives (e.g., coupons for free food at local restaurants) were awarded for their participation.

Measures

In this study, the dependent variables were (a) relationship satisfaction, (b) relationship commitment, (c) alcohol-related problems, and (d) alcohol abuse. The independent variables were (a) differences in drinking frequency and quantity, (b) difference in binge drinking, and (c) drinking partnerships clusters (based on congruency versus discrepancy). All item correlations, means, and standard deviations can be found in Table 1.

Relationship satisfaction and commitment. Satisfaction was assessed with a seven-item satisfaction scale [Hendrick, 1988]. Respondents indicated on a nine-point Likert scale (0=

"Not at all", 8= "Very much") the depth of emotion they experienced in reference to each question (e.g., "In general, how satisfied are you with your relationship?"). Relationship satisfaction scores ranged 22-63 (M=51.00, SD=10.31). Commitment was measured by a seven-item subscale from Sternberg's tripartite love scale [Sternberg, 1988]. Respondents utilized the same nine-point Likert scale to respond to the items (e.g., "I am committed to maintaining my relationship with my partner"). Relationship commitment ranged 8-63 (M=49.22, SD=13.83). Each scale was internally consistent (Cronbach's alpha=.90 and .95, respectively).

Alcohol-related problems. The problems resulting from alcohol consumption in the last 12 months were measured with a list of serious alcohol incidents [Wechsler, Lee, Kuo, & Lee, 2000]. Students utilized a three-point Likert scale (0="Not applicable", 1="Once", 2= "Multiple times") to report the frequency of 12 consequences of their own drinking (e.g., academic difficulties, physical/sexual violence, alcohol overdose). Frequencies were summed to create an index of negative consequences, which ranged 0-21 (M=8.26, SD=6.01). The scale was internally consistent (Cronbach's alpha=.87).

Alcohol abuse. To assess abuse, participants completed the short form of the Michigan Alcoholism Screening Test (SMAST; [Selzer, Vinokur, & van Rooijen, 1975]). The SMAST is a 13-item indicator of alcohol abuse that has 90% sensitivity for identifying alcoholism (e.g., "Do your parents, boyfriend, girlfriend, husband, wife, or other near relatives ever worry or complain about your alcohol use?"; "Are you able to stop drinking alcohol when you want to?" *reverse scored*). For each item, participants indicated whether they had alcohol consumption problems (0="No", 1="Yes"). When summed, the scores ranged 0-10 (M=1.57, SD=2.27). These continuous scores were used in the analyses. Approximately 59% of the participants had a score greater than 1, indicating possible or probable abusive drinking. The scale was internally consistent (Cronbach's alpha=.80).

Alcohol frequency and quantity. Daily diaries were used to assess own frequency and quantity of alcohol consumption by asking participants (a) whether they drank that day and (b) how many drinks were consumed (e.g., "Did you have any alcoholic drinks today?" and "Total number of drinks"). A "drink" was defined as 12 ounces of beer, six-eight ounces of wine, or a shot of hard liquor. Quantity of alcohol consumption was measured by averaging the total number of drinks per day (when drinking occurred) in the 10-day diary period (Daily Mean= 4.01 drinks, SD=2.56, Range=1-14). Frequency was measured by the reported number of days participants consumed alcohol (Mean=2.91 days, SD=2.09, Range=1-10).

Participants also reported on their partners' alcohol consumption and frequency (e.g., "Was romantic partner drinking?" and "Total number of drinks"). Quantity of alcohol consumption for partners was averaged for each day (when drinking occurred) over the 10 days (Daily M=4.51 drinks, SD=2.55, Range=1-13). Partners' reported frequency ranged 0-8 days in the 10-day period (M=1.72, SD=1.81). In order to test hypothesis 2, absolute difference scores were computed for participant-partner quantity and frequency.

Table 1. Bivariate correlations among dependent and independent variables

	1	2	3	4	5	6	7	8	9	10
1. Relationship satisfaction		.87***	-.19	-.28**	-.02	.12	-.35***	-.07	-.21*	.05
2. Relationship commitment			-.25*	-.25*	-.04	.14	-.42***	-.05	-.21*	.05
3. Alcohol-related problems				.49***	.49***	.38***	.50***	.26	.58***	.37***
4. Alcohol abuse					.48***	.40***	.31**	.02	.55***	.38***
5. Participant frequency						.74***	.30**	.22	.88***	.71***
6. Partner frequency							.27**	.18	.68***	.81***
7. Participant quantity								.31*	.57***	.29***
8. Partner quantity									.32*	.43**
9. Participant binge drinking										.72***
10. Partner binge drinking										
Mean	51.00	49.23	8.26	1.57	2.91	1.72	4.01	4.51	1.83	.74
SD	10.31	13.83	6.01	2.27	2.09	1.81	2.56	2.55	2.04	1.31
Range	22-63	8-63	0-21	0-10	1-10	0-8	1-14.20	1-13	0-8	0-5

*$p < .05$, **$p < .01$, ***$p < .001$

Binge drinking. Daily diaries were used to assess binge drinking by asking participants how many drinks were consumed (e.g., "Total number of drinks") each day. Binge drinking was measured by summing the total number of drinks per day in the 10-day diary period and identifying a binge drinking episode if females had 4 or more drinks and males had 5 or more drinks per day. Participants also reported the partners' total number of drinks. Sixty-four percent reported that they had consumed five or more drinks in at least one sitting in the past two weeks. Number of binges in the 10-day period were summed (*M*=1.83 binge drinking episodes, *SD*=2.04, Range=0-8). Binge drinking for partners was calculated the same way over the 10 days (*M*=.74 binge drinking episodes, *SD*=1.31, Range=0-5). In order to test hypothesis 3, absolute difference scores were computed on participant-partner number of binge episodes.

Drinking partnership clusters. In order to test hypothesis 1, the study required identification of the drinking partnerships. Four variables to indicate drinking partnerships were used: (a) participants' drinking frequency; (b) partners' drinking frequency; (c) participants' mean quantity of alcohol consumed per occasion; and (d) partners' mean quantity of alcohol consumed. For comparison purposes, all variables were standardized.

A k-means iterative cluster analysis determined clusters. This procedure seeks to minimize within-cluster variance in the profile variables while maximizing differences between clusters. Paralleling the number of clusters found for married couples, the number of clusters was set to five. Cluster 1 (n=37, 40% of the sample) consisted of participants reporting compatible (e.g., similar), light and infrequent drinking styles with their partners. This group is termed the ***"light and infrequent"*** cluster. Cluster 2 (n=6, 7%) is described as ***"participant heavy and frequent"*** cluster because the participants had higher levels of alcohol consumption (frequency and quantity) than their partners. Cluster 3 (n=27, 29%) is named the ***"moderate"*** drinking cluster because the participants reported that both self and partner drinking was moderate in quantity and frequency. Cluster 4 (n=13, 14%) is called the ***"heavy"*** drinking cluster because participants reported compatible high quantities of drinking. Cluster 5 (n=9, 10%) is designated the ***"frequent"*** drinking cluster and is characterized by compatible high frequency of alcohol consumption.

A repeated measures multivariate analysis of variance revealed significant differences between groups and within groups. Scores on frequency and quantity differed across the five clusters (Wilk's Lambda = .142, *p* < .001), also seen in follow-up univariate tests. Regardless of clusters, participants and partners' reports of quantity and frequency were significantly different, (Wilk's Lambda = .192, *p* < .001), also seen in follow-up univariate tests. There was a significant overall interaction between cluster membership and quantity and frequency (Wilk's Lambda = .335, *p* < .001). In univariate follow-up tests, the interaction term for quantity was significant ($F(4,87) = 51.64, p < .001$).

Follow-up univariate analyses of variance with each of the quantity and frequency variables validated that cluster membership was significantly associated with the four drinking variables. The between cluster analyses indicated significant differences across clusters in (a) participants' quantity, (b) partners' quantity, (c) participants' frequency, and (d) partners' frequency. These results supported the validity of the clustering patterns (see Table 2). There were no significant differences in demographics (e.g., age, relationship length), which suggested that cluster differences were unrelated to such characteristics.

Table 2. Descriptive Statistics for Cluster Membership

Variable	1. Light & Infrequent	2. Participant Heavy & Frequent	Cluster Means (SD) 3. Moderate	4. Heavy	5. Frequent	F	η^2
	(n=37)	(n=6)	(n=27)	(n=13)	(n=9)		
Quantity of Alcohol							
Participant	2.24 abc	7.54 ade1	3.94 bdf2	7.88 cfg	3.63 eg	39.91*	.49
	(1.38)	(1.48)	(1.24)	(2.54)	(1.33)		
Partner	2.03 abc	5.56 ad1	5.34 be2	9.36 cdef	3.49 f	19.48*	.65
	(1.18)	(1.62)	(1.55)	(3.15)	(1.16)		
Frequency of Alcohol Use							
Participant	1.70 abc3	6.00 ad4	2.56 de5	3.08 bf6	6.67 cef	33.89*	.63
	(1.10)	(1.41)	(1.19)	(1.55)	(2.12)		
Partner	.65 ab3	3.83 ac4	1.70 cd5	1.62 e6	4.89 bde	25.03*	.51
	(.82)	(1.60)	(.99)	(1.85)	(2.09)		

Note: Means with matching superscripts in a row differ significantly at $p < .05$ by Neuman-Keuls test. Matching numbers in a column indicate participant/partner significant difference paired t-test.

*$p < .05$. * $p < .001$.

Because there was a significant between by within interaction, tests of partner-participant differences within clusters were calculated. (Although the interaction of cluster by participant-partner on frequency was not significant, within cluster comparisons on frequency provide a parallel to cluster comparisons on quantity. Given that both the between and within terms were significant for frequency, the within cluster differences should be interpreted as additive.) Of the ten sets of within-cluster comparisons of participant and partner on quantity and frequency, only four comparisons were not statistically different: Cluster 1 quantity ("light and infrequent"), Cluster 4 quantity ("heavy"), and Cluster 5 quantity and frequency ("frequent"). The only cluster congruent on both quantity and frequency is Cluster 5 ("frequent"). Two clusters were fully discrepant on quantity and frequency: Cluster 2 ("participant heavy and frequent") and Cluster 3 ("moderate"). Thus, there were two discrepant clusters (2 - "participant heavy and frequent", 3- "moderate") and three fully or partly congruent clusters (1-"light and infrequent", 4-"heavy", 5-"frequent"). Cluster membership, then, is determined by both partners' unique drinking patterns and is more than the sum of couple drinking behaviors.

An advantage of the cluster approach to discrepancy/congruence of drinking partnerships is the identification of patterns that may differ by consumption and frequency. It is important to note that less discrepant couples are not inherently indicative of low levels of alcohol consumption. Partnerships in which both individuals engage in high rates of consumption also have low discrepancy scores. In the present study, almost one third of participants had discrepant drinking styles from their partners. This finding contrasts with Roberts and Leonard's [1998] study, in which they found that only 17% of married couples drank discrepantly. The distributions across clusters in the two studies were significantly different ($\chi^2 = 20.33$, $p < .001$), with discrepant drinking styles occurring more frequently among college dating couples than the married couples. Although the partnerships were distributed differently across clusters in the two studies, the descriptions of clusters were very similar.

RESULTS

Relationship Qualities

Cluster membership. Hypothesis 1 predicted that participants in discrepant drinking clusters would report less romantic satisfaction and commitment than participants in congruent drinking clusters. Support for the hypothesis would be seen if scores for participants in discrepant drinking Cluster 2 ("participant heavy and frequent") and Cluster 3 ("moderate") were lower than participants in the congruent drinking clusters. A multivariate analysis of variance indicated overall significant differences across clusters (Wilk's Lambda = .83, $p < .05$); follow-up univariate F tests were calculated. Cluster means, univariate F tests, percentage of accounted variance, and Newman-Keuls tests of multiple mean comparisons are presented in Table 3. Commitment ($F(4,87) = 3.50$, $p < .05$, eta squared=.14) and satisfaction ($F(4,87) = 2.48$, $p < .05$, eta squared=.10) differed significantly across clusters. Commitment was higher for the "frequent" drinkers (Cluster 5; $M=59.11$), but lower for "heavy" drinkers (Cluster 4; $M=41.00$). Both of these are congruent clusters. Although the effect across clusters was significant for satisfaction, the multiple mean comparisons produced no pair-wise significant comparisons. Thus, the hypothesis that discrepant drinking clusters would be related to less satisfaction and commitment was not supported.

Participant-partner differences in quantity and frequency. Hypothesis 2 predicted that the magnitude of differences in drinking frequency and quantity will be negatively related to relationship quality. Greater difference scores in alcohol quantity were correlated with less commitment ($r(89) = -.37$, $p < .001$) and satisfaction ($r(89) = -.29$, $p < .01$). Also, greater difference scores in frequency were associated with less commitment ($r(89) = -.24$, $p < .05$). Thus, Hypothesis 2 was partially supported.

Participant-partner difference in binge drinking. Hypothesis 3 predicted that the magnitude of difference in number of binge drinking episodes would be related negatively to relationship quality. Greater participant-partner differences in binge episodes were correlated with less commitment ($r(92) = -.38$, $p < .001$) and less satisfaction ($r(92) = -.33$, $p < .001$). Thus, hypothesis 3 was fully supported.

Alcohol-Related Issues

Cluster membership. Cluster membership was based on congruency or discrepancy of participant and partner drinking patterns (i.e., quantity and frequency) within a 10-day time frame. Assessment of the extent to which such patterns are associated with alcohol-related issues will provide a more complete understanding of these drinking partnerships. Thus, we focused on the first research question ("Do participants in compatible (low frequency/quantity) drinking clusters experience fewer alcohol-related problems and alcohol abuse than participants in other (discrepant, heavy, and/or frequent) clusters?"). To address this question, a multivariate analysis of variance was conducted. The analysis indicated a significant between clusters effect (Wilk's Lambda = .62, $p < .001$). Follow-up univariate anovas (see Table 3) found significant differences across the five clusters in the participants' alcohol-related problems ($F(4,85) = 10.41$, $p < .001$, eta squared=.33) and participants' alcohol abuse ($F(4,87) = 5.88$, $p < .001$, eta squared=.21). Specifically, alcohol-related problems were higher for "participant heavy and frequent" discrepant drinkers (Cluster 2; M=15.83), "heavy" (Cluster 4; $M = 11.92$) and "frequent" drinkers (Cluster 5; $M = 11.78$) compared to the "light and infrequent" congruent drinkers (Cluster 1; M=4.77).

In comparison to "light and infrequent" congruent drinkers (Cluster 1; M=1.57), participants' alcohol abuse scores were higher for "participant heavy and frequent" discrepant drinkers (Cluster 2; M=3.17) and "frequent" congruent drinkers (Cluster 5; M=3.78). Alcohol abuse scores for the participants in the "heavy" cluster (Cluster 4; $M = 2.08$) did not differ significantly from those in the other clusters. Although the scores of the discrepant "moderate" cluster were not significantly different from those of the "light and infrequent" cluster, five of the eight comparisons revealed group differences. Respondents in the "participant heavy and frequent" discrepant cluster and congruent "frequent" cluster reported more alcohol problems than respondents in the congruent "light and infrequent" drinking cluster. Alcohol abuse was higher among members of the "participant heavy and frequent" discrepant clusters, members of the congruent "frequent" cluster, and members of the congruent "heavy" cluster than those in the "light and infrequent" cluster. Thus, we found that there were significant associations between cluster membership and alcohol-related issues and results provided an affirmative answer to the research question.

Table 3. Descriptive Statistics for Cluster Membership on Relationship Quality and Problems/Abuse/Binge

Variable	Cluster Means (SD)					F	η^2
	1. Light & Infrequent	2. Participant Heavy & Frequent	3. Moderate	4. Heavy	5. Frequent		
	(n=37)	(n=6)	(n=27)	(n=13)	(n=9)		
Relationship Commitment	51.32 (11.32)	40.17 (15.84)	49.04 (14.84)	41.00 [a] (15.68)	59.11 [a] (7.52)	3.50*	.14
Relationship Satisfaction	52.81 (8.38)	47.33 (7.76)	50.96 (11.22)	44.31 (11.83)	55.78 (10.63)	2.48*	.10
Alcohol-Related Problems	4.77 [abc] (4.96)	15.83 [ad] (2.56)	8.15 [d] (4.96)	11.92 [b] (5.69)	11.78 [c] (5.70)	10.41**	.33
Alcohol Abuse	.57 [ab] (.93)	3.17 [a] (2.48)	1.59 (2.00)	2.08 (2.81)	3.78 [b] (3.67)	5.88**	.21
Binge Occasions							
Participant	.41 [abcd] (.72)	5.33 [aef] (1.63)	1.59 [begh] (1.28)	2.92 [cfg] (1.44)	4.44 [dh] (2.51)	32.98**	.60
Partner	.001 [abc] (.001)	2.67 [ade] (1.86)	.78 [bdf] (.93)	.69 [eg] (1.18)	2.44 [cfg] (1.94)	17.19**	.44

Note: Means with matching superscripts differ significantly at $p < .05$ by Neuman-Keuls test.

* $p < .05$ ** $p < .001$

Participant-partner differences in quantity and frequency. The second research question focused on differences rather than cluster memberships ("Are the magnitudes of differences in participant-partner drinking frequency and quantity associated with alcohol-related problems and alcohol abuse?"). Correlations were calculated to address this research question. These calculations provide additional information over the cluster approach about how couple differences are related to alcohol problems and abuse. Drinking frequency differences were positively associated with alcohol-related problems ($r(88) = .23, p < .05$). Correlations between (a) quantity differences and alcohol-related problems, (b) quantity differences and alcohol abuse, and (c) frequency differences and alcohol abuse were not significant. Thus, we found very weak support for such an association.

Participant-partner difference in binge drinking. The analysis of binge drinking difference provides another avenue for understanding the association between couple drinking and alcohol-related issues. Thus, the third question ("Is the magnitude of participant-partner difference in number of binge drinking episodes associated with alcohol problems and alcohol abuse?") was explored. Binge drinking differences were positively associated with alcohol-related problems ($r(90) = .47, p < .001$) and alcohol abuse ($r(92) = .44, p < .001$). The association between binge drinking participant-partner difference and alcohol-related issues accounted for 22% (alcohol problems) and 19% (alcohol abuse) of the variance.

To learn more about binge drinking, we focused on the fourth research question ("To what extent do the drinking partnership clusters differ in the rate of binge drinking?"). In a repeated measures anova, participants' and partners' number of binge drinking occasions were significantly different across clusters ($F(4,87) = 33.42, p < .001$) and within clusters ($F(1,87) = 108.11, p < .001$). There was a significant interaction between cluster membership and participant/partner reports of binge drinking ($F(4,87) = 10.08, p < .001$). Follow up univariate tests were calculated on participants' binge drinking occasions ($F(4,87) = 32.98, p < .001$, eta squared=.60) and partners' binge drinking occasions ($F(4,87) = 17.19, p < .001$, eta squared=.44) and were significantly different across clusters. Table 3 indicates the results of comparisons made between and within clusters. With one exception, members of the congruent Cluster 1 ("light and infrequent") were significantly lower than members of all other clusters in binge drinking. Furthermore, there was more binge drinking in Cluster 2 (discrepant "participant heavy and frequent") and Cluster 5 (congruent "frequent") compared to Cluster 3 (discrepant "moderate") and Cluster 4 (congruent "heavy"). There was not a significant difference between Cluster 4 and Cluster 5 on binge drinking. Taken together, these findings suggest that cluster membership strongly differentiated among patterns of binge drinking.

CONCLUSION

This chapter assessed the extent to which discrepancy/congruency and differences in drinking were related to relationship qualities and alcohol-related issues. The present study also extended Roberts and Leonard's [1998] work on drinking partnerships to a new population of college students in romantic dating relationships. Consistent with Roberts and Leonard, a five-cluster model emerged that reflected both compatible and discrepant drinking partnerships. The discrepant clusters were not distinct from compatible clusters in romantic quality, but they were distinct in alcohol-related problems. When magnitude of participant-partner differences were examined, greater differences were associated with more alcohol-related issues (alcohol-related consequences, alcohol abuse) and less romantic quality (commitment, satisfaction). These findings are consistent with case studies of young adults who report drinking differences between themselves and nonmarried partners [e.g., Arnett, 2004].

Romantic Quality

In this chapter, the findings revealed that drinking partnerships among unmarried romantic partners were similar to those partnerships found in Roberts and Leonard's research on married couples. Although we expected college drinking partnerships to differ (based on drinking congruence or discrepancy) in romantic qualities (e.g., satisfaction), there was little support for this hypothesis. Indeed, there was an unexpected difference between two congruent clusters, with frequent drinkers reporting more commitment than heavy drinkers. In Roberts and Leonard's [1998] study, married couples with frequent drinking also had higher relationship quality scores. Perhaps these frequently drinking couples (both dating and married) have so integrated drinking into their lives that it does not compromise their relationship functioning. Based on compatibility theory, the partner's similarity in drinking behaviors might serve as a relational bond. Crawford, Houts, Huston, and George [2002] suggest that similarity between couples results in a greater likelihood that couples will engage in activities and spend more time together, which leads to greater satisfaction. If frequent drinking is a primary (and enjoyable) social interaction, then such couples might make positive evaluations of the relationship. As a result of this compatibility, these couples might be more motivated to continue their relationship. Given the cross-sectional design of this study, the long-term consequences of frequent drinking are not known. However, Homish and Leonard's [2007] longitudinal study determined that discrepant drinking partnerships were associated with decreased marital quality over time.

With respect to the difference score method, the magnitude of participant-partner difference in alcohol quantity was associated with less relationship commitment and satisfaction. The difference in alcohol frequency was associated with less commitment. These findings are consistent with Kelly and Halford [2006], who reported that the magnitude of difference between husbands and wives' alcohol consumption was negatively related to wives' marital satisfaction. Differences in binge episodes were also related to lower levels of satisfaction and commitment. As with research on drinking partnerships and dating, there has been little research on the associations between binge drinking and dating romantic relationships. Clapp and Shillington [2001] found that college students were less likely to binge drink on a date than in other relational contexts (e.g., with family or friends). Based on this finding, they argued that dating might be a protective factor that inhibits binge drinking. This contrasts with the current study, in which no such protective factor was evident. Clapp and Shillington did not specify the nature of the dating relationship, so their study could have captured binge drinking tendencies in first dates/early dates. The current study focused on individuals in established relationships (majority of relationships were seven or more months). Thus, individuals might inhibit their binge drinking during early relationship development, but reduce inhibition after they are comfortable in the relationship.

This premise is consistent with the impression management literature in relationship studies [e.g., Benz, Anderson, & Miller, 2005; Ellison, Heino & Gibbs, 2006]. Once impression management has ceased, then true binge drinking habits for both partners (and the magnitude of differences) might emerge.

Couple differences in drinking patterns may generate increased conflict, which is, in turn, related to lower satisfaction and commitment. Fischer et al. [2005] reported that more binge episodes were related to more conversational disagreements and disagreements about drinking. Relationship research highlights the difficult role of conflict management in relationships [cf., Campbell, Simpson, Boldry, & Kashy, 2005; Kline, Pleasant, Whitton, & Markman, 2006]. Compatibility theory also suggests that the reward value of a dissimilar partner is lower than a similar partner [Houts et al., 1996]. Thus, the less well matched the partners are in drinking, the more negative they might become in their relationship interactions. Differences in drinking could mean that the partner disapproves or fails to validate the other's choices. Such failure could weaken the couple bonds. It is possible that the association between binge drinking and alcohol problems is mediated by factors such as conflict and low reward value. Issues with drinking differences between partners that are related to alcohol problems and abuse could then be associated with decreased romantic quality over time [Homish & Leonard, 2007]. Wiesner and Windle's [2006] study illustrated that certain individuals who pursue pathways characterized by higher alcohol consumption may be at higher risk for poorer romantic outcomes. Using conflict and reward value as mediators would help to explain how these outcomes occurred.

Within romantic relationships, college students are exposed to social drinking that carries substantial contextual risks. Individuals who initially drink discrepantly and less than their partners might achieve compatibility (equal to their partners in quantity, frequency, or binges) over time. Such deepening compatibility may reflect a pervasive socialization influence for alcohol risky behaviors. Leonard and Mudar [2004] found that this type of compatibility emerged among newlyweds. In the first year of marriage, wives' increase in drinking matched husbands' earlier, higher drinking levels. It remains to be seen if individuals in dating relationships increase their drinking to match their partners' drinking levels. At the very least, romantic partners exert a strong form of peer socialization through which there are direct (e.g., encouragement to drink) and indirect (e.g., modeling of drinking) avenues of influence [Borsari & Carey, 2001].

Alcohol Problems/Abuse

We examined the associations between discrepant drinking and alcohol problems (i.e., arguments with friends, damaged property) and alcohol abuse (i.e., not able to stop drinking when want to stop). Using the cluster approach, participants in the "participant heavy", "heavy", and "frequent" clusters had more alcohol problems than individuals in the "light and infrequent" cluster. Alcohol abuse was also higher in the "participant heavy" and "frequent" clusters than in the "light and infrequent" cluster. It should be unsurprising that excessive and frequent drinking have implications for abuse. Although not all heavy drinkers will manifest symptoms of abuse, the potential is particularly strong among young adults. Indeed, Grant et al. [2004] reported that the highest rates of past-year alcohol abuse and dependence are found among 18-29 year old adults. Robbins and Bryan [2004] noted that there is a pragmatic effect of time – adolescents who survive risky behaviors (e.g., drinking, unprotected sex) gain the opportunity to repeat the behaviors and suffer additional consequences as they age. Over time, such problems could undermine the achievement of many important developmental tasks. In the college context, heavy drinking can sabotage academic achievement, romantic attachments, and later, developmentally appropriate transitions [White & Jackson, 2004/2005].

The magnitude of participant-partner difference in binge drinking provided strong support for associations between binge drinking incompatibility and alcohol problems/abuse. Taken together, heavy/binge and frequent drinking, as well as discrepant partner drinking, appear to be associated with alcohol-related issues. The results are consistent with prior research, which indicated that college binge drinkers have more school, relationship, employment and legal problems than nonbingers or nondrinkers [Sheffield, Darkes, del Boca, & Goldman, 2005]. Indeed, approximately 600,000 students were physically hurt by another drinking student in a single year [Hingson, Heeron, Zakocs, Kopstein, & Wechsler, 2002]. Such proximity to other drinkers appears to be sufficient to increase the risk of alcohol-related problems. In addition, the presence of romantic partners who drink (or binge drink) more frequently might complicate the risks. The relationship dynamics (e.g., intimacy, shared activities, friendly competition) could exacerbate drinking choices that are harmful to self and/or partners. This premise is consistent with college students' observations about the health risks (e.g., vomiting while sleeping) among romantic partners who binge drink together [Turrisi, Jaccard, Taki, Dunnam, & Grimes, 2001]. Thus, individuals in close romantic relationships may suffer disproportionately the effects of partners' drinking. The closeness that binds them also may lead to harm for one or both partners.

Although number of binge drinking occasions (i.e., heavy and frequent drinking) was associated with alcohol-related problems, quantity of alcohol consumption (in and of itself) was not related to such problems. Perhaps drinking quantity that is infrequent reflects more social drinking, or occurs in response to celebrations and parties. Thus, infrequent and heavy drinking occasions may be accompanied by few alcohol-related problems or abuse. However, when drinking is both heavy and frequent (as evidenced in number of binge drinking episodes), then alcohol-related problems are seen.

Limitations, Strengths and Future Directions

There were several limitations and strengths to the study. One limitation was that information was gathered from only one half of the couple. The respondents' partners did not have an opportunity to report their own drinking patterns or assessment of romantic qualities (e.g., satisfaction). Second, the participants' reports of partners' alcohol use was limited to episodes that occurred in the participants' presence. Thus, the degree of partner drinking that occurred in the absence of the participant (and the total quantity of partner drinking) was not known. If or when partners drank outside of the participants' presence, such drinking would not have been assessed by participants' reports. By failing to measure these occasions, this study may actually be underestimating the extent of dissimilarity in these young adults' drinking. Third, it is possible that participants overestimated self and/or partner drinking in response to social norms [Baer, 2002; Perkins, 2002; Perkins & Wechsler, 1996; Turrisi, 1999]. Fourth, there were uneven group sizes among the clusters and some clusters had small memberships. Although the clustering patterns accurately reflected the data, the numbers of participants within the clusters limited some data analysis options. The smaller subsamples in some clusters may be responsible for the apparently stronger results derived from difference score approaches. Finally, all data were collected within a single time frame (10 days), so causation cannot be determined.

The study's limitations are counterbalanced by its strengths. First, the use of daily records to measure alcohol consumption increased the likelihood of accurate recall. Second, this study identified clusters similar to married clusters [Roberts & Leonard, 1998], suggesting that there is validity to the cluster identifications (even when recorded by only one partner). Third, the research extended the study of cluster partnerships to a younger, unmarried sample. Fourth, this chapter examined the associations of cluster membership with romantic and alcohol-related factors. Fifth, the use of difference scores extended research on discrepant and congruent drinking partnerships. The magnitude of participant-partner difference on binge drinking was consistently related to less satisfaction, less commitment, more alcohol problems and more alcohol abuse. With respect to alcohol-related issues, it appeared that differences in quantity or frequency of drinking were not as important as differences in binge drinking. It would seem that a certain threshold of drinking consumption and frequency was required before drinking differences became related to alcohol issues.

The study of undergraduate drinking partnerships can be improved in several ways. First, collection of data by both romantic partners would provide more detailed information about alcohol consumption episodes. Second, the inclusion of both nonmarried romantic and married couples in the same study would allow a direct comparison of cluster membership by relationship status. Third, longitudinal research could identify long-term romantic intentions [e.g., Carroll, Willoughby, Badger, Nelson, Barry, & Madsen, 2007] and consequences of drinking partnerships. Fourth, a broader range of romantic factors (e.g., emotional support, intimacy) could be explored. Fifth, qualitative interviews would provide insiders' perspectives about relational and alcohol consumption dynamics [e.g., Eyre, Milbrath, & Peacock, 2007; Tilki, 2006]. The mechanisms by which discrepancies in couple drinking are associated with relationship and alcohol issues should be further explored, particularly with respect to the possible mediating roles of conflict and reward value. Such empirical enhancements will no doubt increase our understanding of the nexus of romance, alcohol use and alcohol-related problems in young adulthood.

In sum, several important empirical issues were raised by this study. Does the use of participant-only reports of own and partners' drinking replicate the cluster patterns of research based on two partners' responses? Yes, to a considerable degree, participants' view of the drinking partnerships is comparable to Roberts and Leonard's [1998] clusters based on married couples' responses. Differences between the studies were based on distribution of participants across clusters rather than the cluster characteristics themselves (e.g., heavy drinking, light drinking). The results on binge drinking revealed that the magnitude of participant-partner difference was associated with more problematic relationship and alcohol issues. However, the cluster approach provided additional information. For example, congruent heavy drinkers were less committed than congruent frequent drinkers. Congruent frequent drinkers reported more alcohol problems, binge drinking, and abuse than congruent light and infrequent drinkers. These congruent frequent drinkers may be more committed because of their congruence, but their frequent drinking may lead to a problematic future together. The heavy congruent drinkers are already facing difficulties (e.g., less commitment and more alcohol problems). Thus, our research questions, while strongly supported by the couple differences in the binge drinking analyses, recognized the need to take into account the additional information provided by the cluster approach.

The results of this study have implications for compatibility theory as well. Compatibility of frequent drinking behaviors was associated with greater romantic commitment. This is consistent with the argument that compatibility is not limited to similarity in broad factors (e.g., personality, values), but is evidenced in behaviors [e.g., Crawford et al., 2002]. Indeed, Duck [1990] suggested that couple identity can be defined by daily mundane behaviors. It might be valuable to expand the focus of compatibility to common couple interactions. In comparison to a focus on personality, a focus on behavioral patterns would increase the theory's value in describing the fluid nature of relationships. As noted previously, frequent drinkers might enjoy the compatibility of shared drinking, but their pleasure does not necessarily protect them from long-term risks. Thus, compatibility might not be inherently good and incompatibility (e.g., individual drinks less frequently than his/her partner) might be a healthier choice. The theory could be enhanced by exploring the costs or risks of compatibility.

This chapter provides a starting point for the examination of late adolescent/young adult drinking partnerships (and their consequences). Other than research by Roberts and Leonard [e.g., 1998] and Leadley et al. [2000], little empirical attention has been given to drinking partnerships. Thus, the present study addresses a significant gap in the alcohol literature. Above and beyond the levels of drinking, this chapter demonstrated that couple differences are related not just to romantic issues, but are also reflected in drinking consequences. By continuing to examine drinking partnerships of college students, researchers will identify a broader range of interpersonal consequences faced by undergraduate romantic couples. Expanding the scope of study beyond undergraduates to noncollege young adults would help to enhance understanding of this important developmental time period. If relationship partners cannot resolve the incompatibilities in their drinking patterns, then it is possible that they cannot resolve other relationship problems. Such incompatibility problems may have serious consequences (e.g., quality or longevity) for their relationships [e.g., Horowitz, 1999]. Given the potential severity of such consequences, effective interventions are needed for changing romantic partners' alcohol use behavior patterns.

REFERENCES

Acitelli, L. K., Kenny, D. A., & Weiner, D. (2001). The importance of similarity and understanding of partners' marital ideals to relationship satisfaction. *Personal Relationships, 8,* 167-185.

Arnett, J. J. (2004). *Emerging adulthood: The winding road from the late teens through the twenties.* Oxford, England: Oxford University Press.

Baer, J. S. (2002). Student factors: Understanding individual variation in college drinking. *Journal of Studies on Alcohol, 14,* 40-53.

Benz, J., Anderson, M., & Miller, R. (2005). Attributions of deception in dating situations. *Psychological Record, 55,* 305-314.

Bingham, C. R., & Shope, J. T. (2004). Adolescent problem behavior and problem driving in young adulthood. *Journal of Adolescent Research, 19,* 205-223.

Birch, C. D., Stewart, S. H., & Brown, C. G. (2007). Exploring differential patterns of situational risk for binge eating and heavy drinking. *Addictive Behaviors, 32,* 433-448.

Borsari, B., & Carey, K. B. (2001). Peer influences on college drinking: A review of the research. *Journal of Substance Abuse, 13,* 391-424.

Campbell, L., Simpson, J. A., Boldry, J., & Kashy, D. A. (2005). Perceptions of conflict and support in romantic relationships: The role of attachment anxiety. *Journal of Personality and Social Psychology, 88,* 510-531.

Carroll, J. S., Willoughby, B., Badger, S., Nelson, L. J., Barry, C., & Madsen, S. (2007). So close, yet so far away: The impact of varying marital horizons on emerging adulthood. *Journal of Adolescent Research, 22,* 219-247.

Clapp, J., & Shillington, A. (2001). Environmental predictors of heavy episodic drinking. *American Journal of Drug and Alcohol Abuse,* 27, 301-313.

Cooper, M. L., Frone, M. R., Russell, M., & Mudar, P. (1995). Drinking to regulate positive and negative emotions: A motivational model of alcohol use. *Journal of Personality and Social Psychology,* 69, 990–1005.

Crawford, D., Houts, R., Huston, T., & George, L. (2002). Compatibility, leisure, and satisfaction in marital relationships. Journal of Marriage and the Family, 64, 433-449.

Dawson, D. A., Grant, B. F., & Stinson, F. S. (2004). Another look at heavy episodic drinking and alcohol use disorders among college and noncollege youth. *Journal of Studies on Alcohol,* 65, 477-488.

Duck, S. (1990). Relationships as unfinished business: Out of the frying pan and into the 1990s. *Journal of Social and Personal Relationships,* 7, 5-28.

Ellison, N., Heino, R., & Gibbs, J. (2006). Managing impressions online: Self-presentation processes in the online dating environment. *Journal of Computer-Mediated Communication, 11,* 415-441.

Eyre, S. L., Milbrath, C., & Peacock, B. (2007). Romantic relationship trajectories of African American gay/bisexual adolescents. *Journal of Adolescent Research, 22,* 107-131.

Fischer, J. L., Fitzpatrick, J., & Cleveland, H. H. (2007). Linking family functioning to dating relationship quality via novelty-seeking and harm-avoidance personality pathways. *Journal of Social and Personal Relationships, 24,* 575-590.

Fischer, J. L., Fitzpatrick, J., Cleveland, B., Lee, J-M., McKnight, A., & Miller, B. (2005). Binge drinking in the context of romantic relationships. *Addictive Behaviors, 30,* 1496-1516.

Fischer, J. L., & Lyness, K. P. (2005). Families coping with alcohol and substance abuse. In P.S. McKenry, & S.J. Price (Eds.), *Families and change: Coping with stressful events and transitions* (3rd ed.) (pp. 155-178). Thousand Oaks, CA: Sage.

Gaunt, R. (2006). Couple similarity and marital satisfaction: Are similar spouses happier? *Journal of Personality, 74,* 1401-1420.

Gilmartin, S. K. (2005). The centrality and costs of heterosexual romantic love among first-year college women. *Journal of Higher Education, 76,* 609-633.

Gonzaga, G. C., Campos, B., & Bradbury, T. (2007). Similarity, convergence, and relationship satisfaction in dating and married couples. *Journal of Personality and Social Psychology, 93,* 34-48.

Grant, B., Dawson, D., Stinson, F., Chou, S. P., Dufour, M. C. & Pickering, R. P. (2004). The 12-month prevalence and trends in DSM-IV alcohol abuse and dependence: United States, 1991-1992 and 2001-2002. *Drug and Alcohol Dependence, 74,* 223-234.

Hendrick, S. (1988). A generic measure of relationship satisfaction. *Journal of Marriage and the Family, 50,* 93-98.

Hingson, R. W., Heeron, T., Zakocs, R. C., Kopstein, A., & Wechsler, H. (2002). Magnitude of alcohol-related mortality and morbidity among U. S. college students ages 18-24. *Journal of Studies on Alcohol, 63,* 136-144.

Homish, G. G., & Leonard, K. E. (2007). The drinking partnership and marital satisfaction: The longitudinal influence of discrepant drinking. *Journal of Consulting and Clinical Psychology, 75,* 43-51.

Horowitz, J. (1999). Negotiating couplehood: The process of resolving the December dilemma among interfaith couples. *Family Process, 38,* 303-323.

Houts, R. M., Robins, E., & Huston, T. L. (1996). Compatibility and the development of premarital relationships. *Journal of Marriage and the Family, 58,* 7-20.

Kelly, A., & Halford, W. (2006). Verbal and physical aggression in couples where the female partner is drinking heavily. *Journal of Family Violence, 21,* 11-17.

Kline, G. H., Pleasant, N. D., Whitton, S. W, & Markman, H. J. (2006). Understanding couple conflict. In A. Vangelisti, & D. Perlman (Eds.) *The Cambridge handbook of personal relationships* (pp. 445-462). NY: Cambridge University Press.

Klohnen, E. C., & Luo, S. (2003). Interpersonal attraction and personality: What is attractive-self similarity, ideal similarity, complementarity or attachment security? *Journal of Personality and Social Psychology, 85,* 709-722.

Kurdek, L. A. (1993). Predicting marital dissolution – A 5-year prospective longitudinal study of newlywed couples. *Journal of Personality and Social Psychology, 64,* 221-242.

Leadley, K., Clark, C. L., & Caetano, R. (2000). Couples' drinking patterns, intimate partner violence, and alcohol-related partnership problems. *Journal of Substance Abuse, 11,* 253-263.

Leonard, K. E., & Mudar, P. (2004). Husbands' influence on wives' drinking: Testing a relationship motivation model in the early years of marriage. *Psychology of Addictive Behaviors, 18,* 340-349.

Leonard, K. E., & Roberts, L. J. (1996). Alcohol in the early years of marriage. *Alcohol Health and Research World, 20,* 192-197.

Mason, W. A., & Windle, M. (2002). A longitudinal study of the effects of religiosity on adolescent alcohol use and alcohol-related problems. *Journal of Adolescent Research, 17,* 346-363.

Mudar, P., Leonard, K. E., & Soltysinski, K. (2001). Discrepant substance use and marital functioning in newlywed couples: A brief report. *Journal of Consulting and Clinical Psychology, 69,* 130-134.

Murray, S. L., Holmes, J. G., Bellavia, G., Griffin, D. W., & Dolderman, D. (2002). Kindred spirits? The benefits of egocentrism in close relationships. *Journal of Personality and Social Psychology, 82,* 563-581.

Noller, P., & White, A. (1990). The validity of the Communication Patterns Questionnaire. *Psychological Assessment, 2,* 478-482.

Perkins, H. W. (2002). Social norms and the prevention of alcohol misuse in collegiate contexts. *Journal of Studies on Alcohol Supplement 14,* 164-172.

Perkins, H. W., & Wechsler, H. (1996). Variation in perceived college drinking norms and its impact on alcohol abuse: A nationwide study. *Journal of Drug Issues, 26,* 961-974.

Robbins, R. N., & Bryan, A. (2004). Relationships between future orientation, impulsive sensation seeking, and risk behavior among adjudicated adolescents. *Journal of Adolescent Research, 19,* 428-445.

Roberts, L. J., & Leonard, K. E. (1998). An empirical typology of drinking partnerships and their relationship to marital functioning and drinking consequences. *Journal of Marriage and the Family, 60,* 515-526.

Selzer, M. L., Vinokur, A., & van Rooijen, L. (1975). A self-administered short version of the Michigan Alcoholism Screening Test (SMAST). *Journal of Studies on Alcohol, 43,* 117-126.

Sheffield, F., Darkes, J., del Boca, F., & Goldman M. (2005). Binge drinking and alcohol-related problems among community college students: Implications for prevention policy. *Journal of American College Health, 54,* 137-141.

Sternberg, R. (1988). Triangulating love. In R. Sternberg and M. Barnes (Eds.) *The psychology of love* (pp.119-138). New Haven, CT: Yale University Press.

Stewart, C., & Power, T. G. (2003). Ethnic, social class, and gender differences in adolescent drinking: Examining multiple aspects of consumption. *Journal of Adolescent Research, 18,* 575-598.

Tilki, M. (2006). The social contexts of drinking among Irish men in London. *Drugs: Education, Prevention and Policy, 13,* 247-261.

Turrisi, R. (1999). Cognitive and attitudinal factors in the analysis of alternatives to binge drinking. *Journal of Applied Social Psychology, 29,* 1510-1533.

Turrisi, R., Jaccard, J., Taki, R., Dunnam, H., & Grimes, J. (2001). Examination of the short-term efficacy of a parent intervention to reduce college student drinking tendencies. *Psychology of Addictive Behaviors, 15,* 366-372.

Wechsler, H., & Austin, S.B. (1998). Binge drinking: The five/four measure (letter). *Journal of Studies on Alcohol, 59,* 122-123.

Wechsler, H., & Isaac, N. (1992). "Binge" drinkers at Massachusetts colleges: prevalence, drinking styles, time trends, and associated problems. *The Journal of the American Medical Association, 267,* 2929-2931.

Wechsler, H., Davenport, A., Dowdall, G., Moeykens, B., & Castillo, S. (1994). Health and behavioral consequences of binge drinking in college: A national survey of students at 140 campuses. *Journal of the American Medical Association, 272,* 1672-1677.

Wechsler, H., Dowdall, G. W., Maener, G., Gledhill-Hoyt, J., & Lee, H. (1998). Changes in binge drinking and related problems among American college students between 1993 and 1997; results of the Harvard School of Public Health College Alcohol Study. *Journal of American College Health, 47,* 57-69.

Wechsler, H., Lee, J. E., Kuo, M., & Lee, H. (2000). College binge drinking in the 1990's - A continuing problem: Results of the Harvard School of Public Health 1999 College Alcohol Study. *Journal of American College Health, 48,* 199-210.

Wechsler, H., & Nelson, T.F. (2001). Binge drinking and the American college student: What's five drinks? *Psychology of Addictive Behaviors, 15,* 287-291.

White, H. R., & Jackson, K. (2004/2005). Social and psychological influences on emerging adult drinking behavior. *Alcohol Research and Health, 28,* 182-190.

Wiesner, M., & Windle, M. (2006). Young adult substance use and depression as a consequence of delinquency trajectories during middle adolescence. *Journal of Research on Adolescence, 16,* 239-264.

Wilson, G. D., & Cousins, J. M. (2003). Partner similarity and relationship satisfaction: Development of a compatibility quotient. *Sexual and Relationship Therapy, 18,* 161-170.

Reviewed by H. Harrington Cleveland, Ph.D., Department of Human Development and Family Studies, The Pennsylvania State University, University Park, PA.

In: Binge Drinking Research Progress
Editor: Kevin I. DiGuarde

Chapter 4

BINGE DRINKING IN ADOLESCENTS: RISK AND PROTECTIVE FACTORS

Lorena M Siquiera[1]* *and Lee A Crandall*[2]

¹Departments of Pediatrics, Miami Children's Hospital
²Professor-Department of Epidemiology and Public Health
University of Miami Miller School of Medicine

ABSTRACT

Alcohol use is associated with the leading causes of death and injury in adolescents (i.e. motor vehicle accidents, homicides and suicides). The purpose of the current study is to examine gender and ethnic differences in the risk and protective factors for binge drinking among Hispanic Florida youth utilizing the Florida Youth Substance Abuse Survey 2002. We used a subset of 10,690 Hispanic youth from the original sample of 62,934 students surveyed. Risk and protective factors were first examined in each of five domains, then altogether using logistic regression. Sixteen percent of these students admitted to having binged on one or more occasions in the two weeks prior to the survey and the frequency increased with grade level. Males were more likely to have binged (17% vs. 15%, p<.000). Mexican students were the most likely, Dominicans and Puerto Ricans were the least likely, while Central American and Cubans were intermediate in their frequency of binge drinking. Risk and protective factor analyses suggest that Hispanic youth who grow up in families with poor discipline and have parents with a favorable attitude towards ATOD use are likely to form favorable attitudes towards ATOD use themselves. Males who are sensation seekers and those with low resistance skills are at greater risk of initiating drug use early on, associating with and/or being influenced by friends who use drugs and being binge drinkers. The presence of risk factors in multiple domains endorses the need for a multi-pronged approach to prevention and intervention. Tailoring programs and activities to address risk and protective factors in sub-groups may be an important consideration when participants are homogenous in terms of gender and/or ethnicities.

---

* Correspondence should be addressed to Lorena Siqueira MD, MSPH, Director of Adolescent Medicine, Miami Children's Hospital, 3100 SW. 62ⁿᵈ Court, Ste #205, Miami, Fl 33155, USA. E-mail lorena.siqueira@mch.net

Alcohol is the substance most frequently used by children and adolescents in the United States and its use in youth is a worldwide problem though the extent of use and subsequent problems remain to be documented in many countries (1, 2). The concern with underage drinking has arisen because use of alcohol and other drugs is associated with the leading causes of death and injury in adolescents and young adults (i.e. motor vehicle accidents, homicides and suicides) (3). In 2003, 10.9 million adolescents ages 12 to 20 years reported drinking, with nearly 7.2 million defined as binge drinkers and 2.3 million considered heavy drinkers (4).

The term *binge* has historically been used by clinicians to refer to a prolonged period of excessive drinking in an alcoholic that lasts for days or weeks (5). The combination of prolonged use and the giving up of usual activities formed the core of the clinical definition of binge. Researchers conducting large scale epidemiologic studies have chosen to operationalize the term differently by defining it as the consumption of five or more alcoholic drinks in a row for males and four or more drinks in a row for females, at least once in the preceding two weeks. This term came into use and was popularized following the publication of the Harvard School of Public Health College Alcohol Study (6). Binge drinkers have on occasion been further characterized in some studies as frequent binge drinkers –those who engage in this behavior three or more times in the same period and occasional binge drinkers- those who drink this way less often. A quantitative definition of drinking was chosen because it was noted that binge drinkers engaged in unplanned sexual behavior, got hurt or injured, and experienced five or more alcohol-related problems more often than non-binge drinkers. Binge drinkers were also more likely to produce problems for those around them. Finally, this quantitative definition makes results comparable across studies.

Objections to the use of this term have been raised mainly because it does not take into account several factors known to mediate the effects of alcohol, it does not specify a time period within which the alcohol is consumed, neither does it factor in the drinker's body weight or drinking history. The focus is on the quantity consumed rather than the negative consequences of drinking. In addition, use of this definition will incorrectly imply that drinking below these levels is inherently safe and it is a crude measure for assessing change in alcohol problems (7).

Occasions of binge drinking are common. Among eighth graders in the United States this statistic stands at 12%, among tenth graders at 22%, among twelfth graders at 29%, and among college students at 40% (1). This behavior recedes somewhat after they enter their early 20s, reflected by the 36% rate found in the entire young adult sample and the 26% rate found among 29- to 30-year olds (1). While there may be a decline in binge drinking in young adulthood, the concern is that this behavior will persist into adulthood among some of these adolescents and also that there are serious consequences of this behavior during the high school years.

Adolescent heavy episodic or binge drinkers are more likely than non-binge drinkers to exhibit a wide range of problem behaviors including illicit drug use (8), dropping out of school (9), drunk driving (10), fighting and carrying a weapon (11). Further, adolescent binge drinking is one of the strongest predictors of binging through the college years (12).

Recent national surveys have assessed attitudes towards drinking among high school students (1). Weekend binge drinking is disapproved by fewer seniors (65%), despite the fact that many more seniors see a greater risk in weekend binge drinking (42%) than in having one or two drinks nearly every day (21%). Disapproval of alcohol use is also higher at the lower grade levels than among twelfth graders. For example, 65% of the twelfth graders said they disapprove of weekend binge drinking versus 72% of the tenth graders and 82% of the eighth graders. Over the last one to three years there has been some rise in all three grades in disapproval of weekend binge drinking, and use has begun to decline in this period. The great majority of these teens also see alcohol as readily available: 68% of the eighth graders, 85% of the tenth graders, and 95% of the twelfth graders said they could get it fairly easily or very easily.

CONCEPTUAL FRAMEWORK: RISK AND PROTECTIVE FACTORS

Rather than grounding research in a unitary theoretical approach or trying to establish a single specific cause, most intervention researchers use a risk and protective factor approach. The precursors of drug and alcohol use are termed *risk factors*. Taken together these factors increase one's vulnerability to substance use. The assumption is that there is no single cause of substance use or nonuse and that there are several pathways to individual initiation into use, progression and cessation of use. Programs that seek to prevent drug use utilize interventions that eliminate or reduce the effects of these precursors.

Protective factors are often conceptualized in two ways. The first is the absence of a risk factor. Thus, if being deviant is a risk factor, not being deviant may be considered to be a protective factor. Another approach is to consider them as conceptually distinct entities. Protective factors reduce the effects of risk factors either directly (linear effect) or through a more complex buffering process (interactive effects). Protective factors against adolescent substance use exist within the individual, family and community (13). Brook et al (14) defined two mechanisms by which protective factors may reduce the risk of drug use in adolescents. The first is a 'risk-protective' mechanism such as when the risk posed by drug-using peers is moderated by a strong attachment or bond between parent and adolescent and by parent conventionality. A second mechanism termed 'protective/protective' is when one protective factor potentiates the effect of another. For example, a strong bond between the father and the adolescent enhances the effects of other protective factors such as adolescent conventionality, positive maternal characteristics and marital harmony in preventing drug use. On a cautionary note, these risk and protective factors may not function equally well for adolescents of diverse ethnic groups and this needs further study.

Risk Factors for Alcohol Use

Longitudinal studies specifically focusing on adolescent binge drinking and its correlates are relatively few. Nonetheless, a number of risk factors for alcohol misuse have been identified that may be relevant to understanding the onset and course of binge drinking (13).

There is a substantial *gender* difference among high school seniors in the prevalence of occasions of heavy drinking (23% for females versus 34% for males in 2002), although this difference generally has been diminishing very gradually over time (1). In 1975 there was a 23% difference between genders versus an 11% difference in 2002. While the gap between *genders* in the rate of drinking is narrowing, less frequent and lighter drinking in women may reflect biologic differences. As women on average weigh less than men and have lower body water percentages they get higher blood alcohol levels than males for similar quantities of alcohol consumed (15). As a result they are more likely to develop complications from alcohol use earlier than men for similar patterns of drinking. Some gender related health consequences include an increased rate of breast cancer, complications during pregnancy and the risk of fetal alcohol syndrome in their offspring (16).

Studies of *ethnic* differences in alcohol use have been mainly conducted in adults. The patterns of alcohol use and the prevalence of alcohol-related problems vary among adults from different ethnic groups. Comparing gender differences by ethnic group it has been noted that among adult males, Hispanics consume larger quantities of alcohol more frequently than do whites or African-American and are more likely to experience alcohol related consequences (17). Among females, whites are more likely than Hispanics or African-American to drink and to do so heavily and report alcohol related problems but the gap may be narrowing (18, 19). Some of these patterns have been attributed to biologic differences in absorption and metabolism of alcohol that are probably genetically based. Asians for example, are more likely to have a specific variant of a gene (i.e. allele) and as a result they get unpleasant reactions to low levels of alcohol, consume less alcohol and have lower levels of alcoholism than other ethnic groups (20).

Heterogeneity in drinking patterns is also found among different nationalities within specific ethnic groups (21). Among subgroups of Hispanics, Puerto Rican and Mexican females drink more often and more heavily than Cubans or other Hispanics. Among adult males, frequent and heavy drinking is most prevalent among Mexican Americans and least prevalent for Cubans, with Puerto Ricans and other Hispanics falling in the middle (22). One study that evaluated differences in drinking patterns by the major subgroups of Hispanic adolescents (Mexicans, Puerto Ricans, Cubans and Central/South Americans) using the 1993 National Household Survey on Drug Abuse did not find differences by gender or ethnic subgroup (23). Other studies using school-based samples comparing a smaller number of Hispanic subgroups have noted differences among them (24, 25). For example, Mexican American youth had higher rates of past month use and heavy drinking than Puerto Rican youth in one study (24). While another study noted that Nicaraguan youth were less likely to drink than the other subgroups evaluated (25). We found differences in drinking patterns among adolescent Hispanic sub-groups in Florida (26).

Some suggested reasons for differences in sub-groups include an ethnic group's alcohol norms and attitudes, and the degree to which a group is acculturated to the larger U.S. society. Among Hispanic men, the drinking patterns of those who are more acculturated more closely resemble drinking patterns among the general U.S. population than those of less acculturated Hispanic men (27). A recent study among Hispanic youth indicates that those with no prior history of alcohol use were unaffected by acculturation variables. Youth with a previous history of alcohol use experienced greater likelihood of binge drinking as a function of the acculturation-related variables, but the relationship was complex (28).

Risk factors within the *family* that affect alcohol use include the genetic transmission of the propensity to alcoholism in males, family modeling of drug using behavior, parenting skills and parental attitudes towards children's drug use (14, 29, 30). Parental approval of drinking is a significant predictor of the amount of alcohol consumed by teenagers (14).

Examples of risk factors within the *school and peer* group include associating with deviant peers, doing poorly in school and exposure to a pro-drinking social environment (parental and peer drug use and approval of use) (31, 32). Finally we have risk factors within the *individual*. Some examples include initiating alcohol use at a young age (33, 34), smoking and marijuana use (35, 36), holding positive expectancies about alcohol use, having poor behavior regulation and being deviance prone (37-40).

Study

The purpose of our study was to examine gender and ethnic differences in the risk and protective factors for heavy episodic or binge drinking among Florida youth. We conducted a secondary data analysis on the Florida Youth Substance Abuse Survey 2002 (FYSAS 2002) (40). Data collection for this survey involved the collaboration of four Florida State agencies- (1) the Departments of Children and Families, (2) Health, (3)Education and (4) Juvenile Justice-under the leadership of the Governor's Office of Drug Control. The sampling plan targeted 47,342 middle school students (grades 6-8) and 47,452 high school students (grades 9-12) from all 67 of the state's counties. After invalid responses were removed, valid questionnaires from 62,934 students were included in the dataset. This final sample includes 71% of the targeted middle school sample and 61% of the targeted high school sample.

Florida is more ethnically diverse than the rest of the nation, with a large percentage of its population composed of minorities. Florida's public school membership has higher proportional minority representation than the state's overall population. From 1976 to 2001, the greatest numerical gains in Florida's public school system occurred in the Hispanic population (409% to 505,099 in 2001). This represents a proportional increase from 6.4% to 20.2% of the student membership.

The FYSAS asked for the student's race with the following question: "How do you describe yourself?" Subjects were allowed to make more than one selection from the following choices-American Indian/Native American or Alaska Native, Asian, Black/African American, Spanish/Hispanic/Latino, Native Hawaiian or other Pacific Islander, White/Caucasian, and other. There was a space to specify the 'other' category. They were next asked "Which one of these ethnic groups BEST describes you?" They could choose only one answer. The choices were- Central American (Guatemalan, Nicaraguan, Honduran for example), Cuban or Cuban-American, Dominican, Mexican or Mexican American, Puerto Rican, other Hispanic/Latino or Spanish origin, Haitian, West Indian or Caribbean or none of these. The surveyors then created a variable called 'ethnicity' by cross-tabulating race and ethnic group.

Our interest was in evaluating the risk and protective factors for binge drinking among students in Florida with particular emphasis on the White and Hispanic youth.

Variables

Our dependent variable, binge drinking, was assessed by asking the following question: "Think back over the last two weeks. How many times have you had five or more alcoholic drinks in a row?" The responses were assessed on an ordinal scale as follows: none, one time, two times, 3 to 5 times, 6 to 9 times, 10 or more times. We dichotomized the scale to non-binge='0' and binge drinking='1' for any binging, in some analyses. Independent variables:

The risk and protective factors evaluated in this survey were in four domains that included: (1) community, (2) family, (3) peer/individual and (4) school domains. The variables in these domains and their correlation with binge drinking are listed in Appendix A. Of note, one protective factor 'community opportunities for pro-social involvement' served as a risk rather than a protective factor. This is a composite measure that includes self-reported data on involvement in neighborhood sporting teams and clubs as well as the availability of adults in the neighborhood to talk to about something important. It may be that adolescents who are more socially active are more aware of opportunities both for pro-social involvement *and* for party participation where alcohol may be available.

Analyses

SPSS 10.1 for windows was used to conduct all our statistical procedures (41). We initially conducted frequency analyses on the demographic variables. From each of these domains, we next assessed the correlation among questions specifically related to alcohol and the outcome of binge drinking. We then used logistic regression analyses to evaluate the relationship of the risk and protective factors to the outcome of binge drinking as a dichotomous variable. The independent variables were added in a stepwise forward fashion. Statistical significance was calculated at the 0.05% alpha level. Three regressions were run. Initially the regression was run with the risk and protective factors in each domain, with age, gender, ethnicity and SES as covariates. Then this was repeated for all the variables in the four domains and finally for all the variables by gender.

RESULTS

Demographics

Whites (19%) were the most likely, while African-Americans (10%) were the least likely to have engaged in binge drinking. Hispanics (15%), Native Americans (15%) and Asian Americans (11%) were intermediate to these two groups in their frequency of binge drinking.

White males were more likely to have started drinking at age 10 years or younger than females (19% vs. 13.4%, $\chi^2 = 278.675$, p<.000) and to have binged than white females (20.7% vs. 17.3%, $\chi^2 = 175.49$, p<.000). Similarly, Hispanic males were more likely than Hispanic females to have started drinking (19% vs. 15%, p<.001) at or before age 10 years. Hispanic males were more likely than Hispanic females to have binged in the past two weeks (17% vs. 15%, p<.000) and the difference by gender was more evident among those who had binged on three or more occasions in the last two weeks (7% vs. 5%). Although highly significant because of the large sample size, the actual magnitude of the gender differences was not large.

Binge Drinking by Grade

Sixteen percent of this sample of students admitted to having binged on one or more occasions in the two weeks prior to the survey and the frequency increased with grade level.

Six percent of sixth graders acknowledged having binged in the past and 1% had done so on 10 or more occasions, while 31% of twelfth graders had binged with 2% admitting to having done so on ten or more occasions. Among 12th graders 40.4% of males and 27.2% of females had binged at least once in the two weeks prior to the survey.

Table 1. Demographic Data on the entire FYSAS student sample (N= 62,934)

	N	Valid %
Gender		
Male	28,652	47
Female	32,381	53
Race/Ethnicity		
African-American	11,199	17.8
Hispanic/Latino	8,558	13.6
American Indian	3,025	4.8
Asian	1,336	2.1
Native Hawaiian/Pacific Islander	457	0.7
Other/multiple	3,940	6.3
White, non-Hispanic	37,545	59.7
Age		
10	94	0.2
11	2838	4.5
12	9904	15.8
13	11293	18
14	10585	16.9
15	9312	14.9
16	8166	13
17	6422	10.3
18	3510	5.6
19 or older	471	0.8
Grade		
6th	11,415	18
7th	11,331	18
8th	10,646	17
9th	9,563	15
10th	8,053	13
11th	6,613	11
12th	4,758	8

Binge Drinking and Age of Initiation of Gateway Drug Use

Of those who had engaged in binge drinking, 55% had initiated alcohol use, 60% had smoked cigarettes and 38% had used marijuana before age 13 years. These rates are higher than those for the entire sample, among whom 34% had tried alcohol, 26% had tried cigarettes and 8% had tried marijuana before age 13 years.

Binge Drinking in Hispanic Subgroups

In this sample, Mexican students (17%) were the most likely to have engaged in binge drinking, Dominicans (13%) and Puerto Ricans (13%) were the least likely, while Central American (15%) and Cubans (14%) were intermediate in their frequency of binge drinking to the other three groups (χ^2=18.6, p<.017). However, when analyzing binge drinking in subgroups by gender, the differences were only significant among males (χ^2=25.8, p<.001).

Binge Drinking and Acculturation

Using language spoken at home as a surrogate marker for acculturation we noted no difference in the rates of binge drinking by acculturation among the Hispanic youth (χ^2=3.9, p<.142).

ATTITUDES TOWARDS ALCOHOL AND BINGE DRINKING (SEE TABLE 2)

Binge drinkers had lower perceived risks for drinking and were less likely to think it wrong to drink, or that their parents or adults in their neighborhood would think it was wrong to drink (p<.001). They were more likely to indicate that alcohol was easy to get, that it was cool to drink, that they would drink as adults and that their friends were more likely to drink (p<.001).

Risk and Protective Factors in Four Domains and Binge Drinking

We then conducted a series of logistic regressions using binge drinking as a binary outcome variable. We initially conducted the logistic regression with the independent variables in each of the four domains for White and then Hispanic youth.

Community Domain

We entered all of the protective and risk factors in the Community Domain (CP1-CR8 in Appendix A) using stepwise forward entry along with age, gender, ethnicity and father's level of schooling as a surrogate marker for SES. Of interest, none of the variables in this domain were correlated to each other.

Among Hispanic youth CR3 (Low Neighborhood Attachment), CR4 (Community Disorganization), CR5 (Personal Transitions and Mobility), CR7 (Laws and Norms Favorable to Drug Use and Firearms), CR8 (Perceived Availability of Drugs and Firearms) along with age were significantly related to binge drinking.

Among white youth CR4, 7 and 8 were significant while CR3 and 5 were not.

Table 2. Alcohol related attitudes as risk factors for binge drinking (Chi Square p<.001)

		BINGE DRINKING		
Risk factors	(N)	None	1-5 times	>5 times
How Much Risk:				
1-2 drinks nearly every day				
No Risk	(1447)	77%	16%	7%
Slight Risk	(1839)	76%	21%	3%
Great Risk	(3754)	91%	7%	2%
How Easy to Get Alcohol				
Very Hard	(3983)	95%	4%	1%
Sort of Easy	(1798)	78%	20%	2%
Very Easy	(2180)	67%	27%	6%
How cool if you drink?				
Not	(6374)	91%	7%	1%
Somewhat	(990)	70%	27%	3%
Very	(360)	64%	25%	11%
Would you drink as an adult?				
No	(5962)	97%	2%	1%
Yes	(3842)	48%	41%	11%
How many of your 4 best friends:				
Tried Alcohol				
None	(4693)	96%	3%	1%
Four	(1939)	56%	36%	8%
How Wrong to Drink Alcohol				
Very Wrong	(4450)	96%	3%	1%
A little wrong	(1995)	70%	27%	3%
Not wrong at all	(975)	46%	42%	12%
How Wrong Parents feel				
For you to Drink Alcohol				
Very Wrong	(6573)	89%	8%	1%
A little wrong	(767)	62%	33%	5%
Not wrong at all	(262)	56%	31%	12%

Family Domain

In this domain, among both Hispanics and whites: FR 5 (Poor Family Discipline), FR7 (Family History of Antisocial Behavior), FR8 (Parental Attitudes Favorable toward ATOD Use) and age remained significant when all the variables were entered along with age, gender, ethnicity and SES in a stepwise forward conditional model. Of interest, FP2 (Family Opportunities for Pro-social Involvement) is inversely correlated with FR4 (-0.62, p<.000), while FR4 (Poor family supervision) is positively correlated with FR5 (0.62, p<.000). FR7 was not correlated with any other variable while FR8 was correlated with FR9 (Parental attitudes favorable toward antisocial behavior) (0.63, p<.000).

Individual-Peer Domain

The significant variables in this domain for Hispanic youth included IP 2 (Social Skills), IP4 (Rebelliousness), IP5 (Friend's Delinquent Behavior), IP6 (Friend's Use of Drugs), IP9 (Favorable Attitudes toward ATOD Use), IP10 (Low Perceived Risks of Drug Use), IP11 (Early Initiation of Drug Use and Antisocial Behavior), IP13 (Sensation Seeking), age and gender. IP6 was correlated with IP5 (0.62, p<.000), IP9 (0.55 p<.000) and IP 11 (0.58, p<.000) while IP9 was correlated with IP11 (0.56, p<.000). Among white youth, in addition to the above, IP7 (Peer rewards for antisocial behavior) was significant.

School Domain

When the four variables in this domain were entered along with age, gender, ethnicity and SES, the significant variables for Hispanic youth were SR 3 (poor academic performance) and SR4 (low school commitment). Among white youth, in addition, SR2 (School rewards for pro-social involvement) was a protective factor. None of the variables in this domain were correlated with each other.

FINAL MODELS FOR HISPANIC AND WHITE YOUTH (SEE TABLES 3 AND 4)

We then performed another regression analysis with all of the variables in each of the domains in addition to age, gender, ethnicity and SES and entered them using stepwise forward entry. The final models are displayed in *Tables 3 and 6*. Using a 0.05 level of significance, only one of the five *community* variables remained significant in Hispanic youth: CR7-Laws and norms favorable to drug use and firearms. Intuitively, this variable should have functioned as a risk factor but paradoxically served as a protective factor. Among White youth, CP2-Community Rewards for Pro-social Involvement and CR8-Perceived Availability of Drugs and Firearms both served as risk factors.

In the *family* domain among Hispanic youth three of the nine variables remained in the model: poor family discipline (FR5), parental attitudes favorable to ATOD use (FR8), and a family history of antisocial behavior (FR7). Among White youth, the first two risk factors, FR5 and 8 remained significant.

In the *individual/peer* domain one of the three protective factors, social skills (IP2) was significant in both Hispanic and white youth. Five of the ten risk factors among Hispanics remained significant: friend's use of drugs (IP6), favorable attitudes toward ATOD use (IP9), sensation seeking (IP13), rebelliousness (IP4), and early initiation of drug use and antisocial behavior (IP11). Among white youth IP4-rebelliousness dropped out while IP10-Low Perceived Risks of Drug Use entered the model.

None of the variables in the *school* domain remained significant. Age and gender added to the final model while SES did not.

Table 3: Final Model for Hispanic Youth

Variables in the Equation	Sig.	Exp(B)	95.0% C.I. for EXP(B)	
			Lower	Upper
AGE	.000	1.217	1.148	1.290
Gender	.001	.721	.591	.880
Laws and Norms Favorable to Drug Use and Firearms (CR 7)	.010	.789	.659	.944
Parental Attitudes Favorable toward ATOD Use (FR8)	.001	1.382	1.151	1.661
Poor Family Discipline (FR5)	.041	1.142	1.005	1.296
Family History of Antisocial Behavior (FR7)	.040	1.125	1.006	1.259
Friend's Use of Drugs (IP6)	.000	1.475	1.317	1.653
Favorable Attitudes toward ATOD Use (IP9)	.000	1.458	1.231	1.728
Sensation Seeking (IP13)	.000	1.260	1.160	1.370
Rebelliousness (1P4)	.032	1.199	1.016	1.414
Early Initiation (of Drug Use and Antisocial Behavior) (IP 11)	.001	1.148	1.060	1.244
Social Skills (IP2)	.000	.575	.486	.680

Table 4: Final Model for White Youth

Variables in the Equation	Sig.	Exp(B)	95.0% C.I. for EXP(B)	
			Lower	Upper
AGE	.000	1.253	1.215	1.293
Gender	.000	.753	.682	.832
Community Rewards for Pro-social Involvement (CP2)	.000	1.229	1.154	1.309
Perceived Availability of Drugs and Firearms (CR8)	.024	1.083	1.011	1.160
Parental Attitudes Favorable toward ATOD Use (FR8)	.000	1.286	1.184	1.398
Poor Family Discipline (FR5)	.000	1.197	1.120	1.280
Friend's Use of Drugs (IP6)	.000	1.508	1.425	1.596
Early Initiation (of Drug Use and Antisocial Behavior) (IP 11)	.000	1.465	1.401	1.531
Favorable Attitudes toward ATOD Use (IP9)	.000	1.368	1.256	1.489
Sensation Seeking (IP13)	.000	1.218	1.170	1.269
Low Perceived Risks of Drug Use (IP10)	.000	1.196	1.110	1.290
Social Skills (IP2)	.000	.437	.400	.478

Final Model By Gender

Next we conducted regression analyses separately for males and females among two ethnic groups (see *Tables, 4, 5,7,8)*. Among the original seven *community variables*, one significant variable in the final model for Hispanic youth: CR7 (laws and norms favorable to drug use) remained significant in females only and continued to serve as a protective factor. Among White youths, only one of two factors in the final model remained significant in both genders CP2-Community Rewards for Pro-social Involvement and served as a risk factor.

In the *family domain* among Hispanic youth FR5 (poor family discipline) and FR7 (family history of antisocial behavior) remained significant only in females, while FR8 (parental attitudes favorable towards ATOD use) remained significant only in males. In addition FR4 (poor family supervision) and FP2 (family opportunities for pro-social involvement) became significant in males. This last protective factor served as a risk factor in males. Among White youth: FR5 (poor family discipline) and FR8 (parental attitudes favorable towards ATOD use) remained significant in both genders.

In the *individual/peer domain* IP2 (Social Skills), IP6 (Friend's Use of Drugs) and IP11 (Early Initiation of Drug Use and Antisocial Behavior) remained significant in both genders while IP4 (Rebelliousness) and IP5 (Friend's Delinquent Behavior) dropped out of the model for both genders. In addition, IP9 (Favorable Attitudes toward ATOD Use), dropped out for males and IP13 (Sensation Seeking) dropped out for females. IP8

(Favorable attitudes towards antisocial behavior) entered the model as a protective factor in females. Among white youth the only difference by gender was that IP13-sensation seeking dropped out for females. The factors in the final model were otherwise the same when evaluated by gender.

Table 5. Final model for Male Hispanic Youth (9 variables)

Variables in the Equation	Sig.	Exp(B)	95.0% C.I. for EXP(B)	
			Lower	Upper
D1-Age	.000	1.252	1.152	1.366
Parental Attitudes Favorable toward ATOD Use-FR8	.002	1.531	1.171	2.001
Poor Family Supervision-FR4	.019	1.414	1.059	1.888
Family Opportunities for Pro-social Involvement-FP2	.046	1.336	1.006	1.775
Friend's Use of Drugs (IP6)	.000	1.498	1.268	1.769
Early Initiation (of Drug Use and Antisocial Behavior)-IP11	.000	1.245	1.112	1.315
Sensation Seeking-IP13	.005	1.173	1.049	1.311
Social Skills-IP2	.000	.588	.464	.746

Table 6. Final Model for female Hispanic Youth (7 variables)

Variables in the Equation	Sig.	Exp(B)	95.0% C.I. for EXP(B)	
			Lower	Upper
D1-AGE	.000	1.185	1.090	1.288
Laws and Norms Favorable to Drug Use and Firearms-CR7	*.003*	*.680*	*.525*	*.880*
Poor Family Discipline-FR5	.004	1.291	1.084	1.552
Family History of Antisocial Behavior-FR7	.025	1.197	1.023	1.402
Favorable Attitudes toward ATOD Use-IP9	.000	1.730	1.345	2.224
Friend's Use of Drugs-IP6	.000	1.490	1.268	1.751
Early Initiation (of Drug Use and Antisocial Behavior)-IP11	.000	1.283	1.129	1.459
Social Skills-IP2	*.000*	*.541*	*.425*	*.690*
Favorable Attitudes towards antisocial behavior –IP8	*.038*	*.713*	*.517*	*.982*

In the *school domain*, none of the variables were significant either in the overall model or the one by gender in either ethnic group.

Table 7. Final Model for Male White Youth (9 variables)

Variables in the Equation	Sig.	Exp(B)	95.0% C.I. for EXP(B)	
			Lower	Upper
D1-AGE	.000	1.322	1.263	1.384
Community Rewards for Pro-social Involvement (CP2)	.000	1.220	1.111	1.339
Parental Attitudes Favorable toward ATOD Use (FR8)	.000	1.420	1.254	1.609
Poor Family Discipline-FR5	.001	1.171	1.064	1.289
Friend's Use of Drugs-IP6	.000	1.511	1.389	1.644
Early Initiation (of Drug Use and Antisocial Behavior)-IP11	.000	1.456	1.371	1.546
Favorable Attitudes toward ATOD Use-IP9	.001	1.235	1.093	1.396
Low Perceived Risks of Drug Use-IP10	.009	1.224	1.101	1.360
Sensation Seeking-IP13	.000	1.171	1.107	1.239
Social Skills-IP2	.000	.417	.368	.472

DISCUSSION

In this study of binge drinking in Florida youth, we noted some similarities and many important differences compared to what has been reported in the literature. Males began drinking earlier than females and engaged in binge drinking more frequently than females. By their senior year, Florida youth had higher rates of binge drinking than in national samples with males drinking more than females.

In addition to differences in rates of binge drinking among ethnic groups we also noted differences in binge drinking rates among Hispanic subgroups. Mexican American youth were the most likely to binge drink, Puerto Ricans and Dominicans were the least likely, and Central Americans and Cubans were intermediate in their frequency of binge drinking. The difference in binge drinking among Hispanic sub-groups was not related to the level of acculturation as measured by the language spoken at home.

In evaluating the risk and protective factors for binge drinking we noted that those in the individual/peer and family domains were most significant and differed most by gender. None of the school variables and only one community variable in each of the two ethnic groups studied were significant. 'Laws and norms favorable to drug use and firearms' served as a protective rather than a risk factor in Hispanic females only. It is conceivable that in communities dealing with this situation, parents and other family members have stricter rules for their daughters and supervise them more closely, resulting in this being a protective rather than a risk factor for alcohol use. The protective factor 'Community Rewards for Pro-social Involvement' served as a risk factor for white males and females. As noted previously, alcohol use is integral to socializing in western societies influencing attitudes and availability to minors.

Table 8. Final Model for Female White Youth (8 variables)

Variables in the Equation	Sig.	Exp(B)	95.0% C.I. for EXP(B)	
			Lower	Upper
D1-AGE	.000	1.216	1.165	1.270
Community Rewards for Pro-social Involvement (CP2)	.000	1.234	1.132	1.346
Parental Attitudes Favorable toward ATOD Use (FR8)	.002	1.192	1.065	1.834
Poor Family Discipline-FR5	.000	1.212	1.103	1.331
Early Initiation (of Drug Use and Antisocial Behavior)-IP11	.000	1.508	1.410	1.612
Friend's Use of Drugs-IP6	.000	1.490	1.379	1.611
Favorable Attitudes toward ATOD Use-IP9	.000	1.483	1.316	1.672
Low Perceived Risks of Drug Use-IP10	.009	1.154	1.031	1.284
Social Skills-IP2	*.000*	*.465*	*.409*	*.528*

'Poor family discipline' was a risk factor for both genders and both ethnic groups, followed by parental attitudes favorable to drug use and a family history of antisocial behavior. Previous models suggest that family factors influence the development of individual personality, attitudes and behaviors, which in turn determine one's choice of peers and one's vulnerability to their influence to use drugs (14). So, difficulties in the parent-child bond may be associated with the development of a drug prone personality, which is then associated with selecting friends who use drugs. Our results, even though cross-sectional, appear to endorse this reasoning among these youth.

Among Hispanic females, having a 'favorable attitude towards ATOD use' had the highest impact on the predicted odds for being a binge drinker. This was followed by 'friend's use of drugs,' 'poor family discipline,' 'family history of antisocial behavior' and 'early initiation of drug use'. Among Hispanic males, 'parental attitudes favorable toward ATOD use' most significantly increased the boys' odds of binge drinking, followed by 'friend's use of drugs', 'poor family supervision', 'family opportunities for pro-social involvement', 'early initiation of drug use' and 'sensation seeking'.

Among white females 'early initiation of drug use' had the highest impact on the odds of being a binge drinker followed by 'friend's use of drugs', 'favorable attitudes toward ATOD use', and 'low perceived risks of drug use'. Among white males 'friends use of drugs', had the highest impact followed by 'early initiation of drug use and antisocial behavior', 'favorable attitudes toward ATOD use', 'low perceived risks of drug use' and 'sensation seeking'.

Early initiation of drug use was a risk factor for binge drinking in both genders in both ethnic groups. This may be a reflection of an individual having more risk factors, resulting in earlier initiation of binge drinking.

'Friends' use of drugs' was a risk factor in both genders and highlights the role of peers in substance use (42). Homogeneity between friends reflects both the processes of peer selection and peer influence. In cross-sectional studies, the role of peer influence may be overestimated. That is, by examining peer similarities at only one time point, it is not possible to determine the extent to which similarities between friends existed at the beginning of the relationship and served as a basis for initiating the friendship (selection), or developed over the course of the relationship (influence). Secondly, findings of similarities between adolescents, to some degree, reflect the projection of the respondents' behavior onto their friends. Nevertheless, since social skills (resistance skills) served as a protective factor in both genders, it is likely that lack of resistance skills does allow for the possibility that friends do influence one's intake of alcohol.

Sensation seeking is a personality characteristic that is considered to be unconventional and indicates the need for novel experiences and the willingness to take physical and psychological risks for these experiences (43). The connection of sensation seeking to earlier onset of substance use among teens and young adults and to higher levels of use has been established (44). A large number of studies have also shown that unconventional behaviors (tolerance of deviance, sensation seeking and rebelliousness) are positively related to drug use (45,46). Of great interest, in this study this risk factor appeared to operate only among males.

None of the school related variables remained significant in the overall final model in both ethnic groups and the final model by gender. Academic failure is often cited as a very significant risk factor for substance use in adolescents (13). Poor academic performance and low school commitment were significant risk factors in the initial model. It is possible that in a model that evaluates a number of risk and protective factors together some interactions will be overlooked, and this could account for these results.

In summary, while this is a cross-sectional study and we need to be cautious with attributing causality, our results suggest that youth who grow up in families with poor discipline and have parents with favorable attitudes towards ATOD use, are likely to form favorable attitudes towards ATOD use themselves. Those with low resistance skills and male sensation seekers are at greater risk of initiating drug use early on, associating with and/or being influenced by friends who use drugs and being binge drinkers themselves.

IMPLICATIONS

Since youth (1) form attitudes early in life and (2) obtain their alcohol from adults, a strategy directed at youth alone would be unlikely to be successful. Efforts to curb underage drinking need to target adults and engage the society at large as well. The presence of risk factors in multiple domains endorses the need for a multi-pronged approach to prevention and intervention.

At the individual level these results would suggest that programs for students, in addition to emphasizing the risks of binge drinking should teach resistance skills. However, intervention programs that rely on provision of information alone or those that focus on increasing self-esteem or resisting peer pressure have not been demonstrated to be effective, while public policies like those that raise drinking ages and lower acceptable blood alcohol levels have been successful at lowering mortality.

The National Academies were asked by Congress to develop a strategy to reduce and prevent underage drinking (47). Their suggestion is to build comprehensive programs that emphasize evidenced based education interventions, screening and brief intervention strategies for youth and adults, policy and environmental changes that limit underage access to alcohol and national media campaigns that inform attitudes. This calls for more research and development in each of these areas.

There are several caveats that need to be highlighted. Given that social approval of adult drinking is high, the risk and protective factors that are related to binge drinking may be unique to alcohol use and may not be related to other substance use categories. This will need further evaluation in future studies. Another issue raised by these results is that adolescent substance abuse prevention programs may not be equally effective across genders and ethnicities. Tailoring programs and activities to address risk and protective factors in sub-groups may be an important consideration when participants are homogenous in terms of gender or ethnicities. This sample of Florida youth emphasizes the lack of homogeneity in ethnic groups and the difficulties encountered by lumping them together as in a 'Hispanic' category.

APPENDIX A. CORRELATION OF
VARIABLES I EACH DOMAIN WTH BINGE DRINKING

	RPF Variable	Corr.	P-value
CP1	*Community Opportunities for Pro-social Involvement*	*.026*	*.017*
CP2	*Community Rewards for Pro-social Involvement*	*-.082*	*.000*
CR3	Low Neighborhood Attachment	.039	.000
CR4	Community Disorganization	.148	.000
CR5	Personal Transitions and mobility	.050	.000
CR7	Laws and norms favorable to drug use and firearms	.258	.000
CR8	Perceived availability of drugs and firearms	.330	.000
FP1	*Family Attachment*	*-.122*	*.000*
FP2	*Family Opportunities for Pro-social Involvement*	*-.146*	*.000*
FP3	*Family rewards for pro-social involvement*	*-.143*	*.000*
FR4	Poor family supervision	.187	.000
FR5	Poor family discipline	.229	.000
FR6	Family Conflict	.125	.000
FR7	Family history of antisocial behavior	.319	.000
FR8	Parental attitudes favorable toward ATOD use	.281	.000
FR9	Parental attitudes favorable toward antisocial behavior	.197	.000
IP1	*Religiosity*	*-.071*	*.000*
IP2	*Social Skills*	*-.376*	*.000*
IP3	*Belief in the moral order*	*-.303*	*.000*
IP4	Rebelliousness	.258	.000
IP5	Friend's delinquent behavior	.286	.000
IP6	Friend's use of drugs	.426	.000
IP7	Peer rewards for antisocial behavior	.198	.000
IP8	Favorable attitudes towards antisocial behavior	.312	.000
IP9	Favorable attitudes towards ATOD use	.446	.000
IP10	Low perceived risks of drug use	.177	.000
IP11	Early initiation (of drug use and antisocial behavior)	.412	.000
IP13	Sensation seeking	.332	.000
IP14	Gang involvement	.201	.000
SP1	*School opportunities for pro-social involvement*	*-.110*	*.000*
SP2	*School rewards for pro-social involvement*	*-.145*	*.000*
SR3	Poor academic performance	.143	.000
SR4	Low School Commitment	.240	.000

REFERENCES

[1] Johnston, L. D., O'Malley P., and Bachman, J. G. (2003). *Monitoring the Future national survey results on drug use,* 1975-2002. Volume I: Secondary school students (NIH Publication No. 03-5375). Bethesda, MD: National Institute on Drug Abuse, 520 pp.

[2] www.who.int. Alcohol use and youth.

[3] Substance Abuse and Mental Health Services Administration. *Underage Drinking Prevention: Action Guide and Planner.* Rockville, MD: Substance Abuse and Mental Health Services Administration; 2001. DHHA Publication No. SMA 3259.

[4] Substance Abuse and Mental Health Services Administration. *Results from the 2003 National Survey on Drug Use and Health.* National Findings (Office of Applied Substances, NSDUH Series-25, DHHS Publication No. SMA 04-3964). Rockville, MD: Substance Abuse and Mental Health Services Administration, 2004

[5] Jellnick EM. Phases of alcohol addiction. *Quarterly Journal of Studies of Alcohol.* 1952; 13:673-684.

[6] Weschler H, Davenport A, Dowdall G, Moeykens B, Castillo S. Health and behavioral consequences of binge drinking in college: A national survey of students at 140 campuses. *Journal of the American Medical Association.* 1994; 272:1672-1677.

[7] DeJong W. Finding common ground for effective campus based prevention. *Psychology of Addictive Behaviors.* 2001; 15:292-296.

[8] Office of Applied Studies. (2000). *National Household Survey on Drug Abuse: Main findings 1998* (DHHS Publication No. SMA 00-3381, NHSDA Series H-11). Rockville, MD: Substance Abuse and Mental Health Services Administration.

[9] Hill, K. G., White, H. R., Chung, I. J., Hawkins, J. D., and Catalano, R. F. (2000). Early adult outcomes of adolescent binge drinking: Person- and variable-centered analyses of binge drinking trajectories. *Alcoholism: Clinical and Experimental Research, 24,* 892–901.

[10] Escobedo, L. G., Chorba, T. L., and Waxweiler, R. (1995). Patterns of alcohol use and the risk of drinking and driving among US high school students. *American Journal of Public Health, 85,* 976–978.

[11] Valois, R. F., McKeown, R. E., Garrison, C. Z., and Vincent, M. L. (1995). Correlates of aggressive and violence behaviors among public high school adolescents. *Journal of Adolescent Health, 16,* 26–34.

[12] Wechsler, H., Dowdall, G. W., Davenport, A., and Castillo, S. (1995). Correlates of college student binge drinking. *American Journal of Public Health, 85,* 921–926.

[13] Hawkins JD, Catalano, Miller JY. Risk and Protective Factors for Alcohol and Other drug problems in adolescence and early adulthood: Implications for Substance abuse prevention. *Psychological Bulletin.* 1992; 112:64-105.

[14] Brook JS, Brook DW, Gordon AS, Whiteman M, Cohen P (1990). The psychosocial etiology of adolescent drug use: A family interactional approach. *Genetic Social and General Psychology Monographs,* 116 (whole No.2).

[15] Mello NK. Drug use patterns and premenstrual dysphoria. In: Ray BA, Braude MC, eds *Women and drugs: A New Era for Research*, NIDA research Monograph 65, Rockville, MD: NIDA, 1986.

[16] Pietrantoni M, Knuppel RA. Alcohol use in pregnancy. *Clin Perinatol* 1991; 18:93-111.

[17] Caetano R, Kaskutas LA. Changes in drinking patterns among whites, blacks and Hispanics: 1984-1992. *J Stud Alcohol* 1995; 56:558-565.

[18] Caetano R, Clark CL. Trends in alcohol consumption patterns among whites, blacks and Hispanics: 1984-1995. *J Stud Alcohol* 1998:56:659-668.

[19] Caetano R, Clark CL. Trends in alcohol consumption patterns among whites, blacks and Hispanics: 1984-1995. *Alesm Clin. Exp. Res*; 1998:22534-538.

[20] Makimoto K. Drinking patterns and drinking problems among Asian Americans and Pacific Islanders. *Alcohol Health and Research World* 22:270-275, 1998.

[21] Dawson, D.A. Beyond Black, White and His-panic: Race, ethnic origin and drinking patterns in the United States. *Journal of Substance Abuse* 10:321-339, 1998.

[22] Caetano R Drinking Patterns and alcohol problems in a national sample of U.S. Hispanics In: National Institute on Alcohol Abuse and Alcoholism. *Alcohol use among U.S. ethnic minorities.* Research Monogram No. 18, DHHS Publication No (ADM) 89-1435, Washington Government Printing Office, 1989, pp. 147-162.

[23] Nielsen AL, Ford JA. Drinking Patterns among Hispanic adolescents: Results from a National Household Survey. *J Stud Alcohol* 2000; 62:448-456.

[24] Wallace JM, Bachman JG. Explaining racial/ethnic differences in adolescent drug use: The impact of background and lifestyle. *Social Probl.* 1991; 38: 333-353.

[25] Warheit GJ, Vega WA, Khoury EI, Gill AA, Elfenbein PH. A comparative analysis of cigarette, alcohol and illicit drug use among an ethnically diverse sample of Hispanic, African-American and non-Hispanic white adolescents. *J Drug Issues* 1996; 26:901-922.

[26] Siqueira L, Crandall L.A. Risk and protective factors for binge drinking among Hispanic subgroups in Florida. *Journal of Ethnicity in Substance Abuse* (In Press for 2006 Volume 5 Issue 2).

[27] Caetano, R. Acculturation and drinking patterns among U.S. Hispanics. *British Journal of Addiction* 82:789-799, 1987.

[28] Guilalmo-Ramos V, Jaccard J, Johansspm M, Turrisi R. Binge drinking among Latino Youth: Role of acculturation-related variables. *Psychology of Addictive Behavior* 2004:18:2: 135-142.

[29] Gamerzy N. (1983) Stressors of childhood. In N. Gamerzy and M Rutter (Eds), *Stress, coping and development in children* (pp. 43-84). New York: McGraw-Hill.Abuse and Mental Health Services Administration; 2001. DHHA Publication No. SMA 3259.

[30] Griffin, K. W., Botvin, G. J., Epstein, J. A., Doyle, M. M., and Diaz, T. (2000). Psychosocial and behavioral factors in early adolescence as predictors of heavy drinking among high school seniors. *Journal of Studies on Alcohol, 61,* 603–606.

[31] DeWit, D. J., Adlaf, E. M., Offord, D. R., and Ogborne, A. C. (2000). Age at first alcohol use: A risk factor for the development of alcohol disorders. *American Journal of Psychiatry, 157,* 745–750.

[32] Hawkins, J. D., Graham, J. W., Maguin, E., Abbott, R., Hill, K. G., and Catalano, R. F. (1997). Exploring the effects of age of alcohol use initiation and psychosocial risk factors on subsequent alcohol misuse. *Journal of Studies on Alcohol, 58,* 280–290.

[33] Ellickson, P. L., Tucker, J. S., Klein, D. J., and McGuigan, K. A. (2001). Prospective risk factors for alcohol misuse in late adolescence. *Journal of Studies on Alcohol, 62,* 773–782.

[34] Ellickson, P. L., Hays, R. D., and Bell, R. M. (1992). Stepping through the drug use sequence: Longitudinal scalogram analysis of initiation and regular use. *Journal of Abnormal Psychology*, 101, 441–451.

[35] Duncan, S. C., Duncan, T. E., and Hops, H. (1998). Progressions of alcohol, cigarette, and marijuana use in adolescence. *Journal of Behavioral Medicine*, 21, 375–388.

[36] Lewinsohn, P. M., Rohde, P., and Brown, R. A. (1999). Level of current and past adolescent cigarette smoking as predictors of future substance use disorders in young adulthood. *Addiction, 94*, 913–921.

[37] Barnes, G. M., and Welte, J. W. (1986). Adolescent alcohol abuse: Subgroup differences and relationships to other problem behaviors. *Journal of Adolescent Research, 1*, 79–94.

[38] Fergusson, D. M., Lynskey, M. T., and Horwood, L. J. (1996). Alcohol misuse and juvenile offending in adolescence. *Addiction, 91*, 483–494.

[39] Greenfield, T. K., and Weisner, C. (1995). Drinking problems and self reported criminal behavior, arrests and convictions: 1990 US alcohol and 1989 county surveys. *Addiction, 90*, 361–373.

[40] Colder, C. R., and Chassin, L. (1999). The psychosocial characteristics of alcohol users versus problem users: Data from a study of adolescents at risk. *Development and Psychopathology,*

[41] 2002 Florida Youth Substance Abuse Survey State Report. http://www.state.fl.us/cf

[42] SPSS. http://www.spss.com

[43] Zuckerman, M., 1986. *Sensation seeking and the endogenous deficit theory of drug abuse*. National Institute on Drug Abuse Research Monograph Series No. 74. Neurobiology of Behavioral Control in Drug Abuse. Department of Health and Human Services, pp. 59-70.

[44] Pederson, W., 1991. Mental health, sensation seeking and drug use patterns: a longitudinal study. *Br. J. Addict*. 86, pp. 195-204.

[45] Bauman, KE. and Ennett, ST. Peer influence on adolescent drug use. *American Psychologist*. 1994; 49: 820–822.

[46] Jessor R, Jessor SL. *Problem behavior and psychosocial development: A longitudinal study of youth*. 1977 New York: Academic Press.

[47] National Research Council and Institute of Medicine (2004). *Reducing Underage Drinking: A Collective Responsibility*. Committee on developing a strategy to reduce and prevent underage drinking, Richard J. Bonnie and Mary Ellen O'Connell, Editors. Board on Children, Youth and Families, Division of Behavioral Sciences and Education. Washington DC: The National Academy Press.

In: Binge Drinking Research Progress
Editor: Kevin I. DiGuarde

Chapter 5

PARADIGMS FOR ALCOHOL USE AND CO-OCCURRING BEHAVIORAL HEALTH RISK FACTORS AMONG WOMEN OF CHILDBEARING AGE

James Tsai[1]*, R. Louise Floyd[1] and Mary J. O'Connor[2]

1) Prevention Research Branch, Division of Birth Defects and Developmental Disabilities, National Center on Birth Defects and Developmental Disabilities, Centers for Disease Control and Prevention (CDC), Atlanta, GA 30333, USA
2) Department of Psychiatry and Biobehavioral Sciences, David Geffen School of Medicine at the University of California, Los Angeles, 760 Westwood Plaza, Room 68-265A, Los Angeles, CA 90024, USA

ABSTRACT

Alcohol use often co-occurs with one or more other behavioral health risk factors that can place women and their offspring at heightened risk for morbidity and mortality. Women with co-occurring alcohol use and behavioral health risk factors, such as tobacco use, illicit drug use, and mental illness are especially vulnerable. These women are not only at increased risk for hazardous reproductive outcomes, but also physical and psychological illness, disability and premature death, interpersonal conflicts, violence and legal problems, unemployment, and poverty. Despite evidence that co-occurring multiple behavioral health risk factors are prevalent and often associated with more severe adverse health outcomes and higher social economic costs, a majority of health promotion and intervention programs are designed to target only one risk factor of concern. Given that many of these behavioral health risk factors are interrelated and amenable to

* Address all correspondences and reprint requests to:
Dr. James Tsai
National Center on Birth Defects and Developmental Disabilities
Centers for Disease Control and Prevention
1600 Clifton Road, Mailstop-E86
Atlanta, GA 30333 USA
Fax: 404-498-3940; E-mail address: jxt9@cdc.gov

interventions, and that many patients frequently present for treatment with two or more behavioral risk factors in various health care settings, establishing paradigms of assessment and intervention for multiple behavioral health risk factors could be more successful in preventing initiation of high-risk behavior, improving targeted health conditions, decreasing the likelihood of co-morbidity, enhancing treatment adherence, preventing relapse, and subsequently maintaining long-term behavioral changes. Prevention of alcohol-related morbidity and mortality among women of childbearing age needs to incorporate the success of evidence-based strategies that address interrelated risk factors across more than one domain.

Keywords: alcohol, tobacco, illicit drug, mental illness, co-occurring, women, prevention

1. INTRODUCTION

Prenatal alcohol use is a leading preventable cause of neurobehavioral and developmental abnormalities among children [1, 2]. Alcohol use can co-occur with one or more other behavioral health risk factors [3-7], thereby placing women and their offspring at heightened risk for morbidity and mortality [8-11]. Women with co-occurring alcohol use and other behavioral health risk factors, such as tobacco use, illicit drug use, and mental illness are especially vulnerable [11-14]. These women are not only at increased risk for hazardous reproductive outcomes [15-20], but also physical and psychological illness, disability and premature death, interpersonal conflicts, violence and legal problems, unemployment, and poverty [11, 21, 22].

Ample evidence from several decades of research has shown that alcohol use and many behavioral health risk factors (e.g. tobacco use, illicit drug use, or mental illness) can each independently contribute to serious health consequences for women and their children [11, 12, 23-25]. Despite evidence that co-occurring multiple behavioral health risk factors are prevalent and associated with more severe adverse health outcomes and higher socioeconomic costs [11, 21, 26, 27], a majority of health promotion and intervention programs are designed to target only one primary risk factor of concern. To date, many theories of single-behavior modification have advanced rapidly [28-30]. However, much work for multiple risk factors theory development, refinement, and intervention data support remains [28-30]. The mechanisms for many behavioral changes are still poorly understood [28, 29, 31]. Given that many behavioral health risk factors are interrelated and amenable to interventions [23, 32], and that many patients frequently present for treatment with two or more behavioral risk factors in various health care settings [3, 4, 33-35], conceptualizing the occurrences of multiple behavioral health risk factors may contribute to enhanced assessment and intervention for preventing initiation of high-risk behavior, improving targeted health conditions, decreasing the likelihood of co-morbidity, enhancing treatment adherence, preventing relapse, and subsequently maintaining long-term behavioral changes [5, 11, 22, 36-45]. The aim of this chapter is to summarize the evidence of co-occurring alcohol use and selected behavioral health risk factors among women of childbearing age in order to delineate epidemiologic perspectives that can advance the prevention of alcohol-related morbidity and mortality among this population [31, 46, 47].

2. ALCOHOL USE AMONG WOMEN OF CHILDBEARING AGE

2.1. Prevalence

Based on the Behavioral Risk Factor Surveillance System (BRFSS) data collected annually by the Centers for Disease and Control and Prevention (CDC) [48], the estimated prevalence for binge drinking and any use of alcohol among women aged 18–44 years during 2001−2006 is shown in Figure 1. In 2006, the BRFSS adopted an advisory from the National Institute on Alcohol Abuse and Alcoholism's (NIAAA) National Advisory Council on Binge Drinking, in which a new definition of binge drinking was proposed lowering the number of drinks for women from five or more to four or more on a single occasion. That change reflected the understanding that women need fewer number of drinks to reach a binge blood alcohol concentration (BAC) level than do men [49]. Using the new definition, the prevalence for binge drinking was estimated at 14.7% and any use of alcohol was estimated at 50.0% among women aged 18–44 years for the year 2006. These findings, along with the results from a number of previous studies [50-54], have confirmed that binge drinking among women of childbearing age in the United States continues to be a significant concern [55].

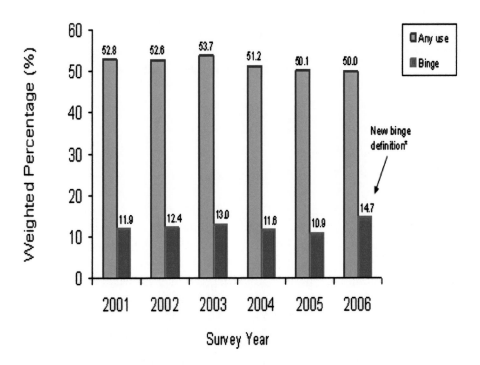

Binge drinking definition for BRFSS survey year 2001-2005: ≥ 5 drinks on one occasion.
*Binge drinking definition for BRFSS survey year 2006 and later: ≥ 4 drinks on one occasion.

BRFSS United States, 2001-2006.

Figure 1. Estimated prevalence of alcohol use among women aged 18-44 years.

2.2. Women and Drinking

Alcohol affects women differently, even in small amounts, than it affects men [56]. The Surgeon General of the United States advises that women who are pregnant or who might become pregnant should abstain from alcohol use in order to eliminate the chance of giving birth to a baby with any of the harmful effects of fetal alcohol spectrum disorders (FASDs) [51, 57]. In addition, a pregnant woman who has already consumed alcohol during her pregnancy should stop in order to minimize further risk [57]. For nonpregnant women, the NIAAA defines a safe level of drinking as no more than one drink (i.e., one 12-ounce bottle of beer or wine cooler, one 5-ounce glass of wine, or 1.5 ounces of 80-proof distilled spirits) per day [58]. However, most women of childbearing age do not recognize their pregnancy until 5–6 weeks after conception, a critical period when the fetus is most vulnerable to developmental and neurological damage [59, 60]. Even though no level of maternal drinking is considered safe because alcohol is a potent teratogen [57, 58, 61], the actual risk of having fetal alcohol syndrome (FAS) or less severe neurobehavioral and developmental abnormalities due to prenatal alcohol use depends on many factors, including the pattern, average volume, timing, and duration of alcohol use [53]. Certain alcohol drinking patterns (e.g. binge drinking) are particularly hazardous, because they can increase the peak BAC experienced by the fetus, and thereby affect the occurrence and severity of alcohol-induced developmental brain injury [62]. Less intense alcohol use levels have been associated with the risk of having less obvious but still measurable effects on children's development and behavior [63, 64]. In addition to being associated with FASDs, binge drinking also is associated with a wide range of other morbidities and mortality for women, including unintentional injuries, interpersonal violence, alcohol poisoning, cardiovascular disease, sexually transmitted diseases, unintended pregnancy, and sudden infant death syndrome [55, 65].

2.3. Interplay of Alcohol Use and Other Risk Factors

Certain characteristics are predictive of excessive drinking among women, such as having parents, siblings, relatives, or partners with alcohol problems; a history of depression; or childhood physical or sexual abuse [56]. Because health and behavior are an interplay of biological, behavioral, and social influences [10], alcohol use can interact with other biological and psychosocial determinants. These include race and ethnicity, socioeconomic status, malnutrition, alcohol metabolism and genetic sensitivity to alcohol, environmental settings, policy, and psychosocial factors [53, 66-68]. Therefore, multifaceted considerations are essential to address interventions for changing drinking behaviors [69].

3. PARADIGMS FOR ALCOHOL USE AND CO-OCCURRING RISK FACTORS

Behavioral health risk factors, such as alcohol, tobacco, illicit drug use, and mental illness, can result in substantial morbidity and mortality, as well as significant societal and economic costs [11, 25]. Women who engage in high-risk drinking, often have one or more of other risk factors that can inhibit successful changes in their drinking behavior. This section discusses several patterns of co-occurring risk factors frequently presented by women in many health care settings [1, 3, 4, 33, 35].

3.1. Co-Occurring Alcohol and Tobacco Use

Alcohol use and tobacco use are among the top causes of preventable morbidity and mortality in the United States [8-10, 70]. Women who use alcohol and tobacco concurrently often face many challenges in their cessation efforts [71, 72]. Well-established evidence has shown that drinking alcohol is highly associated with tobacco use [38, 72-76]. Clinical intervention studies have found that as many as 70%−90% of women who report alcohol use are also smokers [1, 2, 38]. Prevalence for concurrent alcohol and tobacco use was estimated at about 20%−25% among women of childbearing age in a recent population representative study [72]. Other studies also have shown that women who smoke are much more likely to drink, and women who drink are much more likely to smoke [53, 76]. They also have shown that women who smoke are more likely to engage in binge drinking at higher quantity levels [53, 76], or have non-binge patterns of heavier drinking [43]. In particular, young women who smoke are at increased risk of engaging in frequent binge drinking as a means of self-medicating to avoid a problem [76].

Although data specific to women of childbearing age are lacking, results from a number of clinical studies have shown that alcohol users are more addicted to nicotine, because they often smoke more cigarettes with higher nicotine level per day [77], and are less motivated to quit [78]. One study showed that alcohol users were less able to resist cigarette smoking after consuming alcohol compared with a placebo group of users who drank nonalcoholic beverages [38]. Other studies have found that concurrent alcohol and tobacco users often need to smoke in order to cope with the urge of alcohol drinking because of cross-substance craving [79, 80]. Not surprisingly, one recommendation advised smokers during the initial stages of attempting to quit also to avoid alcohol use [81]. Despite earlier concerns that addressing both addictions concurrently would be too difficult for patients and would adversely affect the recovery from alcoholism [82], accumulating evidence suggests otherwise. This and other evidence has revealed that concurrent smoking cessation intervention does not pose a risk to alcoholism treatment, as it does not disrupt alcohol abstinence and might actually enhance the likelihood of longer-term sobriety [42, 70, 82-86]. Furthermore, smoking-related craving and pleasantness decrease after a period of prolonged abstinence [87]. Regardless of whether alcohol use is targeted first, then tobacco addiction, or both alcohol and tobacco use are targeted simultaneously [36, 88], evidence suggests that combining intervention strategies might be the most effective way to address concurrent alcohol and tobacco addictions [70, 82, 83, 86, 88].

Given that serious health consequences and staggering economic costs are associated with alcohol and tobacco use, prevention of alcohol-related morbidity and mortality should consider the role that concurrent alcohol and tobacco use might play in alcohol abstinence and relapse. Clinicians in primary care and women's health care settings have frequent opportunities to identify and intervene with women who are at various risks, include that of an alcohol-exposed pregnancy [52]. Health care providers need to be informed about the heightened risk for hazardous drinking among occasional and daily smokers [89]. Several studies have suggested that smoking status can be used as a clinical indicator for alcohol misuse and as a reminder for alcohol screening in general [89], or as a clinical marker for greater risk of relapse among those who were in alcohol or other substance use treatment [42]. Screening for alcohol use in primary care settings is recommended by clinical care guidelines but is not adhered to as strongly as screening for smoking [89]. A number of federal agencies, including CDC, the NIAAA and the Substance Abuse and Mental Health Services Administration (SAMHSA), are making efforts to increase the practice of screening and brief intervention for both alcohol and tobacco use by health care providers [52]. Because there is considerable interest and receptiveness to the idea of a dual-recovery approach among many women who are concurrent alcohol and tobacco users [84, 85, 90, 91], clinicians who provide screening for tobacco and alcohol use should also discuss the option of a dual-cessation approach with these women.

3.2. Co-Occurring Alcohol and Illicit Drug Use

The National Survey on Drug Use and Health (NSDUH) conducted by SAMHSA defines illicit drug use as the use of marijuana or hashish, cocaine, inhalants, hallucinogens, heroin, or prescription drugs used non-medically [92]. The NSDUH reported that, for the years 2002–2003, approximately 4.3% of pregnant women and 10.6% of non-pregnant women aged 15–44 years used illicit drugs during the month prior to survey [92]. During the same period, the prevalence for co-occurring alcohol and marijuana use was 8.7%, and for co-occurring alcohol and cocaine use was 1.2% for the 12 months prior to interview among women in a general population [93]. In contrast, clinical studies showed that illicit drug use by alcohol abusers ranged from 30%–60% for cocaine, 20%–50% for marijuana, 12%–20% for benzodiazepines, and 7%–10% for heroin [93, 94]. Among the many possible combinations of concurrent substances used, alcohol use has been most strongly associated with cocaine use [93, 95], and has had most consistent adverse effects on neonatal outcomes, particularly fetal growth retardation [20]. Furthermore, results from a number of other studies have showed that women become addicted to alcohol, tobacco, or other drugs faster than men, and suffer more serious health consequences [13, 14]. Consequently, women are more susceptible to adverse reproductive outcomes, sexually transmitted diseases, mental illness, injury and violence [11, 14, 20, 96, 97].

Researchers have proposed a "gateway or stepping-stone" theory to describe the progression from the earlier use of alcohol or tobacco to marijuana, and later use of other types of illicit drugs such as cocaine, heroin, and MDMA (3,4-methylenedioxymethamphetamine), which subsequently leads to profound and severe addiction [44, 45, 98, 99]. Several epidemiologic studies have provided further evidence of such sequential links [43-45]. For example, users of tobacco and alcohol have been shown to be more likely than nonusers to try marijuana, or use marijuana when given an opportunity [44, 45]. Moreover, users who have prior experience of using marijuana have been shown to be more likely to use cocaine than those with no history of marijuana use [44, 45]. Because concurrent use of alcohol and cocaine can produce greater euphoria and the perception of psychological well-being than the use of cocaine alone [100], these enhanced effects might encourage more subsequent concurrent use, leading to greater toxicity [100]. Because alcohol has been shown to be used more heavily by many concurrent users to ameliorate the intense discomfort associated with reducing or ceasing of cocaine use [101], not surprisingly, concurrent use of alcohol and cocaine has been linked to an increased risk of developing secondary alcoholism [102].

Given that many of the interrelationships between alcohol and illicit drug use are still not well understood, those dual addictions continue to complicate intervention efforts [103]. For example, data have shown that alcohol use has been linked to more severe cocaine use, poor retention in substance use treatment, and poor recovery outcome [104]. Even though a number of clinical intervention studies have found that alcohol use at baseline had no effect on treatment outcome for cocaine abuse [104], a lower level of alcohol use both at and after a few weeks of treatment has been predictive of future cocaine abstinence. Thus, the ability to reduce alcohol use during early treatment is considered an important prognostic factor [104, 105]. Because drinking alcohol is linked closely to relapse episodes [105], prevention of cocaine relapse should include interventions designed to reduce drinking or abstinence from all substances use during treatment, including alcohol [104]. Individuals with dual addictions often have more psychological and social problems [106]. Current intervention should include an assessment of motivation and readiness, identification of specific co-occurring patterns, and recommendations on optimal lifestyle changes, along with psychosocial and educational interventions and pharmacotherapy based on individual factors [106, 107]. Risk reduction should also consider advice on effective contraception use until the treatment of dual addictions is successful [1, 2].

3.3. Co-Occurring Alcohol Use and Mental Illness

In one clinical study, approximately one in seven women was identified with and treated for depression during the period from 39 weeks prior to through 39 weeks after pregnancy [108]. Alcohol use has also been linked with both general psychological distress and specific psychiatric disorders among women [34, 109, 110], especially mood disorders [111-113]. For example, a number of clinical studies have found that up to 70% of pregnant women experience some symptoms of depression [114], and up to 50% of pregnant women might actually meet the diagnostic criteria for depression during their pregnancy [115, 116]. Studies also have revealed that women who are socially anxious are significantly more likely to use alcohol to get greater anxiety relief in social situations [66, 117, 118]. Furthermore, women with higher levels of depression often continue to use alcohol despite knowing they are pregnant and clinician advice against alcohol use [119]. Such use can result in serious adverse birth outcomes, including one or more fetal alcohol-related conditions [1, 15, 16].

Co-occurring alcohol misuse and specific psychiatric disorders have broad clinical and public health significance, as they are often associated with more severe adverse health outcomes and higher socioeconomic costs [11, 21]. Many of the earlier barriers to appropriate treatment for patients with co-occurring disorders occurred because they were treated in two separate systems (i.e., mental health or substance abuse) [11, 35]. Patients with co–occurring disorders are frequently referred back and forth between health service systems for the purpose of treating the "primary cause" of their problems, resulting in their noncompliance with medication regimens, poor treatment responses, frequent hospital admissions, and relapses with both conditions, thus placing them at heightened risk of morbidity and mortality [11, 40, 120].

There is well-established evidence to indicate that concurrent disorders are frequently underdiagnosed and inadequately treated, despite the fact that these co-occurring conditions are prevalent [33-35, 120]. Clinicians in various healthcare settings, including alcohol misuse treatment and mental health clinics, have frequent opportunities to identify women who have various risks related to drinking alcohol. Optimally, health care providers should be well-informed about the heightened risks and complications of co-occurring conditions, particularly among women with serious psychological distress who are heavier alcohol users. Health care providers also should provide intervention for them using proper assessment, counseling, or referral for integrated dual diagnosis and treatment as appropriate. Although more results of integrated treatment are forthcoming, research has shown that most existing efficacious treatments for reducing psychiatric symptoms also tend to work among dually diagnosed patients, and many efficacious treatments for reducing substance use work with dually diagnosed patients [121]. Furthermore, evidence-based programs have consistently shown that the key to effective treatment of co-occurring conditions is the integration of mental health and substance abuse treatment services in a cohesive and unitary system of care [22, 35, 40, 122, 123]. Other similar options might include adding needed intervention services at existing facilities that currently treat a single disorder for patients with less severe dual conditions [33]. Prevention strategies for reducing alcohol-related morbidity and mortality among women of childbearing age (e.g. alcohol-exposed pregnancies) should consider the role of co-occurring conditions and include integrated services for dual diagnosis and treatment when appropriate.

4. DISCUSSION

Alcohol use can co-occur with other behavioral health risk factors (e.g. tobacco use, illicit drug use, and mental illness), thereby placing women and their offspring at heightened risk for morbidity and mortality. Patterns of alcohol use and co-occurring risk factors are exceedingly complex. Their associated health consequences are affected by biological, behavioral, and social influences at multiple levels in multiple domains. In addition to personal factors, influences from peers, families, communities, and social policies or norms, as well as early life experiences and allostatic loads resulting from cumulative adverse social or economic effects, can all affect women's drinking behavior and associated health consequences [10, 124-126]. Nevertheless, addressing these co-occurring risk factors in clinical and public health settings can prevent current and future behavioral health risks. These include preventing initiation of high-risk behaviors, improving existing health conditions, decreasing the likelihood of co-morbidity, enhancing treatment adherence, preventing relapse, and subsequently maintaining long-term behavioral changes [5, 11, 22, 36-45]. Although several patterns of co-occurring alcohol use and behavioral health risk factors (i.e., tobacco, illicit drug use, mental illness) have been discussed, it must be pointed out that there are many other possible combinations of behavioral health risk factors that can also have important public health significance for women of childbearing age [7, 78, 83, 127] For example, when tobacco use co-occurs with illicit drug use (i.e., marijuana and cocaine use) or mental illness, smoking cessation can be indicated and beneficial for people already in recovery, as it can protect against relapse back into illicit drug use [134, 135]. Also, alcohol has been linked to unwanted sex, unplanned pregnancy, alcohol-exposed pregnancy, sexually transmitted diseases, sexual assault and violence, infertility, stillbirth and miscarriage among women [8, 47, 136-139]. Additionally, as reported by one population representative study, there was a higher estimated prevalence of binge drinking by women who were current smokers, and who were not taking daily multivitamins or pills containing folic acid which has been linked to adverse birth outcomes [53, 140]. Therefore, identifying women who are consuming alcohol and who have co-occurring behavioral health risk factors and intervening with them is one important strategy for reducing alcohol-related morbidity and mortality.

Currently, several United States federal agencies, including CDC, NIAAA, and SAMHSA, are making efforts to combine prevention messages and to fund more research using interventions that address multiple risk factors. Because many women frequently present with alcohol use and other interrelated and amenable risk factors in various healthcare settings, multiple risk factor screening should be feasible, although the actual screening instrument will depend on several factors, including purpose, primary risk factor of concern, target population, health care settings, and a number of other practical considerations [141]. Present strategies for alcohol-related risk reduction include broad-based implementation of screening and brief intervention in primary care and women's health care settings [52, 53, 142-145]. Until more results from intervention studies on co-occurring multiple behavioral health risk factors are forthcoming to guide specific multiple risk factor screening and intervention, prevention of alcohol-related morbidity and mortality among women of childbearing age should consider the role of concurrent risky behaviors, and encourage dual cessation as appropriate, as there is evidence of efficacy and no indication of harm.

While results of multiple risk factor intervention among women of childbearing age are becoming available, population-based epidemiologic studies can provide important evidence to inform the development of prevention research and programs for target populations or subgroups. Presently, there is a lack of information about the co-occurring patterns, distribution, and determinants for alcohol use and many co-occurring behavioral health risk factors among nationally representative populations of women of childbearing age. The lack of adequate scientific data is a barrier for advancing population-based prevention efforts among women of childbearing age. Efforts to strengthen such epidemiologic foundations are necessary in order to identify those women who might benefit from enhanced intervention strategies in many clinical and public health settings.

5. CONCLUSION

Excessive drinking among women of childbearing age continues to be an important public health concern. Such drinking increases the risk for alcohol-related problems or complicates the management of other health concerns. Prevention of alcohol-related morbidity and mortality among women of childbearing age needs to incorporate the success of evidence-based strategies that address interrelated risk factors across more than one domain.

ACKNOWLEDGMENTS

The authors thank the anonymous reviewers for their valuable comments and suggestions.

No financial conflict of interest was reported by the authors of this paper.

Disclaimer: The findings and conclusions in this report are those of the authors and do not necessarily represent the official position of the Centers for Disease Control and Prevention.

REFERENCES

[1]   Floyd RL, Sobell M, Velasquez M, Ingersoll K, Nettleman M, Sobell L, et al. Preventing alcohol-exposed pregnancies–a randomized controlled trial. *Am J Prev Med* 2007;32(1):1-10.

[2]   Ingersoll K, Floyd L, Sobell M, and Velasquez MM. Reducing the risk of alcohol-exposed pregnancies: a study of a motivational intervention in community settings. *Pediatrics* 2003;111(5 Part 2):1131-5.

[3]   Coups EJ, Gaba A and Orleans CT. Physician screening for multiple behavioral health risk factors. *Am J Prev Med* 2004;27(2 Suppl):34-41.

[4]   Fine LJ, Philogene GS, Gramling R, Coups EJ, and Sinha S. Prevalence of multiple chronic disease risk factors. 2001 National Health Interview Survey. *Am J Prev Med* 2004;27(2 Suppl):18-24.

[5]   Nigg CR, Allegrante JP and Ory M. Theory-comparison and multiple-behavior research: common themes advancing health behavior research. *Health Educ Res* 2002;17(5):670-9.

[6]   Chiolero A, Wietlisbach V, Ruffieux C, Paccaud F, and Cornuz J. Clustering of risk behaviors with cigarette consumption: A population-based survey. *Prev Med* 2006;42(5):348-53.

[7]   Poortinga W. The prevalence and clustering of four major lifestyle risk factors in an English adult population. *Prev Med* 2007;44(2):124-8.

[8]   Bradley KA, Badrinath S, Bush K, Boyd-Wickizer J, and Anawalt B. Medical risks for women who drink alcohol. *J Gen Intern Med* 1998;13(9):627-39.

[9]   DHHS. U.S. Department of Health and Human Services. Healthy people 2010. 2nd ed. With understanding and improving health and objectives for improving health. 2 vols. Washington: U.S. Government Printing Office. 2000.

[10]   IOM. Institute of Medicine. Committee on Health and Behavior: Research, Practice and Policy, Board on Neuroscience and Behavioral Health. National Academic Press, Washington, D.C. 2001.

[11]   DHHS. U.S. Department of Health and Human Services. Report to congress on the prevention and treatment of co-occurring substance abuse disorders and mental disorders. Rockville, MD: Substance Abuse and Mental Health Services Administration.; 2002.

[12]   Cnattingius S. The epidemiology of smoking during pregnancy: smoking prevalence, maternal characteristics, and pregnancy outcomes. *Nicotine Tob Res* 2004;6 Suppl 2:S125-40.

[13] CASA. Women Under the Influence. The National Center on Addiction and Substance Abuse at Columbia University (CASA) *The Johns Hopkins University Press* 2005.

[14] Lejuez CW, Bornovalova MA, Reynolds EK, Daughters SB, and Curtin JJ. Risk factors in the relationship between gender and crack/cocaine. *Exp Clin Psychopharmacol* 2007;15(2):165-75.

[15] Diego MA, Jones NA, Field T, Hernandez-Reif M, Schanberg S, Kuhn C, et al. Maternal psychological distress, prenatal cortisol, and fetal weight. *Psychosom Med* 2006;68(5):747-53.

[16] Kelly R, Russo J, Holt V, Danielsen B, Zatzick D, Walker E, et al. Psychiatric and substance use disorders as risk factors for low birth weight and preterm delivery. *Obstet Gynecol* 2002;100(2):297-304.

[17] Juhl M, Nyboe Andersen AM, Gronbaek M, and Olsen J. Moderate alcohol consumption and waiting time to pregnancy. *Hum Reprod* 2002;16(12):2705-9.

[18] Kesmodel U, Wisborg K, Olsen SF, Henriksen TB, and Secher NJ. Moderate alcohol intake in pregnancy and the risk of spontaneous abortion. *Alcohol Alcohol* 2002;37(1):87-92.

[19] Henriksen TB, Hjollund NH, Jensen TK, Bonde JP, Andersson AM, Kolstad H, et al. Alcohol consumption at the time of conception and spontaneous abortion. *Am J Epidemiol* 2004;160(7):661-7.

[20] Schempf AH. Illicit drug use and neonatal outcomes: a critical review. *Obstet Gynecol Surv* 2007;62(11):749-57.

[21] DHHS. U.S. Department of Health and Human Services. Mental Health: A Report of the Surgeon General—Executive Summary. Rockville, MD: U.S. Department of Health and Human Services. Substance Abuse and Mental Health Services Administration.; 1999.

[22] Drake RE, Essock SM, Shaner A, Carey KB, Minkoff K, Kola L, et al. Implementing dual diagnosis services for clients with severe mental illness. *Psychiatr Serv* 2001;52(4):469-76.

[23] Poudevigne M and O'Connor P. A review of physical activity patterns in pregnant women and their relationship to psychological health. *Sports medicine* 2006;36(1):19-38.

[24] WHO. The Word Health Report: Reducing Risks, Promoting Healthy Life. World Health Organization (WHO), Geneva. URL: http://www.who.int/whr/2002/en/ Pdf file URL: http://www.who.int/entity/whr/2002/en/whr02_en.pdf. 2002.

[25] Galea S, Nandi A and Vlahov D. The social epidemiology of substance use. *Epidemiol Rev* 2004;26:36-52.

[26] Rehm J, Taylor B and Room R. Global burden of disease from alcohol, illicit drugs and tobacco. *Drug Alcohol Rev* 2006;25(6):503-13.

[27] Harwood R, Fountain D and Livermore G. The economic costs of alcohol and drug abuse in the United States, 1992. *Bethesda, MD: National Institute on Alcohol Abuse and Alcoholism (NIAAA) and National Institute on Drug Abuse (NIDA)* 1998.

[28] Rothman A. "Is there nothing more practical than a good theory?": Why innovations and advances in health behavior change will arise if interventions are used to test and refine theory. *Int J Behav Nutr Phys Act* 2004;1(1):11.

[29] Weinstein ND. Misleading tests of health behavior theories. *Ann Behav Med* 2007;33(1):1-10.

[30] Noar SM, Chabot M and Zimmerman RS. Applying health behavior theory to multiple behavior change: Considerations and approaches. *Prev Med* 2007.

[31] Morgenstern J. Perspectives and future directions. *Alcohol Clin Exp Res* 2007;31(s3):87s-90s.

[32] Orleans CT. Addressing multiple behavioral health risks in primary care. Broadening the focus of health behavior change research and practice. *Am J Prev Med* 2004;27(2 Suppl):1-3.

[33] Hendrickson E, Schmal M and Ekleberry S. Treating co-occurring disorders: A handbook for mental health and substance abuse professionals. Haworth Press; 2004.

[34] Kessler RC, Chiu WT, Demler O, Merikangas KR, and Walters EE. Prevalence, severity, and comorbidity of 12-month DSM-IV disorders in the National Comorbidity Survey Replication. *Arch Gen Psychiatry* 2005;62(6):617-27.

[35] Ries R. Co-occurring alcohol use and mental disorders. *J Clin Psychopharmacol* 2006;26 (Suppl 1):S30-6.

[36] Hyman DJ, Pavlik VN, Taylor WC, Goodrick GK, and Moye L. Simultaneous vs Sequential Counseling for Multiple Behavior Change. In; 2007. p. 1152-1158.

[37] Atkins D and Clancy C. Multiple risk factors interventions. Are we up to the challenge? *Am J Prev Med* 2004;27(2 Suppl):102-103.

[38] McKee SA, Krishnan-Sarin S, Shi J, Mase T, and O'Malley SS. Modeling the effect of alcohol on smoking lapse behavior. *Psychopharmacology (Berl)* 2006;189(2):201-10.

[39] Goldstein M, Whitlock E and DePue J. Multiple behavioral risk factor interventions in primary care. Summary of research evidence. *Am J Prev Med* 2004;27(2 Suppl):61-79.

[40] Mueser K, Noordsy D, Drake R, and Fox L. Integrated treatment for dual disorders: a guide to effective practice New York, NY: The Guilford Press; 2003.

[41] Stenbacka M, Beck O, Leifman A, Romelsjo A, and Helander A. Problem drinking in relation to treatment outcome among opiate addicts in methadone maintenance treatment. *Drug Alcohol Rev* 2007;26(1):55-63.

[42] Kohn CS, Tsoh JY and Weisner CM. Changes in smoking status among substance abusers: baseline characteristics and abstinence from alcohol and drugs at 12-month follow-up. *Drug Alcohol Depend* 2003;69(1):61-71.

[43] Jensen MK, Sorensen TI, Andersen AT, Thorsen T, Tolstrup JS, Godtfredsen NS, et al. A prospective study of the association between smoking and later alcohol drinking in the general population. *Addiction* 2003;98(3):355-63.

[44] Wagner FA and Anthony JC. Into the world of illegal drug use: exposure opportunity and other mechanisms linking the use of alcohol, tobacco, marijuana, and cocaine. *Am J Epidemiol* 2002;155(10):918-25.

[45] Wilcox HC, Wagner FA and Anthony JC. Exposure opportunity as a mechanism linking youth marijuana use to hallucinogen use. *Drug Alcohol Depend* 2002;66(2):127-35.

[46] Huebner RB and Tonigan JS. The Search for Mechanisms of Behavior Change in Evidence-Based Behavioral Treatments for Alcohol Use Disorders: Overview. *Alcohol Clin Exp Res* 2007;31(s3):1s-3s.

[47] Floyd RL, O'Connor MJ, Sokol RJ, Bertrand J, and Cordero JF. Recognition and prevention of fetal alcohol syndrome. *Obstet Gynecol* 2005;106(5):1059−64.

[48] CDC. Behavioral Risk Factor Surveillance System Survey Data 2001-2006, Atlanta, Georgia. Atlanta, Georgia: U.S. Department of Health and Human Services; 2007.

[49] NIAAA. Binge drinking defined. Newsletter, Winter 2004, Number 3. National Institute on Alcohol Abuse and Alcoholism, National Institute of Health, U.S. Department of Health and Human Services. Rockville, Maryland; 2004.

[50] CDC. Alcohol use among women of childbearing age−United States, 1991−1999. *MMWR Morb Mortal Wkly Rep* 2001;51:273−6.

[51] CDC. Alcohol consumption among women who are pregnant or who might become pregnant−United States, 2002. *MMWR Morb Mortal Wkly Rep* 2004;53(50):1178−81.

[52] Tsai J, Floyd RL and Bertrand J. Tracking binge drinking among U.S. childbearing-age women. *Prev Med* 2007b;44(4):298-302.

[53] Tsai J, Floyd RL, Green PP, and Boyle CA. Patterns and average volume of alcohol use among women of childbearing age. *Matern Child Health J* 2007a;11(5):437-45.

[54] Caetano R, Ramisetty-Mikler S, Floyd LR, and McGrath C. The epidemiology of drinking among women of child-bearing age. *Alcohol Clin Exp Res* 2006;30(6):1023-30.

[55] Mokdad A, Brewer R, Naimi T, and Warner L. Binge drinking is a problem that cannot be ignored. *Prev Med* 2007;44(4):303-4.

[56] NIAAA. Alcohol: A Woman's Health Issue. NIH Publication No. 04–4956. National Institute on Alcohol Abuse and Alcoholism (NIAAA). Rockville, MD. Available URL: http://pubs.niaaa.nih.gov/publications/brochurewomen/women.htm. 2005.

[57] DHHS. Office of the Surgeon General. Surgeon General's Advisory on Alcohol Use in Pregnancy. U.S. Department of Health & Human Services. Washington, DC. Availabe URL: http://www.lhvpn.net/hhspress.html. 2004.

[58] NIAAA. Frequently Asked Questions for the General Public. Available URL: http://www.niaaa.nih.gov/FAQs/General-English/default.htm. *National Institute on Alcohol Abuse and Alcoholism (NIAAA), Bethesda, MD* 2007.

[59] Floyd RL, Decoufle P and Hungerford DW. Alcohol use prior to pregnancy recognition. *Am J Prev Med* 1999;17(2):101-7.

[60] Tough S, Tofflemire K, Clarke M, and Newburn-Cook C. Do women change their drinking behaviors while trying to conceive? An opportunity for preconception counseling. *Clin Med Res* 2006;4(2):97-105.

[61] Welch-Carre E. The neurodevelopmental consequences of prenatal alcohol exposure. *Adv Neonatal Care* 2005;5(4):217-29.

[62] Maier SE and West JR. Drinking patterns and alcohol-related birth defects. *Alcohol Res Health* 2001;25(3):168−74.

[63] Day NL, Leech SL, Richardson GA, Cornelius MD, Robles N, and Larkby C. Prenatal alcohol exposure predicts continued deficits in offspring size at 14 years of age. *Alcohol Clin Exp Res* 2002;26(10):1584−91.

[64] Sood B, Delaney-Black V, Covington C, Nordstrom-Klee B, Ager J, Templin T, et al. Prenatal alcohol exposure and childhood behavior at age 6 to 7 years: I. dose-response effect. *Pediatrics* 2001;108(2):E34.

[65] Naimi TS, Brewer RD, Mokdad A, Denny C, Serdula MK, and Marks JS. Binge drinking among US adults. *JAMA* 2003;289(1):70−5.

[66] Thomas SE, Randall CL, and Carrigan MH. Drinking to cope in socially anxious individuals: a controlled study. *Alcohol Clin Exp Res* 2003;27(12):1937-43.

[67] Naimi TS, Brewer RD, Miller JW, Okoro C, and Mehrotra C. What do binge drinkers drink? Implications for alcohol control policy. *Am J Prev Med* 2007;33(3):188-93.

[68] Bobo JK and Husten C. Sociocultural influences on smoking and drinking. *Alcohol Res Health* 2000;24(4):225-32.

[69] Willenbring ML. A broader view of change in drinking behavior. *Alcohol Clin Exp Res* 2007;31(10 Suppl):84s-86s.

[70] NIAAA. Alcohol Alert: Alcohol and Tobacco. No. 71. National Institute on Alcohol Abuse and Alcoholism (NIAAA). Rockville, MD. 2007.

[71] Breslau N, Peterson E, Schultz L, Andreski P, and Chilcoat H. Are smokers with alcohol disorders less likely to quit? *Am J Public Health* 1996;86(7):985-90.

[72] Falk D, Yi H and Hiller-Sturmhöfel S. An epidemiologic analysis of co-occurring alcohol and tobacco use and disorders: findings from the National Epidemiologic Survey on Alcohol and Related Conditions. *Alcohol Res Health* 2006;29(3):162-71.

[73] Kranzler HR, Amin H, Cooney NL, Cooney JL, Burleson JA, Petry N, et al. Screening for health behaviors in ambulatory clinical settings: does smoking status predict hazardous drinking? *Addict Behav* 2002;27(5):737-49.

[74] John U, Hill A, Rumpf HJ, Hapke U, and Meyer C. Alcohol high risk drinking, abuse and dependence among tobacco smoking medical care patients and the general population. *Drug Alcohol Depend* 2003;69(2):189-95.

[75] John U, Meyer C, Rumpf HJ and Hapke U. Probabilities of alcohol high-risk drinking, abuse or dependence estimated on grounds of tobacco smoking and nicotine dependence. *Addiction* 2003;98(6):805-14.

[76] Weitzman ER and Chen YY. The co-occurrence of smoking and drinking among young adults in college: national survey results from the United States. *Drug Alcohol Depend* 2005;80(3):377-86.

[77] Burling AS and Burling TA. A comparison of self-report measures of nicotine dependence among male drug/alcohol-dependent cigarette smokers. *Nicotine Tob Res* 2003;5(5):625-33.

[78] Ceballos NA, Tivis R, Lawton-Craddock A, and Nixond SJ. Nicotine and cognitive efficiency in alcoholics and illicit stimulant abusers: implications of smoking cessation for substance users in treatment. *Subst Use Misuse* 2006;41(3):265-81.

[79] Rohsenow DJ, Colby SM, Martin RA, and Monti PM. Nicotine and other substance interaction expectancies questionnaire: relationship of expectancies to substance use. *Addict Behav* 2005;30(4):629-41.

[80] Drobes D, Beylotte F, Scott M, Saladin M, Randell C, and Anton R. Cross-reactivity to alcohol and smoking cues. *Alcohol Clin Exp Res* 2000;24:147a.

[81] Fiore M, Bailey W and Cohen S. Treating tobacco use and dependence. Clinical practice guideline. U.S. Department of Health and Human Services. Public Health Service, Rockville, MD. 2000.

[82] Gulliver SB, Kamholz BW and Helstrom AW. Smoking cessation and alcohol abstinence: what do the data tell us? *Alcohol Res Health* 2006;29(3):208-12.

[83] Ziedonis DM, Guydish J, Williams J, Steinberg M, and Foulds J. Barriers and solutions to addressing tobacco dependence in addiction treatment programs. *Alcohol Res Health* 2006;29(3):228-35.

[84] Ellingstad TP, Sobell LC, Sobell MB, Cleland PA, and Agrawal S. Alcohol abusers who want to quit smoking: implications for clinical treatment. *Drug Alcohol Depend* 1999;54(3):259-65.

[85]   Burling TA, Ramsey TG, Seidner AL, and Kondo CS. Issues related to smoking cessation among substance abusers. *J Subst Abuse* 1997;9:27-40.

[86]   Prochaska JJ, Velicer WF, Prochaska JO, Delucchi K, and Hall SM. Comparing intervention outcomes in smokers treated for single versus multiple behavioral risks. *Health Psychol* 2006;25(3):380-8.

[87]   Littel M and Franken IH. The effects of prolonged abstinence on the processing of smoking cues: an ERP study among smokers, ex-smokers and never-smokers. *J Psychopharmacol* 2007;21(8):873-82.

[88]   Kodl M, Fu SS and Joseph AM. Tobacco cessation treatment for alcohol-dependent smokers: when is the best time? *Alcohol Res Health* 2006;29(3):203-7.

[89]   McKee SA, Falba T, O'Malley SS, Sindelar J, and O'Connor PG. Smoking status as a clinical indicator for alcohol misuse in US adults. *Arch Intern Med* 2007;167(7):716-21.

[90]   Seidner AL, Burling TA, Gaither DE, and Thomas RG. Substance-dependent inpatients who accept smoking treatment. *J Subst Abuse* 1996;8(1):33-44.

[91]   Joseph AM, Nelson DB, Nugent SM, and Willenbring ML. Timing of alcohol and smoking cessation (TASC): smoking among substance use patients screened and enrolled in a clinical trial. *J Addict Dis* 2003;22(4):87-107.

[92]   NSDUH. Substance use during pregnancy: 2002 and 2003 Update. *Office of Applied Studies, Substance Abuse and Mental Health Services Administration (SAMHSA). The National Survey on Drug Use and Health* 2005;June 2, 2005.

[93]   Midanik LT, Tam TW and Weisner C. Concurrent and simultaneous drug and alcohol use: results of the 2000 National Alcohol Survey. *Drug Alcohol Depend* 2007;90(1):72-80.

[94]   Petry NM. A behavioral economic analysis of polydrug abuse in alcoholics: asymmetrical substitution of alcohol and cocaine. *Drug Alcohol Depend* 2001;62(1):31-9.

[95]   DHHS. Results from the 2005 National Survey on Drug Use and Health: National Findings. Department of Health and Human Services (DHHS) Substance Abuse and Mental Health Services Administration (SAMHSA). Office of Applied Studies (OAS). Rockville, MD. 2006.

[96]   Macdonald S, Erickson P, Wells S, Hathaway A, and Pakula B. Predicting violence among cocaine, cannabis, and alcohol treatment clients. *Addict Behav* 2007.

[97]   Curry MA. The interrelationships between abuse, substance use, and psychosocial stress during pregnancy. *J Obstet Gynecol Neonatal Nurs* 1998;27(6):692-9.

[98]   Tullis LM, Dupont R, Frost-Pineda K, and Gold MS. Marijuana and tobacco: a major connection? *J Addict Dis* 2003;22(3):51-62.

[99]   Kandel DB, Yamaguchi K and Chen K. Stages of progression in drug involvement from adolescence to adulthood: further evidence for the gateway theory. *J Stud Alcohol* 1992;53(5):447-57.

[100] McCance-Katz EF, Kosten TR and Jatlow P. Concurrent use of cocaine and alcohol is more potent and potentially more toxic than use of either alone--a multiple-dose study. *Biol Psychiatry* 1998;44(4):250-9.

[101] Magura S and Rosenblum A. Modulating effect of alcohol use on cocaine use. *Addict Behav* 2000;25(1):117-22.

[102] Carroll KM, Rounsaville BJ and Bryant KJ. Alcoholism in treatment-seeking cocaine abusers: clinical and prognostic significance. *J Stud Alcohol* 1993;54(2):199-208.

[103] Gossop M, Marsden J and Stewart D. Dual dependence: assessment of dependence upon alcohol and illicit drugs, and the relationship of alcohol dependence among drug misusers to patterns of drinking, illicit drug use and health problems. *Addiction* 2002;97(2):169-78.

[104] Mengis MM, Maude-Griffin PM, Delucchi K, and Hall SM. Alcohol use affects the outcome of treatment for cocaine abuse. *Am J Addict* 2002;11(3):219-27.

[105] McKay JR, Alterman AI, Rutherford MJ, Cacciola JS, and McLellan AT. The relationship of alcohol use to cocaine relapse in cocaine dependent patients in an aftercare study. *J Stud Alcohol* 1999;60(2):176-80.

[106] Flannery B, Morgenstern J, McKay J, Wechsberg W, and Litten R. Co-occurring alcohol and cocaine dependence: recent findings from clinical and field studies. *Alcoholism: clinical and experimental research* 2004;28(6):976-81.

[107] Lamberg L. Road to recovery for cocaine users can start in primary care setting. *JAMA* 2004;292(15):1807-1809.

[108] Dietz PM, Williams SB, Callaghan WM, Bachman DJ, Whitlock EP, and Hornbrook MC. Clinically identified maternal depression before, during, and after pregnancies ending in live births. *Am J Psychiatry* 2007;164(10):1515-20.

[109] DHHS. U.S. Department of Health and Human Services. The Numbers Count: Mental Disorders in America. A summary of statistics describing the prevalence of mental disorders in America. Rockville, MD: Substance Abuse and Mental Health Services Administration, Center for Mental Health Services, National Institutes of Health, National Institute of Mental Health.; 2006.

[110] DHHS. Women Hold Up Half the Sky: Women and Mental Health Research. A brief overview of research into mental illness in women. National Institute of Mental Health (NIMH), National Institute of Health (NIH). NIH Publication No. 01-4607; 2001.

[111] APA. Diagnostic and Statistical Manual on Mental Disorders, 4th Edition, Text Revision (DSM-IV-TR). American Psychiatric Association. Washington, DC: American Psychiatric Association; 2000.

[112] DHHS. Alcohol and Health. The Ninth Special Report to Congress from the U.S. Department of Health and Human Services. NIH Publication No. 97-4127. Washington DC: U.S. Department of Health and Human Services; 1997.

[113] Li T-K, Hewitt BG and Grant BF. Alcohol use disorders and mood disorders: A National Institute on Alcohol Abuse and Alcoholism perspective. *Biol Psychiatry* 2004;56(10):718-720.

[114] Llewellyn AM, Stowe ZN and Nemeroff CB. Depression during pregnancy and the puerperium. *J Clin Psychiatry* 1997;58 Suppl 15:26-32.

[115] Kurki T, Hiilesmaa V, Raitasalo R, Mattila H, and Ylikorkala O. Depression and anxiety in early pregnancy and risk for preeclampsia. *Obstet Gynecol* 2000;95(4):487-90.

[116] McKee MD, Cunningham M, Jankowski KR, and Zayas L. Health-related functional status in pregnancy: relationship to depression and social support in a multi-ethnic population. *Obstet Gynecol* 2001;97(6):988-93.

[117] Meshberg-Cohen S and Svikis D. Panic disorder, trait anxiety, and alcohol use in pregnant and nonpregnant women. *Compr Psychiatry* 2007;48(6):504-10.

[118] Ham LS, Bonin M and Hope DA. The role of drinking motives in social anxiety and alcohol use. *J Anxiety Disord* 2007;21(8):991-1003.

[119] O' Connor M and Whaley S. Health care provider advice and risk factors associated with alcohol consumption following pregnancy recognition. *J Stud Alcohol* 2006;67(1):22-31.

[120] Kranzler HR and Rosenthal RN. Dual diagnosis: alcoholism and co-morbid psychiatric disorders. *Am J Addict* 2003;12 Suppl 1:S26-40.

[121] Tiet QQ and Mausbach B. Treatments for patients with dual diagnosis: a review. *Alcohol Clin Exp Res* 2007;31(4):513-36.

[122] Sciacca K and Thompson C. Program development and integrated treatment across systems for dual diagnosis: mental illness, drug addiction, and alcoholism (MIDAA). *J Ment Health Adm* 1996;23(3):288-297.

[123] Velasquez MM, Carbonari JP and DiClemente CC. Psychiatric severity and behavior change in alcoholism: the relation of the transtheoretical model variables to psychiatric distress in dually diagnosed patients. *Addict Behav* 1999;24(4):481-96.

[124] Leatherdale S. What modifiable factors are associated with cessation intentions among smoking youth? *Addictive Behaviors* 2008;33(1):217-223.

[125] Lu MC and Halfon N. Racial and ethnic disparities in birth outcomes: a life-course perspective. *Matern Child Health J* 2003;7(1):13-30.

[126] Geronimus AT, Hicken M, Keene D, and Bound J. "Weathering" and age patterns of allostatic load scores among blacks and whites in the United States. *Am J Public Health* 2006;96(5):826-33.

[127] Flynn HA, Walton MA, Chermack ST, Cunningham RM, and Marcus SM. Brief detection and co-occurrence of violence, depression and alcohol risk in prenatal care settings. *Arch Womens Ment Health* 2007;10(4):155-61.

[128] Vandelanotte C, Reeves MM, Brug J, and De Bourdeaudhuij I. A randomized trial of sequential and simultaneous multiple behavior change interventions for physical activity and fat intake. *Prev Med* 2007.

[129] Poortinga W. Associations of physical activity with smoking and alcohol consumption: a sport or occupation effect? *Prev Med* 2007;45(1):66-70.

[130] Blumenthal J, Babyak M, Doraiswamy P, Watkins L, Hoffman B, Barbour K, et al. Exercise and pharmacotherapy in the treatment of major depressive disorder. *Psychosom Med* 2007;69(7):587-96.

[131] Husky MM, Mazure CM, Paliwal P, and McKee SA. Gender differences in the comorbidity of smoking behavior and major depression. *Drug Alcohol Depend* 2007.

[132] Vandiver V. Health promotion as brief treatment: Strategies for women with co-morbid health and mental health conditions. *Brief Treat Crisis Interv. 2007;7(3):161-175. Oxford University Press* 2007.

[133] Richardson CR, Faulkner G, McDevitt J, Skrinar GS, Hutchinson DS, and Piette JD. Integrating physical activity into mental health services for persons with serious mental illness. *Psychiatr Serv* 2005;56(3):324-31.

[134] Sullivan MA and Covey LS. Current perspectives on smoking cessation among substance abusers. *Curr Psychiatry Rep* 2002;4(5):388-96.

[135] Hall S. Nicotine Interventions with Comorbid Populations. *American journal of preventive medicine* 2007;33(6, Supplement 1):S406-S413.

[136] Goldstein AL, Barnett NP, Pedlow CT, and Murphy JG. Drinking in conjunction with sexual experiences among at-risk college student drinkers. *J Stud Alcohol Drugs* 2007;68(5):697-705.

[137] Ellickson PL, Collins RL, Bogart LM, Klein DJ, and Taylor SL. Scope of HIV risk and co-occurring psychosocial health problems among young adults: violence, victimization, and substance use. *J Adolesc Health* 2005;36(5):401-9.

[138] Hines DA and Straus MA. Binge drinking and violence against dating partners: the mediating effect of antisocial traits and behaviors in a multinational perspective. *Aggress Behav* 2007;33(5):441-57.

[139] Hurley M, Parker H and Wells DL. The epidemiology of drug facilitated sexual assault. *J Clin Forensic Med* 2006;13(4):181-5.

[140] CDC. Use of vitamins containing folic acid among women of childbearing age—United States, 2004: Centers for Disease Control and Prevention; 2004 Sept 17.

[141] Babor T, Sciamanna C and Pronk N. Assessing multiple risk behaviors in primary care. Screening issues and related concepts. *Am J Prev Med* 2004;27(2 Suppl):42-53.

[142] Chang G. Screening and brief intervention in prenatal care settings. *National Institute on Alcohol Abuse and Alcoholism (NIAAA).* 2006; Available at: http://pubs.niaaa.nih.gov/publications/arh28-2/80-84.htm.

[143] Fleming M. Screening and brief intervention in primary care settings. *National Institute on Alcohol Abuse and Alcoholism (NIAAA).* 2006; Available at: http://pubs.niaaa.nih.gov/publications/arh28-2/57-62.htm.

[144] USPSTF. US Preventive Services Task Force. Screening and behavioral counseling interventions in primary care to reduce alcohol misuse: recommendations statement. *Ann Intern Med* 2004;140:554-6.

[145] Whitlock EP, Orleans CT, Pender N, and Allan J. Evaluating primary care behavioral counseling interventions: an evidence-based approach. *Am J Prev Med* 2002;22(4):267-84.

In: Binge Drinking Research Progress
Editor: Kevin I. DiGuarde

ISBN 978-1-60692-065
© 2009 Nova Science Publishers, Inc.

Chapter 6

FETAL ALCOHOL SPECTRUM DISORDERS: AN OVERVIEW

Kieran D. O'Malley[*]
Jackson School of International Studies

INTRODUCTION

The association between prenatal alcohol exposure and its teratogenic effect on the developing fetus was first observed in Nantes, France by paediatrician Paul Lemoine in 1968. He described similar dysmorphic facial features and growth delays in 127 infants of mothers who had drank alcohol during their pregnancies. The clear central nervous system sequelae and associated physical manifestations from prenatal alcohol were elaborated upon and named the Fetal Alcohol Syndrome in two classic papers from Seattle by David Smith, Ken Jones, Christy Ulleland and Ann Streissguth in 1973. The Seattle group described eight unrelated infants from three different ethnic groups all born to mothers who were chronic alcoholics. Thus, it was established that prenatal alcohol exposure caused facial dysmorphology, growth delays and central nervous system abnormalities The current diagnostic criteria for Fetal Alcohol Syndrome still incorporates this triad of clinical effects, namely, dysmorphic facial features, growth retardation and central nervous system abnormalities. The essential principles of the teratogenic effects of prenatal alcohol involve;

i)   The dosage of alcohol (the agent) even a low dosage may be teratogenic,
ii) The timing(trimester) of the exposure during pregnancy. Each trimester of pregnancy has specific teratogenic effects, the 1st trimester, facial dysmorphology and growth deficiencies and the 2nd and 3rd trimester exposure has the most insidious effect on CNS development, especially the neurotransmitter development.
iii) Medical factors particular to the mother (or host). These include the chronicity of alcoholism in the mother and her general nutritional status, as well as the protective

factor of her specific genetic endowment. The group of infants and children who did not show the full Fetal Alcohol Syndrome were initially described as displaying Fetal Alcohol Effects (FAE).

Over twenty years later in 1996 the U.S. Institute of Medicine described 3 different conditions related to prenatal alcohol exposure, Full FAS, Partial FAS and Alcohol Related Neurodevelopmental Disorder (ARND). The ARND condition replacing the older FAE descriptive term. More recently the full clinical range of clinical effects associated with a range of alcohol exposure have been described under the umbrella title of FAS Spectrum Disorder initially described and documented by O'Malley and Hagerman in 1998, and subsequently refined to Fetal Alcohol Spectrum Disorder(s) (FASD) by O'Malley and Streissguth.in 2000. A recent consensus statement from NOFAS (National Organization of Fetal Alcohol Syndrome) and the FASD Centre of Excellence in FASD in Washington DC, April 15th 2004 states: " Fetal Alcohol Spectrum Disorders (FASD) is an umbrella term describing the range of effects that can occur in an individual whose mother drank alcohol during pregnancy. These effects may include physical, mental, behavioral, and /or learning disabilities with possible lifelong implications. The term FASD is not intended for use as a clinical diagnosis."

Thus the essence of understanding patients with FASD is to appreciate that they are not just the children of alcoholics (COA) or adult children of alcoholics (ACOA), where many of the behaviors and psychiatric disorders are learned and reflective of the chaotic and/or abusive home-rearing environment. The FASD population of patients are presenting clinical features related to the teratogenic effect of alcohol on the developing brain, irrespective of the home-rearing environment. FASD are now recognized as chronic developmental and neuropsychiatric disorders with two conditions, Fetal Alcohol Syndrome (FAS) and Alcohol Related Neurodevelopmental Disorder (ARND). Although FASD are true developmental disorders, as Streissguth and colleagues have shown in 1996, at least 70-75% of the patients have a normal IQ and it is the deficit in functional ability that is the kernel of the disability. Clinical experience is showing that the functional disability is more commonly related to the co-morbid neurospychiatric disorder (O'Malley 2005).

Recent interest has evolved in exploring the epigenetic component to Fetal Alcohol Spectrum Disorders. Epigenetics deals with regulatory mechanisms of gene activity and inheritance that are independent of changes in the nucleotide sequence of DNA(Pembrey 2002). The epigenetic mechanisms are in turn controlled by genes whose products encode the enzymes needed for DNA methylation, RNA regulatory apparatus and histone modifications to name a few. Already epigenetic factors have been shown to have a role in medical diseases, as well as in psychiatric diseases such as Schizophrenia and Alcohol Dependence (Song et al. 2003, Waterland et al. 2003, Tchurikov 2005). Current research has shown an association between alcohol dependence and GABA (A) receptors which is modulated by genetic imprinting (Song et al. 2003). Genetic imprinting is the phenomenon whereby one or two alleles are preferentially expressed, dependent on its parent of origin. The association between

* Kieran D.O'Malley M.B., D.A.B.P.N.(P); Lecturer / Adjunct Faculty, Dept. of Psychiatry and Behavioral Sciences and Henry M. Jackson School of International Studies, 22727 84th Ave W. Edmonds, WA 98026; Contact: omalley.kieran@gmail.com

psychiatric disorders, including alcohol dependence, and FASD has been documented by Baer et al. in1998 and Barr et al. 2006.

Genetic imprinting is one of the key areas of epigenetics that is currently being studied in FASD. The essence of genetic imprinting involves the encoding of gene methylation patterns which have been shown to differ between paternally and maternally derived alleles (Tchurikov 2005). Subsequently, the transmission of gene expression from parental to daughter cells commonly occurs through DNA methylation. The level of DNA methylation sharply decreases during early embryogenesis of mammals. However, it recovers later due to what is called de-novo methylation. A number of regulatory proteins, including DNA methyl transferases (DNMT), histone modifying enzymes (acetylases and deacetylases) and methyl CpG binding proteins, have been identified as involved in this epigenetic process(Tchurikov 2005).

The DNA methylation has been shown to be decreased in response to folate, zinc methionine/choline insufficiencies often associated with excessive alcohol intake. The relevance of the DNA hyomethylation in FASD relates to the possibility that this could result in the activation of genes that are normally inactivated. This key balance between gene silencing and gene activation has been postulated as the mechanism underpinning inappropriate gene transcription. Thus the major liver pathway of oxidative metabolism of ethanol which involves production of acetaldehyde by cytosolic alcohol dehydrogenase is accompanied by the reduction of NAD to NADH. This reduction alters the cellular redox state by decreasing the NAD/NADH ratio, and may result in gene activation with subsequent changes in gene expression. Many of these ideas are still speculative and further research will uncover their veracity. Nevertheless, at the present time there is a scientific belief that medical disorders, cancer or diabetes and psychiatric disorders, schizophrenia or alcohol dependence, may have their roots in epigenetic factors in the pregnant adult woman as well potentially her offspring. This would make FASD a mutagenic disorder, and necessitate a re-visitation of the effect of alcohol on the male spermatozoa involved in fertilization especially it's possible effect on male DNA or RNA(Anway et al. 2005).

EPIDEMIOLOGY

There have been differing analysis of the incidence and prevalence of FASD. Varying prevalence figures have been estimated for FAS from Cleveland, 4.6 per 1000 live births, 1.3 to 4.8 per 1000 live births in Roubaix, France and 2.8 per 1000 live births in Seattle. However, a recent estimate of the prevalence of FAS and ARND was 9.1 per 1000 live births in Seattle (Sampson et al. 1997). In contrast a recent extensive survey, of 922 first-grade students, aged 5 to 7 years, in 12 elementary schools in a South African community produced an incidence of more than 40 cases of FAS per 1,000 births among this population.

The varying rates have been attributed to higher maternal alcoholism, and binge drinking in particular, in some geographical areas. Also some researchers have postulated that there may be genetic differences in susceptibility to alcohol based on the individual's liver metabolism, specifically the alcohol dehydrogenase and acetaldehyde dehydrogenase pathways which metabolize alcohol. The challenges for more consistent mapping of incidence and prevalence of FASD will depend on the increasing awareness of the more common subtype ARND which is traditionally underestimated or even ignored because of the absence of facial dysmorphic features.

The University of Washington's Secondary Disability Study in 1996 showed no gender difference in parent or caregiver report of ADHD in 6 to 11.9 year old children with either FAS or FAE (ARND). This is significant as boys commonly show ADHD symptoms 4 to 5 times more commonly than girls. This suggests that the ADHD resulting from prenatal alcohol exposure is distributed equally between the genders. (O'Malley et al. 2006)

There have been no scientific studies showing an increase in mortality due to FASD. However, it is beginning to be recognized clinically that depression with suicidal attempts and impulsivity can lead to premature deaths in young adult FASD patients (Huggins and O'Malley 2004).

ETIOLOGY AND PATHOGENESIS

The etiology of FASD is clearly the teratogenic effect of prenatal alcohol exposure on the developing fetus. It remains to be seen if prenatal alcohol exerts its long term clinical effect as a mutagen. Nevertheless, the developmental and neuropsychiatric clinical presentation of this teratogenic effect has been shown to be effected by *genetic factors* which modulate a woman's susceptibility to having a baby with FASD. Studies have demonstrated that certain genetic traits have a protective effect on alcohol abusing pregnant women decreasing her likelihood of having a baby with full FAS. Also *environmental factors,* influence the clinical presentation of FASD. So a child raised in a stable and nuturant home, or in a stable environment when 8 to 12 years of age displays less adverse risk outcomes (Streissguth, et al., 2004). Whereas a child exposed to early abandonment, multiple foster home placements, or physical or sexual abuse shows much more complicated overlapping psychiatric disorders. Some of which include Post Traumatic Stress Disorder or Reactive Attachment Disorder.

The diffuse CNS effects of prenatal alcohol begin with the nerve cell. There may be direct toxic effect on nerve cells, producing cell death with massive apoptotic neurodegeneration in the developing brain (Olney, et al. 2000). It can also and disrupt astrocyte, glial cell and neuronal migration and maturation (Phillips, 1994, Guerri and Renau-Piqueras, 1997, Streissguth, 1997). Other work has studied the effect of alcohol on inhibiting L1, an immunoglobulin cell adhesion molecule that promotes cell–cell adhesion, cell migration and synaptic plasticity (Sutherland, et al., 1997, Ikonomidou, et al. 2000).Finally, recent research has pointed out the selective loss of complexin proteins in the frontal cortex of rats prenatally exposed to alcohol which may have parallels in future human studies (Barr, et al. 2005).The possible role of complexin protein in psychiatric disorders has been explored by Sawada and colleagues in 2002 and 2005.

Structural brain damage in severe FASD has been reviewed using autopsy reports of early infant deaths. Diffuse structural brain changes reported included severe brain malformations with hydrocephalus, microcephaly, enlarged ventricles, cerebellar hypoplasia, corpus callosal agenesis, and hetertopias (pockets of arrested migration of groups of cells (Streissguth 1997, Hagerman 1999).

Brain imaging (MRI, CAT SCAN) techniques have enabled mapping of brain abnormalities in patients with less severe forms of FASD. Microcephaly is consistently seen.

The corpus callosum appears to be the area of the brain most commonly affected by prenatal alcohol. Researchers have demonstrated morphological changes in the shape of the corpus callosum. The caudate, which is important for working memory and executive function cognition is the area most affected in the basal ganglion. The cerebellum can be smaller, especially the anterior cerebellar vermis (vermal bodies I through V) compared to controls. Lastly, the hippocampus has been shown to be decreased in shape and volume (Mattson, et al. 1994, Riley, et al. 1995, Sowell, et al., 1996, Swayze, et al. 1997, Hagerman 1999, Bookstein, et al. 2001).

Neurotransmitter development is disrupted by prenatal alcohol exposure. Deficits have been found in the dopaminergic, noradrenergic, serotonergic, GABAergic, cholinergic, glutaminergic and histaminergic. The dopaminergic and noradrenergic system deficits most likely are connected with the ADHD presentation of patients with FASD. Previous rat research has demonstrated that the D1 receptors of the mesolimbic dopamine system are more affected by prenatal alcohol than the nigrostriatal or tegmental dopamine D1 receptor system. Ongoing research is analyzing the clinical effect of the prenatal alcohol disruption of the balance between the inhibitory, GABA, and the excitatory Glutaminergic neurotransmitters (Hannigan 1996).

Neurophysiological abnormalities have been demonstrated to be sequelae of prenatal alcohol exposure. They were initially described by Lemoine and colleagues in 1968. Recent work in the 1990's has reported the increased prevalence of temporal lobe dysrhythmia and complex partial seizure disorder in FASD children and adolescents. All these patients responded to carbamazepine (O'Malley and Barr 1998). Animal research has shown the kindling of seizures due to the effect of prenatal alcohol on the GABA ergic cells in the hippocampus which lowers the seizure threshold.(Bonthius et al. 2001) This is borne out in humans where it appears GABA agents have good efficacy for FASD patients with seizure disorder.

DIAGNOSTIC CLINICAL FEATURES OF FASD

Developmental Impairments

The developmental disability of FASD is a Complex Learning Disorder affecting multiple domains of functioning including working memory, attention, impulsivity, learning, interpersonal relatedness, social skills and language development. The patient's complex Learning Disorder is coded under AXIS II in DSM- IV T-R. It often includes a Mathematics Disorder (315.1), and/ or Disorder of Written Expression (315.2) and/or Reading Disorder(315.0), and. evidence of a Mixed Receptive/Expressive Language Disorder(315.32) with specific deficits in social cognition and social communication. Sometimes a more generic coding of Cognitive Disorder NOS (249.9) or Learning Disorder NOS (315.9) may suffice as initial clinical descriptions.

A standardized intellectual functioning assessment is the first step in assessing the cognitive function i.e., WPPSSI or WISC –IV. The deficits in functional development are best quantified by standardized instruments such as the Vineland Adaptive Behavioral Scale (VABS). This shows varying deficits in daily living skills, socialization and communication.

It is important to remember that 70 to 75% of patients with FASD are not mentally retarded, so the developmental disability is commonly seen in the context of a normal I.Q.

Developmental disability in FASD is also seen in gross and fine motor delays which can be coded Developmental Coordination Disorder(315.4).

Neuropsychiatric Impairment

Neither of the current diagnostic nomenclature DSM-IV T-R or ICD- 10 acknowledge the neurodevelopmental or neuropsychiatric disorders resulting from prenatal alcohol exposure. However, there is a general category called Mental Disorders due to a General Medical Condition which can be used to describe FASD and their co-morbid psychiatric presentation. Each descriptor has a code which can then be used for re-imbursement through the different medical insurance companies, for example:

- Mood Disorder due to general medical condition of prenatal alcohol exposure with evidence of FAS (293.83)
- Anxiety Disorder due to general medical condition of prenatal alcohol exposure with evidence of PFAS(293.84)
- Psychotic Disorder due to general medical condition of prenatal alcohol exposure with evidence of ARND (293.8x)
- Personality Change due to general medical condition of prenatal alcohol exposure with evidence of ARND (310.1). The personality changes include, Labile, Disinhibited, or Paranoid.

ICD-10. has similar categories which can be used as descriptors for patients with FASD, and also facilitate re-imbursement. In this instance the terms are:

- Catatonic Disorder due to a general medical condition of prenatal alcohol exposure with evidence of FAS
- Personality Change due to a general medical condition of prenatal alcohol exposure with evidence of ARND

Patients with FASD can present clinical symptoms from infancy/young childhood. The clinical presentation is described using the Zero to Three Diagnostic Classification (Zero to three 1994). This classification has been developed to describe psychiatric disorders in the under three year old population, which is not included in the more commonly used DSM IV T-R classification. AXIS I disorders cover the major psychiatric disorders in the infant or young child. The AXIS II component analyses the relationship between the mother or care provider and the infant or young child. The psychiatric diagnoses reflect the CNS sensory integration problems that are pathognomonic of FASD in infancy. The Zero to Three classification is less widely known in primary care environments, but has been developed since 1994 and is well validated and used commonly in the early childhood mental health world (DC:O-3R 2005).

Infants and young children with FASD commonly demonstrate Regulation Disorders of Sensory Processing which are characterized by difficulties in tolerating environmental stimuli, co-ordinating basic motor movements or in approaching and interacting with others in their immediate environment. Three types of Regulation Disorder are seen:

i)   Hypersensitive : Type A Fearful / Cautious or Type B Negative Defiant may present in the FASD infant or young child by becoming upset very easily, crying, irritable with no clear cause .i.e. sometimes the force of the water jet from a shower may precipitate an episode of marked distress.

ii) Hypopsensitive /Underresposive (either Withdrawn and Difficult to engage or Self-Absorbed) may be evidenced by the appearance of marked avoidance and withdrawal in social situations. Also the young child may show little reactive to visual or auditory cues

iii) Sensory Stimulation –Seeking /Impulsive may be seen in the infant or young child's pervasive high motor activity and almost ceaseless motion. Often the infant or young child shows dangerous impulsivity and is quite accident prone.

Other psychiatric disorders which can be seen are: Disorders of Affect of Infancy and Early Childhood are diagnosed when the infant or young child shows emotional incontinence with overwhelming crying or giddiness.

Anxiety Disorders of Infancy and Early Childhood are diagnosed if the infant or young child has a panic attack with hyperventilation in a common social situation i.e., a mother takes a toy away from the young child.

Finally the psychiatric disorders may be of a Secondary nature due to environmental stressors such as Reactive Attachment Disorder of Infancy or Early Childhood related to separation from birth mother or multiple foster home placements.

The AXIS II diagnostic frame of the Zero to Three Classification is equally important in obtaining a holistic clinical picture of the infant or young child with FASD, as it addresses the immediate safety, security and organization in the nurturing environment.

All the relationships listed are relevant, but the commonest ones are:

1.   Overinvolved; where the mother/careprovider often interferes with the infant or young child's goals or desires i.e., inhibits the young child's developmental progress by doing everything for him/her.

2.   Underinvolved, where the mother/careprovider is insensitive to the infant or young child's needs.

3.   Anxious/Tense, where the mother/careprovider is very anxious in parenting and appears to create anxiety in the child because of inconsistent parenting cues about basic issues such as feeding.

4.   Angry/ Hostile, where the actual handling of the infant or young child is quite rough or abrupt with very little patience. Also where there appears to be resentment of the infant or young child's developmental needs.

5.   Disorganized, where the birth mother may have FASD herself and is cognately disorganized, impulsive and is unpredictable in parenting. Thus this type of relationship highlights the risk of parental neglect due to cognitive, neurodevelopmental reasons.

While all of these types be observed in the infant/ young child dyadic relationship, none specifically characterizes this relationship. Nevertheless, the Disorganized paradigm is frequently observed due to the birth mother having one of the FASD herself, or due to severe Regulatory Disorder in the infant or young child with FASD which also creates major parenting challenges.

LATER CHILDHOOD, ADOLESCENCE AND YOUNG ADULTHOOD

The psychiatric course of FASD in childhood and adulthood has been documented by a number of studies in the USA and Canada using standardized psychiatric assessments such as the SCID or psychiatric specialist clinical evaluation. This is truly where it is seen that FASD is the great 'masquerader' as it presents itself in the form of many common psychiatric disorders.

The most common AXIS I (Primary Psychiatric) disorders were, ADHD, Mood Disorder, Anxiety Disorder, Alcohol or Drug Dependence, PDD and Psychotic Disorder The largest series of 57 patients showed that 64% had two AXIS I diagnoses and 19% patients had three AXIS I diagnose (Famy et al. 1998,O'Malley 2001).

So diagnostic codes such as: ADHD, Predominantly Inattentive Type, due to prenatal alcohol exposure with evidence of ARND (314.00) or Major Depressive Disorder, Recurrent with mood- incongruent psychotic features due to prenatal alcohol exposure with evidence of FAS (296.3x) may be used to describe the FASD. Recent clinical observation has delineated a subgroup of adult FASD patients who display Schizoaffective Disorder features either Depressed type or Bipolar type.

As well, the psychiatric disorder may be Secondary due to environmental stressors, such as PTSD after physical or sexual abuse.

The most common AXIS II (Personality) Disorders seen were, Avoidant, Dependent, Schizoid, Passive/Aggressive and Borderline. Furthermore, at least 50 % of those with AXIS 11 Personality Disorders had more than one .Thus it appears that patients with FASD demonstrate multiple personality diagnoses not conforming to the classical DSM IV –T-R clusters A, B or C.

Overall there was no significant difference between the AXIS I and AXIS II diagnoses in the FAS or ARND subtypes of FASD populations. Thus the presence or absence of facial dysmorphology or growth features did not seem to be clinically correlated to the psychiatric presentation of this neurodevelopmental disorder.

SUMMARY

The clinical features of FASD may be divided into to two broad categories (Tables 1 and 2):

1.   Fetal Alcohol Syndrome (FAS).
2.   Alcohol Related Neurodevelopmental Disorder (ARND) (adapted from Stratton and colleagues, Institute of Medicine, classification).

The neuropsychiatric condition most problematic to diagnose and understand is the Alcohol Related Neurodevelopmental Disorder (ARND). However, with a clear significant history of prenatal alcohol exposure it should be possible to grade the clinical severity of the possible ARND.

Mild ARND (Also known as Alcohol Related Neurobehavioral Disorder in Dysmorphology assessments), evidence of Complex Learning Disorder, commonly including Mathematics Disorder, with or without Mixed Receptive/ Expressive language disorder, evidence of Psychiatric Disorder such as ADHD, inattention type with Impulsivity or Mood or Panic disorder, deficits in adaptive functioning and or executive functioning.

Moderate ARND Evidence of Complex Learning Disorder with or without borderline intellectual functioning or mental retardation. Chronic psychiatric disorder unresponsive to standard medication. or behavioral/psychological management approaches. neuropsychological deficits in working memory, executive functioning, judgment and decision-making, significant deficits in adaptive functioning.

Severe ARND (Also known as Static Encephalopathy in Dysmorphology assessments) Evidence of structural brain dysfunction or seizure disorder.

(Sources: Stratton et al. 1996, Streissguth 1997, Astley and Clarren 1997, Coggins et al. 1998, Streissguth and O'Malley 2000, Kapp and O'Malley 2001)

Table 1. Anatomic and Functional Characteristic's of FAS vs ARND (O'Malley 2005)

	FAS	ARND
Confirmed maternal alcohol exposure	Yes	Yes
Evidence of a characteristic pattern of facial anomalies	short palpebral fissures flat upper lip flattened philtrum flat midface	No characteristic pattern of facial anomalies
Evidence of Growth retardation	low birth weight (less than 3rd percentile for height and weight), decelerating weight over time not due to nutrition, disproportional low weight to height.	No or little growth retardation
Structural Brain Abnormalities	decreased cranial size at birth, microcephaly, partial or complete agenesis of the corpus callosum, cerebellar hypoplasia,decreased hippocampal size	decreased cranial size at birth, microcephaly, partial or complete agenesis of the corpus callosum, cerebellar hypoplasia, decreased hippocampal size
neurophysiological abnormalities	complex partial seizure disorder, absence seizure, other seizure	complex partial seizure disorder, absence seizure, or other seizure
Gross Motor Function	poor tandem gait, positive romberg test, balance problems	poor tandem gait, positive romberg test, balance problems
Fine Motor Function	Constructional apraxia, ideomotor apraxia, poor hand-eye co-ordination, intentional tremor, motorically disorganized in the under 5 year age group	Constructional apraxia, ideomotor apraxia, poor hand- eye co-ordination, intentional tremor, motorically – disorganized in the under 5 year age group
Sensory Function	abnormal sensation upper or lower limbs, neurosensory hearing loss, abnormal visual, auditory, gustatatory, olfactory or tactile sensations, including hallucinations, includes craving touch and can make the patient a victim of a false accusation of sexually inappropriate behavior	abnormal sensation upper or lower limbs,neurosensory hearing loss, abnormal auditory, visual, gustatatory, olfactory, or tactile sensations, including hallucinations, includes craving touch and can make the patient a victim of a false accusation of sexually inappropriate behavior

As well, this age group of patients with FASD experience a host of social dysfunctions or what have been called Secondary Disabilities through their lifespan. (Streissguth et al. 1996). For example, inappropriate sexual behaviors occurred in 45%, 43% had a disrupted school experience and 42% have had trouble with the law (including incarceration). Other authors have commented on the psychiatric and social dysfunction in adolescents and adults with FASD in the absence of clear diagnostic criteria, decreased awareness even among psychiatrists, and standardized therapeutic interventions (Nowicki 1992, Brown 1993, Streissguth and O'Malley 2000) See Table 3.

Table 2. Behavioral, Cognitive and Language Characteristics of FAS vs ARND

	FAS	ARND
Behavioral	attentional problems, visual and auditory poor impulse control working memory problems poor adaptive functioning	attentional problems, visual and auditory poor impulse control working memory problems poor adaptive functioning
Cognitive	complex learning disorders With inability to link cause and effect Specific deficits in mathematical skills Marked split between verbal and performance IQ, over 12-15 points Poor capacity for abstraction and metacognition, deficits in school performance poor insight impaired judgment	complex learning disorders with inability to link cause and effect specific deficits in mathematical skills marked split between verbal and performance IQ, over 12-15 points poor capacity for abstraction and metacognition deficits in school performance poor insight impaired judgment
Language	Deficits in higher level receptive and expressive language i.e. the patient does not fully comprehend the "gist".of a social situation -impairment in social interaction -problems in social perception,cognition and communication -problems in expressing emotions, Alexithymia,where the patient does not have the words to express feelings and acts them out, or expresses them, physically (O'Malley 2004).	deficits in higher level receptive and expressive language i.e.the patient does not fully comprehend the "gist" of a social situation -impairment in social interaction -problems in social perception, cognition and communication -problems in expressing emotions, Alexithymia, where the patient does not have the words to express feelings and acts them out,or expresses them, physically.

Table 3. Psychiatric and Social Dysfunction with FASD

Problem	Percentage of Patients with FASD
Mental Health/Psychiatric Problems	94%
Problems with Employment	80%
Patient in Dependent Living	80%
Inappropriate Sexual Behavior	45%
Disrupted School Experience	43%
Trouble with the Law	42%
Confinement for a Crime	35%
Mental Hospital Admission	23%
Drug/ Alcohol In-Patient Treatment Admission	15%

Adapted from Streissguth et al. 1996, Gideon et al. 2003.

CO-MORBIDITY IN FASD: DUAL AND TRIPLE DIAGNOSIS

Co-morbidity is the rule rather than the exception in patients with FASD. It often begins in infancy, continues through the lifespan, and may change over time due to environmental stressors.

The infants, children, adolescents and adults with FASD present the features of a *Dual Diagnosis* condition i.e., Developmental Disorder with co-morbid Neuropsychiatric Disorder. The psychiatric disorder may also have a familial component due to the presence of Depression, Bipolar Disorder or Schizophrenia in the birth mother or birth father. Patients with common developmental disabilities such as Autistic Spectrum Disorder, Down's Syndrome or Aspergers Disorder have a range of psychiatric disorders from 40 to 60%, whereas, the patients with FASD have a prevalence of psychiatric/ mental health disorders through the lifespan of 90-94%. Therefore, the developmental disorder of the FASD inevitably co-morbidly occurs with a neuropsychiatric disorder.

There has been extensive animal research on prenatal alcohol exposure which has formed a basis for the understanding of the aetiology of the co-morbid neuropsychiatric disorders in FASD. The co-morbid ADHD, for example, may originate in the effect that pre natal alcohol has on the developing dopaminergic neurotransmitter system. Previous animal studies have demonstrated that prenatal alcohol interferes with the development of the mesolimbic dopamine D1 receptors which have been shown to regulate attention, impulsivity, and to some extent, affect

The co-morbid Mood Disorders may relate to prenatal alcohol modulating the development of the suprachiasmatic nucleus (SCN), the master circadian pacemaker, as well as disrupting the developing serotonergic neurotrasmitter system.(Sher 2003)

Co-morbid Anxiety Disorders, including Panic Attacks, may have their origins in the prenatal alcohol disruption of the balance between the developing excitatory (glutaminergic) and inhibitory (GABAergic) neurotransmitters (Ikonomidou, et al. 2000).

As an added clinical complication the co-morbid conditions are often not unitary. So FASD may present with developmental disorder features of PDD or Asperger's Disorder and it may be hard to unravel where the FASD ends and the other begins. Similarly the neuropsychiatric presentation of FASD may not just be one psychiatric disorder but a combination of AXIS I and AXIS disorders, i.e., ADHD with co-morbid Mood Disorder and personality features of avoidant and dependent.(O'Malley 2003)

A number of authors have pointed out that in the adolescent and adult years FASD can present features of a *Triple Diagnosis* i.e., Developmental Disorder with co-morbid Neuropsychiatric Disorder and co-morbid Alcohol or Substance Use Disorder. (commonly Alcohol Dependence). Prenatal alcohol exposure has been shown to increase the prevalence of co-morbid alcohol abuse in adolescents and young adults with FASD by as much as threefold. This is higher than the influence of family history of alcoholism. This alcohol craving due to chemical sensitization of the developing brain by prenatal alcohol had been demonstrated repeatedly in animal work. This work has also postulated that the co-morbid alcohol abuse and dependence related to the prenatal priming of dopamine transmission in the Nucleus Accumbens among other basal ganglion structures (Baer et al. 2003, Kapp and O'Malley 2001).

DSM IV –TR criteria: Alcohol Abuse (305.00) Alcohol Dependence (303.90) Polysubstance Dependence (304.80).

It is important to assess the probability of FASD in adolescents or adults with Alcohol or Substance Use Disorder as the standard group counseling approach is commonly not a good fit for this developmental population. As the Alcohol Dependence in FASD may have an organic etiology, medication such as Naltrexone may be a critical part of the Alcohol/Substance Dependence management. Furthermore, careful diagnostic attention to the co-morbid Alcohol or Substance Dependence issues in this neurodevelopmental population offers an opportunity to connect with more appropriate advocacy and clinical services, such as the Parent Child Assistance Programme developed by Grant, Streissguth and colleagues for substance abusing women and children, who also have FASD.(Grant et al. 1999)

Table 4. Alcohol Related Birth Defects (ARBD) With FASD

Body Part	Alcohol Related Birth Defect
EYE	• Visual impairment • Strabismus • Ptosis • Optic nerve hypoplasia • Refractive problems secondary to small eye globes • Tortuosity of the retinal arteries
EAR	• Conductive hearing loss secondary to recurrent otitis media • Sensory- neural hearing loss • Central auditory processing abnormalities related to brain damage in brainstem and cortical areas that process auditory information
TEETH	• Orthodontic Problems
HEART	• Aberrant great vessels • Atrial septal defects • Ventricular septal defects • Tetralogy of Fallot
KIDNEY	• Ureteral duplications • Hydronephrosis • Horseshoe kidneys • Hypoplastic kidneys • Aplastic or Dysplastic kidneys
SKELETAL	• Clindodactyly • Hypoplastic nails • Shortened fifth digits • Radioulnar synostosis • Kippel-Feil syndrome • Pectus excavatum and pectus carinatum • Hemivertebrae • Scoliosis

Table adapted from Stratton et al. 1996, Streissguth 1997, Hagerman 1999, Koren et al. 2003.

Finally, it is equally critical to remember that prenatal alcohol cause effects on organ and system development in the body so co-morbid medical problems are relatively common. These co-morbid medical problems vary in prevalence from 5% for renal abnormalities to 50% with visual impairment. Collectively they are called *Alcohol Related Birth Defects* (ARBD) and include structural abnormalities in the eye, ear, heart, kidney, liver and skeletal system. These conditions are coded under AXIS III of the DSM IV –T-classification. The co-morbid medical problems are important in general medical differential diagnosis as they are not primary medical disorders. Also they are important to be aware of in the monitoring of psychotropic medication n patients with FASD (Table 4).

DIFFERENTIAL DIAGNOSIS

The commonest clinical conditions which need to be considered and out-ruled are:

1. Genetic Disorders
2. Medical Disorders

1.a. **Genetic syndromes with dysmorphic features.** Some genetic disorders with dysmorphic features may have faces that resemble FAS or PFAS. A genetic assessment of the patient is prudent if there are atypical dysmorphic features.

-   Velo-Cardio Facial Syndrome (VCFS); can show flattening of mid facial features structures that are similar to FAS. However, children with VCFS do not generally have a thin upper lip or flat philtrum, but have a long face, large nose with a large tip, high nasal root, small ears and narrow squinting eyes.
-   Fragile X Syndrome: These patients have a long face with a slightly increased head circumference, a large jaw with large protruding ears.
-   -Downs Syndrome (Trisomy 21); have the pathognomonic mongoloid features, with also upward slanting eyes, epicanthus and wide nasal bridge
-   -Williams Syndrome; show elfin-like faces with full prominent cheeks, a widemouth and a flat nasal bridge, but do not have the classical FAS dysmorphic facial, features.

b. **Genetic Syndromes without dysmorphology**. These syndromes would not be mistaken for FAS, PFAS, but it might be hard to differentiate such syndromes from ARND. These syndromes include:

-   -Autistic Spectrum Disorder, and Pervasive Developmental Disorder
-   -Aspergers Disorder

These children or adolescents may display poor social relatedness, obsessive pre-occupations with topics such as computers, hyper or hypo/hyper-responsiveness to sensory stimuli and soft neurological signs with motor clumsiness and coordination problems. They might well be differentiated by the well documented history of prenatal alcohol exposure in the effected patient. The organically-driven pervasive impulsivity and ADHD symptomatology which exists throughout the lifespan is also a discriminating clinical feature of the ARND patient population.

Nevertheless, it has been recognized for over 10 years that patients with FASD can present with either Autistic or Asperger's Disorder symptoms as their primary clinical presentation (Nanson, et al. 1990).

2. Medical disorders, presenting psychiatric disorders that may be confused with, or even potentially mask, the FASD diagnosis. These medical disorders should be considered and out ruled before a diagnosis of a neuropsychiatric disorder associated with the FASD is considered.

The medical disorders can begin in infancy as a result of hypoxia in labour or a difficult delivery. It is always important to review other prenatal toxins such as nicotine, cocaine or even prescription drugs such as the SSRIs. All of these medical conditions can lead to a wide variety of non-specific motor, cognitive and behavioral problems which need to be distinguished from ARND. As well as that, certain seizure disorders, more commonly Complex Partial or Absence, may have their origins in prenatal alcohol exposure and be a primary neurological presentation of the ARND. Acute medical disorders such as hyperthyroiditis, infectious diseases, encephalitis or even meningitis may present acute psychiatric symptomatology, either of a delirium or psychotic nature, which may mask the underlying ARND.

Finally some chronic medical conditions can present complex neuropsychiatric or neurological disorders, including panic disorder, psychosis, dementia and seizures, that need to be considered in the differential assessment of a patient with possible ARND. They include; metabolic or endocrine disorders i.e., uremia, liver or thyroid disease, infectious diseases, including HIV associated early-onset dementia, or even a cerebral tumour (for a complete list see O'Malley 2003).

ASSESSMENT OF FASD

Infants, children, adolescents and adults with FASD present problems of a Dual Diagnosis nature e.g., developmental disability due to prenatal exposure to alcohol and psychiatric disorder (of a primary or secondary nature). However as well, adolescents and adults with FASD may present a Triple Diagnosis clinical picture, namely a combination of developmental disability, psychiatric disorder and an addictive disorder. The Addictive disorder being related to the chemical sensitization of the developing brain by prenatal alcohol exposure (Baer et al. 1998, Baer et al. 2003)

The first step is to evaluate the Developmental Disability that is a legacy of the prenatal alcohol exposure. When assessing a child or even adolescent with possible FASD it is important to be sensitive to their capacity to make up stories because of their deficits in working memory .So the patient can confabulate to fill in the gaps in a personal history narrative. As well the patient may be very suggestible to leading questions. This is especially problematic if the assessment is in the context of a `sexually compromising behavior or legal situation. No patient should be assessed without collateral information from parent or caregiver. Also, as so many of these children and adolescents are in social service custody, it is essential to obtain clear, unambiguous directions from the state social worker as to the role, context and expectations of the clinical assessment.

The clinical dysmorphology and developmental disability assessment used at the University of Washington FAS-DPN clinic is one appropriate screening method. This assessment involves a review of the mother's pregnancy history, a clinical dysmorphological examination, see FAS and PFAS criteria in clinical features section, cognitive and language assessment, Occupational Therapy assessment using the mini-neurological examination.

Infant assessment is more specialized and needs an infant trained primary care physician. with particular attention to basic growth, height and head circumference parameters. The assessment obviously involves the parent or caregiver in a true dyadic assessment to quantify the all interactional and attachment issues. This assessment can often bring forth the `immediate unpredictability and management problems with the infant and the need for ancillary professional support. or even respite care.

This screening assessment quantifies and subtypes the Developmental Disability resulting from the prenatal alcohol exposure. The distinction between the subtypes of FASD is the initial stage of diagnostic evaluation i.e., FAS or ARND.

Table 5. Medical Consultation for Patients with FASD

1. Diagnostic Assessment of the Dual Diagnosis, i.e. Developmental Disability and Psychiatric Disorder, with referral to psychiatrist if probable psychiatric disorder.
2. Blood assays CBC, LFT, TSH, B. glucose, serum creatinine, blood lead
3. Electrocardiogram especially if taking medication.
4. OT assessment especially under 5 and early childhood. Assess for sensory integration and gross / fine motor function.
5. Arrange Intellectual Testing WPPSSI or WISC IV as age appropriate. WAIS in adult to quantify if developmental disability is associated with mental retardation.
6. Sleep Deprived EEG if clinical evidence of possible seizure disorder, especially if intermittent explosiveness or episodes of 'drifting off' seen as ADHD, inattention type
7. Medical consultations as needed e.g., neurologist, paediatrician for general health care if marked developmental disability
8. Public Health referral for pregnant teenager or young adult with FASD. Connection to advocate for help with the arrival of new baby and prevent alcohol/ drug usage in pregnancy.
9. Screening of FASD teenager or young adult for alcohol usage in pregnancy using BARC, TWEAK, or GGT. Haemaglobin Acetaldehyde Adduct. Blood tests.

Sources: Stratton et al. 1997, Streissguth and O'Malley 2000, 2003, O'Malley 2003.

It is also imperative to quantify the co-morbid Psychiatric Disorder. A thorough psychiatric evaluation should be done by a mental health professional or, ideally, a child/adolescent psychiatrist. This assessment should include a complete review of previous medication dosage response and general medical status. This evaluation includes specific attention to issues of Reactive Attachment Disorder or Post Traumatic Stress Disorder, as patients with FASD are at high risk for abandonment, removal from birth parents, multiple foster care placements, or early-onset physical or sexual abuse .As these children and even adolescents often have problems expressing their feelings in words (Alexithymia) non-verbal assessment techniques such as drawing, painting, structured and unstructured play or sandtray are necessary assessment skills (Gardner 1993).

The medical status is important because of the prevalence of Alcohol Related Birth Defects (ARBD), which are a legacy of prenatal alcohol exposure. Prenatal alcohol can affect the skeletal system, cardiac, renal and liver as well as the eye development. The holistic diagnostic assessment which quantifies the Dual Diagnosis i.e., Developmental Disability and Psychiatric Disorder helps greatly in relieving some of the caregiver burden as. adoptive or foster parents are often are blamed as the cause of the child's behavioral problems due to their poor parenting. It also gives direction to ongoing advocacy with both birth and adoptive or foster parents as the assessment clarifies the role of organic brain dysfunction in the child or adolescent's clinical presentation (see Tables 5 and 6).

Table 6. Psychiatric and Psychological Assessment of FASD

1. Clarification of Dual Diagnosis i.e., developmental disability, FAS or ARND subtype and psychiatric presentation i.e., ADHD or Mood Disorder

2. Consideration of Triple Diagnosis in Adolescent or Adult .i.e. Addictive Disorder

3. Medication review with attention to previous drug response and presumptive co-morbid psychiatric diagnoses.

4. Intellectual Testing if not already performed or over 3 years old. WPPSI –R, WISC IV as age appropriate, or WAIS in adult.

5. Speech and Language testing with emphasis on Discourse Analysis (especially social cognition and social communiation).

6. Family Functioning Assessment essential to establish impact of child/ adolescent with FASD on the family system .

7. MRI of brain to assess corpus callosum, hippocampus or cerebellum, especially if low IQ, marked split, over 15 in Verbal/ performance IQ, unresponsiveness to medication. Or case where patient is in forensic/ jail system.

8. Vineland Adaptive Behavior Scales (VABS) to quantify functional disability in activities of daily living, socialization and communication., especially useful if IQ over 70.

9. Neuropsychological testing especially useful for patient with ARND and normal or above average IQ. This establishes the neurocognitive deficits in executive functioning, working memory, impulsivity and personal and social judgment.

10. Case management planning with involvement of social worker to establish support for family/ caregiver, including regular planned respite care and, in-home support or 1on 1 mentorship for teenager (includes job coach).

11. School management meeting to advocate for adequate special education services, especially vocational and work experience in junior high and high school years

12. If Adult case management meeting with DDD or PDD services to establish guardianship, payee (or trusteeship) Pts. with FASD are more likely to qualify for mental health disability funding as their IQ is often over 70.

Sources: King et al. 1998, O'Malley and Streissguth 2000and 2003, Lemay et al. 2003, Goren et al. 2003.

VIGNETTES

The age, gender and ethnicity of these patients have been altered to protect their identity.

1. DM is a 12-year-old Caucasian boy of Irish/ Scottish heritage, is in custody of his birth father and stepmother. His birth mother drank heavily throughout his pregnancy and also had a pattern of binge drinking, at least 5 –6 beers at the weekend. The birth mother is still drinking and only sees DM in supervised visits. Both his parents had finished high school and his father was a house painter (see table 7).

Although he was born by Breech presentation at 38 weeks gestation he had no birth anoxia and no history of neonatal problems. His birth weight was 7 lbs. His developmental milestones were normal for sitting, standing and walking, but he had a history of speech delay and had seen a speech therapist for 2 years from 7 to 9 years of age. A WISC III done at 9 years showed a 24-point difference between verbal and Performance IQ. His verbal IQ was 70 and his Performance IQ was 94 Reading was at 7th percentile, Spelling at the 4th percentile and Mathematics at the 1st percentile.

He was diagnosed as ADHD by a pediatrician at 7 years of age and was treated with methylphenidate for 5 years with mixed success; The dosage of the medication kept increasing and at psychiatric assessment when 12 years of age he was taking 45 mgs of methylphenidate a day, or almost 2 mgs per kilogram. His height and weight were at the 3 rd percentile and head circumference at the 50th percentile. He had FAS dysmorphic features and fulfilled the criteria for full FAS. Patients with FASD are particularly at risk for the negative growth and sleep effects of psychostimulants, especially methylphenidate. X ray for bone age showed that his bone age was 3 years behind his chronological age. Growth hormone was low, less than 0.1. MRI of the brain showed ' thinning of the posterior body and splenium of the corpus callosum'.

Clinically, the patient did not present a clear ADHD picture, but more of a Mood disorder with psychomotor slowing, inattention and some impulsivity. His methylphenidate was discontinued and he was started on liquid fluoxetine 1 cc (4 mgs) initially, He showed good response to this medication and his schoolwork improved. He also became more verbal and was encouraged to use art and clay work to express his feelings. His growth parameters are beginning to show an upward slope and he is being followed by a paediatric endocrinologist. He had marked orthodontic problems seen in prenatal alcohol exposure as ARBD

2. JC is a 17 year old Polish teenager with ARND who lives with his birth mother in a two room inner city apartment. His mother was a 6 beer binge drinker every week-end throughout his pregnancy. She had a long history of Bipolar Disorder, but no sustained Psychiatric follow-up care, and had taken no psychotropic medications during the pregnancy. Currently JC and his mother were living on welfare with little health care insurance. JC has always been a loner and has never fitted into the school environment. He has been bullied and teased for many years and avoids school for varying periods. JC has problems expressing his feelings and many of his absences from school have been for psychosomatic pains and aches with no organic etiology discovered. His school attendance has affected his academic record. He is bright and a WISC III at 15 years gave him a verbal IQ of 129 and a Performance IQ of 120 with Full scale 126. Subtests showed Mathematics at 5th percentile and marked problems in Spelling. His Ht was 25th percentile, Wt 50th percentile and Head circumference at the 98th percentile. He had no FAS dysmorphic features. He presented a mixed clinical picture of

ADHD, inattention type with co morbid mood disorder. The patient has not responded to methylphenidate but has responded to l-tryptophan at night. He now sleeps better and has more energy for school and concentrates better. The school are now aiding JC in planning a work experience programme as they understand from his VABS testing that his functional ability is quite a bit lower than his cognitive ability and he needs practical, 'hands on' experience for his next stage in life .His profile is not unlike a patient with high functioning Autism or Aspergers Disorder.

Table 7. Questions Used to elicit BARC Score

Estimate the following (write 0 if it never happened	Month or so before pregnancy	During this pregnancy
Number of times per month that you drank 5 or more drinks on one occasion		
Number of times per month that you consumed 3-4 drinks on an occasion		
Number of times per month that you consumed just 1-2 drinks on an occasion		
Did you drink alcohol almost every day, even if only a small quantity? (circle answer)	Yes No	Yes No

Note: The fourth question is redundant, but is suggested as a check on the first three questions, and seems to reflect the tone of many of the respondents.

1. Fetal Alcohol Syndrome (FAS) (adapted Stratton et al. 1996)

A. Confirmed maternal alcohol exposure

B. Evidence of a characteristic pattern of facial anomalies that includes features such as short palpebral fissures (2 SD or greater below mean), and abnormalities in the premaxillary zone (i.e. flat upper lip, flattened philtrum and flat midface)

C. Evidence of Growth retardation, as in at least one of the following:
- low birth weight
- decelerating weight over time not due to nutrition (less than 3rd percentile for height and weight),
- disproportional low weight to height.

D. Evidence of CNS neurodevelopmental abnormalities, such as:
- structural brain abnormalities, i.e.decreased cranial size at birth, microcephaly (head circumference less than 3 rd percentile), partial or complete agenesis of the corpus callosum, cerebellar hypoplasia,
- neurophysiological abnormalities, complex partial seizure disorder, absence seizure, other seizure,
- neurological hard or soft signs(as age appropriate):
  - motor:
    - gross motor function; poor tandem gait, positive romberg test, balance problems,

- fine motor function, fine motor problems with evidence of constructional apraxia, poor hand-eye co-ordination motorically disorganized in the under 5 year age group,
  - sensory:
    - abnormal sensation upper or lower limbs,
    - neurosensory hearing loss,
    - abnormal visual, auditory, gustatatory, olfactory or tactile sensations, including hallucinations, includes craving touch and can make the patient a victim of false accusation of sexually inappropriate behavior
    - Regulatory disorder, type 1, 11 or 111, in under 5 year age (see table 1).

2. Alcohol Related Neurodevelopmental Disorder (ARND)
A. Confirmed maternal alcohol exposure
B. No characteristic pattern of facial anomalies
C. No or little growth retardation
D. Evidence of CNS neurodevelopmental abnormalities, such as:
- structural brain abnormalities i.e., decreased cranial size at birth
- microcephaly, partial or complete agenesis of the corpus callosum, cerebellar hypoplasia, decreased hippocampal size
- neurophysiological abnormalities i.e., complex partial seizure disorder, absence seizure, or other seizure
- neurological hard or soft signs (as age appropriate),
  - motor:
    - gross motor problems, poor tandem gait, positive romberg sign, balance problems
    - fine motor problems, poor eye-hand co-ordination, intentional tremor, motorically –disorganized in the under 5 year age group
  - sensory:
    - abnormal sensation upper or lower limbs,
    - neurosensory hearing loss,
    - Abnormal auditory, visual, gustatatory, olfactory, or tactile sensations,(including hallucinations), including craving touch and can make the patient a victim of false accusation of sexually inappropriate behavior
    - Regulatory Disorder, Hypersensitive or Hyposensitive, in the under 5-year age group
- and/or evidence of complex pattern of behavior, cognitive or language abnormalities that are inconsistent with developmental level and cannot be explained by familial background or environment alone:
  - Behavioral:
    - attentional problems, visual and auditory
    - poor impulse control

- working memory problems
- poor adaptive functioning
  - Cognitive:
    - complex learning disorder with inability to link cause and effect
    - specific deficits in mathematical skills
    - marked split between verbal and performance IQ, over 12-15 points
    - poor capacity for abstraction and metacognition
    - deficits in school performance
    - poor insight
    - impaired judgment
  - Language:
    - deficits in higher level receptive and expressive language i.e., the patient does not fully comprehend the "gist" of a social situation
    - impairment in social interaction
    - problems in social perception, cognition and communication
    - problems in expressing emotions, Alexithymia, where the patient does not have the words to express feelings and acts them out,or expresses them, physically (see Table 1)

REFERENCES

Anway MD (2005) Epigenetic transgenerational actions of endocrine disruptors and male fertility. *Science*, 308: 1466-1469

*Astley SJ and Clarren SK (1997) *Diagnostic Guide for Fetal Alcohol Syndrome and Related Conditions*. Seattle, WA: University of Washington.

Baer, JS,Barr, HM, Bookstein, FL, Sampson, PD, Streissguth, AP (1998) Prenatal alcohol exposure and family history of alcoholism in the etiology of adolescent alcohol problems. *Journal of Studies on Alcohol*, Vol. 59, No. 5, 533-543

Baer JS, Sampson PD, Barr HM, Connor PD and Streissguth AP (2003) A 21- year longitudinal analysis of the effects of prenatal alcohol exposure on young adult drinking. *Arch Gen Psychiatry*, Vol. 60, April 377-385.

Barr, AM, Hofman, CE, Phillips, AG, Weinberg, J, Honer, WG (2005) Prenatal ethanol exposure in rats decreases levels of complexin proteins in the frontal cortex, *Alcohol Clin Exp Res,* Vol 29, No. 11, 1915-1920

Barr HM and Streissguth AP (2001) Identifying maternal self- reported alcohol use associated with fetal alcohol spectrum disorders. *Alcohol Clin Exp Res*, Vol 25, No. 2, 283-287.

Bonthius, DJ, Woodhouse, J, Bonthius, NE, Taggard, DA, and Lothman, EW (2001) Reduced seizure threshold and hippocampal cell loss in rats exposed to alcohol during the brain growth spurt. *Alcohol Clin Exp Res*, Vol. 25, No. 1, 70-82

Bookstein FL, Sampson PD, Streissguth AP, Connor PL (2001) Geometric morphometrics of corpus callosum and subcortical structures in fetal alcohol effected brain. *Tetratology,* 4, 4-32.

Brown, Hilary J (1993) Sexuality and intellectual disability: The new realism. *Current Opinion in Psychiatry*, 6, 623-628.

Coggins TE, Olswang LB, Carmichael Olson H and Timler GR (2003) On becoming socially competent communicators: The challenge for children with fetal alcohol exposure, *International review of research in mental retardation*, Vol. 27, 121-150.

**DC:0-3R (2005) Diagnostic classification of mental health and developmental disorders of infancy and early childhood: Revised Edition, Zero to Three Press, Washington, DC

Famy, C Streissguth, AP & Unis, A (1998) Mental illness in adults with fetal alcohol syndrome or fetal alcohol effects. American Journal of Psychiatry, 155, 552-554

*Gardner H (1993) *Multiple Intelligence. The Theory in Practice*. Harper Collins, New York.

Guerri, C, Renau-Piqueras, J (1997) Alcohol, astroglia and brain development. Mol Neurobiol 15 (1), 65-81

*Grant TM, Ernst CC, and Streissguth AP (1999) Intervention with high-risk alcohol and drug abusing mothers: 1.Administrative strategies of the Seattle model of paraprofessional advocacy. *Journal of Community Psychology*, 27, 1-18.

Hagerman RJ (1999) *Neurodevelopmental Disorders. Diagnosis and Treatment. Fetal Alcohol Syndrome,* 3-59, Oxford University Press, New York, Oxford.

Huggins, J & O'Malley KD (2006) Suicidal risk in fetal alcohol spectrum disorders, Letter to the Editor, Can J Psychiatry

Ikonomidou, C, Bittigau, P, Ishimaru, MJ, Wozniak, DF, Koch, C, Genz, K, Price, MT, Stefovska, V, Horster, F, Tenkova, T, Dikranian, K, Olney, JW (2000) Ethanol- induced apoptotic neurodegeneration and fetal alcohol syndrome. *Science*, Vol. 287, 1056-1059

Jones KL, Smith DW, Ulleland CN and Streissguth A P (1973a) Pattern of malformations in offspring of chronic alcoholic mothers *Lancet,* June, 1267-1270.

Jones KL and Smith DW (1973b) Recognition of the fetal alcohol syndrome in early infancy. *Lancet*, 2, 999-1101.

**Kapp FME and O'Malley KD (2001) *Watch for the Rainbows. True stories for educators and caregivers of children with fetal alcohol spectrum disorders*; 64-83, Publisher Frances Kapp Education, Calgary, Canada.

King BH, State MW, Bhavik S, Davanzo P, Dykens (1998) Mental Retardation: A review of the past 10 years. Part I, in *Reviews in Child and Adolescent Psychiatry, AACAP*, 126-133.

Koren G, Nulman I, Chudley AE, Loocke C (2003) Fetal Alcohol Spectrum Disorder. *CMAJ,* 169 (11) 1181-1185.

Lemay J-F, Herbert AR, Dewey DM, Innes AM (2003) A rational approach to the child with mental retardation for the paediatrician. *Paediat Child Health*, vol. 8, No. 6, 345-356.

Lemoine P, Harousseau H and Borteyru JP (1968) Les enfants de parents alcoholiques: Anomalies observees a propos de 127 cas. *Quest Med*, 21, 476- 482.

Li TK (2000) Pharmacogenetics of response to alcohol and genes that influence alcohol drinking. *J Stud Alcohol*. 61, 5-12.

Mattson, SN, Riley, EP, Jernigan, TL, Garcia, A, Kaneko, WM, Ehlers, CL, Jones, KL (1994) A decrease in the size of the basal ganglia following prenatal alcohol exposure: a preliminary report. *Neurotoxicol Teratol*, 16: 283-289

Nanson, J, Hiscock, M (1990) Attention deficits in children exposed to alcohol prenatally. Alcoh Clin Exp Res : 14: 656-661

**Nowicki S and Duke MP (1992) *Helping the Child Who Doesn't Fit In*. Peachtree Publishers. Atlanta, Georgia.

Olney, JW, Farber, NB, Woziak, DF, Jevtovic, -Todorovic,V, Ikonomidou, C (2000) Environmental agents that have the potential to trigger massive neurodegeneration in the developing brain. *Environ Health Project*, 108(Suppl.3), 383-388

*O'Malley KD, Hagerman RJ (1998) Developing Clinical Practice Guidelines for Pharmacological Interventions with Alcohol-affected Children. *Proceedings of a special focus session of the Interagency Co-ordinating Committee on Fetal Alcohol Syndrome.* Chevy Chase Ma, Sept 10TH and 11th, Centers for Disease Control and National Institute of Alcohol Abuse and Alcoholism (Eds.), USA, 145-177.

O'Malley, KD (2001) The National FAS Conference, CDC, Medication in FASD . Uses in primary, secondary and tertiary prevention, Invited Paper April 25-28th, Atlanta

*O'Malley KD and Streissguth AP (2003) Clinical intervention and support for children aged zero to five years with fetal alcohol spectrum disorder and their parents / caregivers. In: Tremblay RE, Barr RG, Peters RdeV, eds. *Encyclopedia on Early Childhood Development (online)*, Montreal, Quebec: Centre for Excellence for Early Childhood development: 1-9 Available at, http://www/excellence-earlychildhood.ca/documents/OMalley-StreissguthANGxp.pdf.

*O'Malley KD and Storoz L (2003) Fetal alcohol spectrum disorder and ADHD: diagnostic implications and therapeutic consequences. *Expert Review of Neurotherapeutics*, July, Vol. 3. No. 4, 477-489.

O'Malley, KD (2003) Youth with Comorbid Disorders. Chapter 13, 276- 315, in *The Handbook of Child and Adolescent Systems of Care*, Pumariega AJ and Winters NC (eds.) Jossey- Bass, San Francisco.

*O'Malley, KD (2005) *Behavioural Phenotype of Fetal Alcohol Syndrome, Alcohol related neurodevelopmental disorder*. 9th International Symposium, Society for Study of Behavioural Phenotypes, Cairns, Australia, October 6th to 8th, 36-37

O'Malley, KD, Barr, HM, Connor, PD and Streissguth, AP (2006) *The frequency of psychiatric problems in children with fetal alcohol spectrum disorders (FASD)*, Submitted Pediatrics

Pembrey, ME (2002) Time to take epigenetic inheritance seriously. *European Journal of Human Genetics*, 10: 669-671

Phillips, DE (1994) *Effects of alcohol on glial cell development in vivo: morphological studies*, In FE Lancaster (Ed.), Alcohol and glial cells (Vol. 27) Bethesda: NIH: NIAAA

Riley, EP, Mattson, SN, Sowell, ER, Jernigan, TL, Sobel, DF,Jones, KL (1995) Abnormalities of the corpus callosum in children prenatally exposed to alcohol. *Alcohol Clin Exp Res*, 19 (5), 1198-1202

Sampson, PD, Streissguth AP, Bookstein FL, Little RE, Clarren SK, Dehaene P, Hanson Jr. JW (1997) Incidence of fetal alcohol syndrome and prevalence of alcohol-related neurodevelopmental disorder. *Teratology*, 56 (6): 317-326.

Sawada, K, Young, CE, Barr, AM, Longworth, K, Takahashi, S, Arango, v, Mann, JJ, Dwork, AJ, Falkai, P, Phillips, AG, Honer, WG (2002) Altered immunoreactivity of complexin proteins in prefrontal cortex in severe mental illness. *Mol Psychiatry*, 7:484-492

Sawaka, K, Barr, AM, Nakamura, M, Arima, K, Young, CE, Dwork, AJ, Falkai, P, Phillips, AG, Honer, WG (2005) Hippocampal complexin proteins and cognitive dysfunction in schizophrenia. *Arch Gen Psychiatry*, 62:263-272

Sher, L. (2003) Developmental alcohol exposure, circadian rhythms, and mood disorders. *Can J. Psychiatry,* vol. 48, No. 6, 428

Song, J et al. (2003) Association of GABA (A) receptors and alcohol dependence and the effects of genetic imprinting. *Am J Med* Genet B Neuropsychiatry Genet,117 (1): 39-45

Sowell, ER, Jernigan, TL, Mattson, SN, Riley, EP, Sobel, DF, Jones, KL (1996) Abnormal development of the cerebellar vermis in children prenatally exposed to alcohol: size reduction in lobules I-V, *Alcohol Clin Exp Res*, 20, 31-34

*Stratton KR, Rowe CJ and Battaglia FC (1996) *Fetal Alcohol Syndrome: Diagnosis, epidemiology, prevention and treatment in medicine* . National Academy Press, Washington DC.

Streissguth, A.P and Little, R.E (1994) "Unit 5: Alcohol, Pregnancy, and the Fetal Alcohol Syndrome": *Second Edition of the Project Cork Institute Medical School Curriculum (slide projection series) on Biomedical Education*: Alcohol Use and Its Medical Consequences, produced by Dartmouth Medical School.

*Streissguth, A.P., Barr, H.M., Kogan, J. and Bookstein, F.L. (1996). Understanding the occurrence of secondary disabilities in clients with fetal alcohol syndrome (FAS) and fetal alcohol effects (FAE). *Final Report, August, C.D.C. Grant R04.*

**Streissguth AP (1997) *Fetal alcohol syndrome. A guide for families and communities.* Brookes Publishing, Baltimore.

*Streissguth AP and O'Malley KD (2000) Neuropsychiatric implications and long-term consequences of fetal alcohol spectrum disorders. *Seminars in Clinical Neuropsychiatry*, 5, 177-190.

*Streissguth, AP, Bookstein, FL, Barr, HM, Sampson, PD, O'Malley KD, Kogan Young (2004) Risk factors for adverse risk outcomes in fetal alcohol syndrome and fetal alcohol effects. *Developmental and Behavioral Pediatrics*, Vol. 25. No. 4, 228-238

Sutherland, RJ, Mc Donald, RJ, Savage, DD (1997) *Prenatal exposure to moderate levels of ethanol can have long–lasting effects on synaptic plasticity in adult offspring.* Hippocampus. 7: 232-238

Swayze, VW, Johnson, VP, Hanson, JW, Piven, J, Sato, Y, Giedd, JN, Mosnick, D, Moore, L (1997) Magnetic resonance imaging of brain abnormalities in fetal alcohol syndrome. *Pediatrics*, 99(2), 232-240

Tchurikov, NA (2005) Molecular mechanisms of epigenetics. *Biochemistry (Moscow),* 70: 406- 423

Waterland, RA, Jirtle, RA (2003) Transposable elements: targets for early nutritional effects on epigenetic gene variation, *Mol Cell Biol*, 23: 5293-5300

* Recommended for primary care physicians or psychologists
** Recommended for families

In: Binge Drinking Research Progress
Editor: Kevin I. DiGuarde

ISBN 978-1-60692-065
© 2009 Nova Science Publishers, Inc.

Chapter 7

BINGE DRINKING - A COMMENTARY

Jan Gill[*], *Julie Murdoch and Fiona O'May*

Queen Margaret University,
Edinburgh, Scotland, UK, EH21 6UU

INTRODUCTION

The term binge drinking is in common usage. Having gained some degree of international credibility, it is employed frequently in reports emerging from research and national agencies, but also within the media and popular press. Implicitly it is linked with the negative consequences of the excesses of alcohol consumption, particularly within the younger members of the population.

This chapter will consider the evolution of the term in the recent past, how it is interpreted and will discuss its value as society in general seeks to curb the excesses of alcohol consumption and address the short and longer term harm that ensues.

HOW HAS THE TERM BINGE DRINKING (BD) EMERGED IN THE RECENT RESEARCH LITERATURE AND HOW IS IT DEFINED?

BD has been used by some within the alcohol research literature to describe a pattern of drinking which involves the intake of a large amount of alcohol within a relatively short period of time. Implicitly it is associated with negative health and behavioural repercussions i.e., it carries a 'risk'. Early work by Cahalan et al. (1969) suggested that drinking beyond 5 US drinks (i.e. 70 g alcohol) on one occasion was linked to particular harm. This definition was adapted to include a time frame of drinking; i.e., 5 drinks in a row within a two week period (O'Malley et al., 1984). An additional modification resulted from an appreciation of the differences between the genders in terms of body water composition and alcohol metabolic rates and the '4 drinks in a row for females and five drinks for males in a row

---

[*] E-mail address: jgill@qmu.ac.uk

within the past two weeks' (Wechsler et al. 1994) classification emerged from work related to the USA College Alcohol Study. However several authors were critical because of the lack of specificity associated with the phrase ' in a row' and also because it failed to relate the biological consequences of BD to the blood alcohol levels known to be linked to intoxication e.g., Beirness et al. (2004) and Lange and Voas (2001). In 2004 the NIAAA National Advisory Council in the US attempted to address these concerns by defining BD as ' a pattern of drinking alcohol that brings blood alcohol concentration (BAC) to 0.08 gram percent or above. For the typical adult, this pattern corresponds to consuming 5 or more [US] drinks (male) or four or more drinks (female) in about two hours' (p. 3). (The council distinguished this pattern of drinking from a "bender" – two or more days of 'sustained heavy drinking'.)

Further clarification of the term binge drinking is evident within the literature. For example sub-classes of binge drinkers have been categorised. Weschler et al. (1994) suggested that those who binge drank one or two times in the last two weeks were 'infrequent' bingers while three or more times in the same time period categorised 'frequent' bingers. Valencia-Martin et al. (2007) sub-divided binge drinkers into 'frequent' (3 or more binge drinking episodes) or 'sporadic' (one or two episodes) but within a 30 day time period. Cranford et al. (2006) replaced the two week timeframe with 'one year' claiming that it was more effective at detecting 'risky drinkers'.

Townshend and Duka (2002) calculated a 'binge score' for their study based on questionnaire responses linking to pattern of drinking viz; speed of drinking, number of times drunk in the last 6 months and the percentage of times a drinking episode led to a participant's drunkenness. From their findings these authors suggest that their binge drinking score was more effective at distinguishing the binge from the non-binge drinker than the 5/4 measure of Weschler et al. (1994) which was more associated with the quantity of alcohol drunk.

What claims are made for the usefulness of measuring individual consumption by this means?

There are two particular questions to address. Firstly what are the potential adverse effects and risks, of this form of drinking and secondly, does the 5/4 definition of BD with its various caveats, represent a useful measure with which to predict risk?

On the first point, it could be argued that the intake of a large amount of alcohol over a relatively short period of time could pose at least six categories of risk for a drinker; (i) immediate behavioural effects e.g., driving while under the influence, committing an act of vandalism etc, (ii) longer term behavioural effects e.g., dropping out of studies as a result of frequent absence from class, disqualification from driving, (iii) damaging effects on close friends, acquaintances or partners, (iv) short term physiological/health effects e.g., passing out, vomiting, immediate injury, (v) long term health actions e.g., on the liver resulting from regular exposure to large doses of alcohol and (vi) a predisposition to chronic forms of alcohol abuse.

If the incidence of BD can be accurately quantified and there is evidence linking this measurement to 'risk', then the argument for the early identification of this pattern of drinking and the subsequent development of appropriate harm reduction strategies seems clear.

The literature concerning the short and longer term physiological/ health risk is slowly accumulating. Additionally several reports have emerged to suggest that BD may incur an increased risk of developing a harmful pattern of consumption in later life (Bonomo et al., 2004; McCarty et al., 2004; Jefferis et al., 2005). Midanik et al. (1996) reported that the drinking of five or more drinks in a row 'ever' within the previous year was characterised by a greater risk of driving after drinking, alcohol-related employment problems and ICD-10 alcohol dependence. Among students, Weschler et al. (1994) reported that the odds of driving after drinking, of experiencing five or more alcohol-related problems in the past year, increased for binge drinkers compared to non-binge drinkers. Crucially the odds for the frequent binge drinkers were greater than those of the infrequent binge drinkers.

(For further discussion of alcohol misuse and its repercussions among university college students see Perkins, 2002; Wechsler and Austin, 1998; Wechsler and Nelson, 2006; Wechsler et al., 1995, 2002) .

Certainly the 5/4 measure has gained some degree of credence within national survey tools e.g., the National Institute on Alcohol Abuse and Alcoholism (NIAAA), US National Institute of Health, Centers for Disease Control and Prevention, and the World Health Organisation. Wechsler and Nelson (2006) have argued that the 'purpose of the binge measure is for public health surveillance and not to diagnose alcohol use disorders for individuals' (p923) and 'as a screen to identify students who may need additional clinical assessment for intervention' (p922). They also suggest that the term BD is a summary measure which can be employed to predict the risk of some 'negative outcome' for populations and that it will permit comparison of drinking behaviour across research studies. (A point discussed further below.)

Naimi et al. (2003) argue that the term is useful to 'communicate concepts of risk to the general public' (p1636) suggesting that BD almost always leads to intoxication and subsequent impairment. They cite evidence that most drinkers engage in binge drinking behaviour with the intention of becoming drunk.

On what grounds has the term BD been criticised?

The first problem refers to semantics. This criticism was articulated by the editor of a major US academic journal (Schuckit, 1998) who argued that the term binge drinking was historically more commonly associated with the phenomenon seen in the clinical field where a person drinks over ' an extended period of time (often operationalized as at least 2 days) during which a person repeatedly administers a substance to the point of intoxication, and gives up his/her usual activities and obligations in order to use the substance' (p123). Consequently, he suggested, simply to avoid confusion, that the term *binge drinking* should be reserved for this extended drinking behaviour while the drinking pattern described by Wechsler et al. (1994), undoubtedly of importance should, (it is suggested in guidance later issued by the journal), be referred to as 'heavy drinking'/ 'heavy use' or 'heavy episodic drinking'/'heavy episodic use'. There are many individuals, particularly within the clinical field who endorse the view of Schuckit (1998) and several alternative terms have appeared within the literature over the years (see Table 1).

Table 1 Examples of terms employed within the literature to describe the sessional drinking of alcohol.

Term	Reference
Spree drinking	Brown and Gunn (1977)
Heavy episodic binge drinking	Nezleck et al. (1993)
Frequent binge drinking	Schulenberg et al. (1996)
Heavy sessional drinking	Measham (1996)
Risky single occasion drinking	Murgraff et al. (1999)
Concentrated Drinking Episode	Gill (2002)
Heavy Episodic Drinking	Makela and Mustonen (2007)

Despite these concerns the term binge drinking continues to be used to describe the sessional intake of alcohol. This is particularly evident in the media (a current search of the UK 'Times' newspaper index reveals almost 500 'hits' for 'binge drinking' in the last three years) but also within official government publications and research literature. Critically this disparity extends also to the quantitative definition.

For example the World Health Organisation (WHO, 2004) define binge drinking as a 'risky single drinking occasion' (p28) but also use the descriptor 'heavy episodic drinkers' to present international prevalence figures while the Alcohol Advisory Council of NZ (2005) define 'binge drinking' in the following manner; 'when you drink a lot more than usual on any one occasion'. In terms of amount of alcohol they advise 'No more than 6 drinks per occasion for men, no more than 4 for women'.

In Australia the NHMRC (2001) report that 'Daily consumption should not exceed 4 standard drinks for men two for women, 4-6 should be viewed as hazardous for men, 2-4 for women'. In their later publication (NHMRC, 2007) the NHMRC make the following comment on the term binge drinking BD; 'This term is avoided as far as possible...because its meaning is ill defined and unclear'(p19). Statistics Canada (2004) define episodes of heavy drinking as five or more drinks on a single occasion. There is no gender distinction.

Within the UK, two measures of sessional intake have been described and both have been expressed in terms of the prevailing guidelines for safe drinking. The first (Moore et al., 1994) equated binge drinking with the sessional consumption of more than half of the *weekly* limits of consumption advocated by the Health Education Council (HEC,1985) i.e., half of 21 standard UK drinks for men, 14 for women. A later definition also emerged following the move within the UK to recommending 'Sensible Drinking' *daily* limits of consumption (Department of Health, 1995) i.e., daily limits of 3-4 standard drinks for men, 2-3 for women. Critically, it was suggested in this document that guidance on daily amounts could be 'helpful in deciding how much to drink on a single occasion and thus help people to avoid drunkenness' (p24). Following this reasoning many national agencies in the UK and researchers define BD as drinking more than double the recommended daily limit on any one day in the past week (8 standard UK drinks for men, 6 for women).

Many UK agencies add caveats to their definitions of binge or sessional drinking; the General Household Survey (Rickards et al. 2004) follows the above quantitative definition but describe it as 'heavy drinking that would be likely to lead to intoxication'. The Parliamentary Office of Science and Technology (2005) state that binge drinking 'refers to the consumption of excessive amounts of alcohol within a limited time period. Such behaviour [BD] leads to a rapid increase in blood alcohol concentration (BAC) and consequently drunkenness' (p1). Alcohol Concern (2003) define BD as 'Drinking sufficient alcohol to reach a state of intoxication on one occasion or in the course of one drinking session' (p2).

However Anderson and Baumberg (2006) in their extensive report prepared for the European Commission, preface evidence relating to binge drinking levels in Europe with the following statement 'this chapter uses the term 'binge drinking' only when looking at reported drinking occasions above a given cut-off level of drinking, while 'intoxication' and 'drunkenness' are used to refer to self reports about how the individual perceived their state after drinking' (p93). They also state that drinking '5 or more 'standard drinks' on a single occasion is the most common definition of binge drinking but make no gender distinction.

Eurobarometer (2003) was also prepared for the European Commission and had the remit of interviewing over sixteen thousand European Union (EU) citizens aged 15 years or over. Participants were asked how often in the last month they had drunk the equivalent of one bottle of wine, 5 pints/bottles of beer or five measures of spirit on one drinking occasion. This was seen as 'excessive alcohol consumption'. A later study, Eurobarometer (2007) interviewed over twenty eight thousand EU citizens and defined the size of drinks more precisely (a 150 ml glass of wine, one 330 ml can of beer or 40 ml of spirit). These definitions were used to monitor consumption at '5 or more drinks on one occasion'. No gender distinction was made nor was it specifically defined as 'binge drinking'.

Using national definitions of the alcohol content of standard drinks, Table 2 describes the information presented in the above references contrasted with the definition of binge drinking proposed by Wechsler at al (1994). The limits of sessional intake for men vary from 40g to 80g for men, 20-80g for women.

Table 2. Examples of International definitions of BD/Sessional intake of Alcohol.

Publication	Limit of sessional intake of alcohol (g) for men	Limit of sessional intake of alcohol (g) for women
US (Wechsler et al.,1994)	70	56
Alcohol Advisory Council New Zealand (2005)	60	40
NHMRC Australia (2001)	40-60	20-40
Statistics Canada (2004)	68 (both genders)	
UK (Moore et al., 1994)	80	56
UK (Rickards et al.,(2004)	48-64	32-48
Eurobarometer (2003)	80 (beer) or 72 (wine) or 40 (spirit) (both genders)	
Eurobarometer (2007)	53 (beer) or 72 (wine) or 64 (spirit) (both genders)	

While there is evidence of some reluctance to adopt the term BD to describe sessional drinking, there is nevertheless clear disagreement as to how it should be quantified. This is also evidenced in Table 3 which summarises the disparity in the descriptors of sessional drinking employed within recent international research literature.

PROBLEMS WITH QUANTIFYING SESSIONAL DRINKING

Thus the prevailing evidence suggests that use of the term BD as a descriptor of the sessional intake of alcohol is still favoured by the authors of some reports and scientific studies. Secondly, irrespective of favoured terminology, it is clear that there is considerable variation in the parameters used to define this pattern of drinking quantitatively and thereby, the associated dose of alcohol. The last point is crucial when the potential risk of this form of drinking is considered.

In truth this lack of consensus, in different guises, has bedevilled alcohol research for some time. There is a lack of clarity and agreement associated with much drinking measurement terminology and this can seriously restrict meaningful comparison between study findings. The terms 'safe' drinking, 'moderate' drinking, 'heavy' drinking can have a multiplicity of definitions. Additionally, when attempts are made to compare research evidence in terms of reported levels of sessional intake of alcohol the ineptitude of the term 'drink' is clearly evident. There is much disparity between how alcohol drinks are quantified and then reported in studies e.g., the terms millilitres, grams, fluid ounces of pure alcohol, fluid ounces of drink, standard units of drink are all employed. While it is true that the number of alcoholic drink varieties available to consumers has increased greatly, many researchers do little to facilitate the comparison of the drink quantities which they report. The elastic term 'drink' survives often without definition in spite of the fact the alcohol content of national standard drinks varies from 6 g in Austria to 19.75 g in Japan (over threefold) (ICAP,1998). Additionally, the '5/4 drinks' definition proposed by Wechsler et al. (1994) to define binge drinking, is often applied without modification. The appeal by Brick (2006) to report all drinks and overall consumption in terms of grams of alcohol seems appropriate and somewhat overdue.

Many surveys designed to investigate sessional intake depend on the accurate account of a participant's drinking quantities usually from the previous week. The accuracy of this measure is threatened by poor recall (and given that the endpoint of an evening is often intoxication, this is an important detail), poor understanding of drink sizes and the extensive range of 'designer drinks' with differing alcohol contents. Another problem which may contribute to the inaccurate quantification of the sessional intake of alcohol is the fact that self-poured drinks tend to be 'generous measures'. Gill and Donaghy (2004) and Gill and O'May (2007) suggested from studies conducted within the UK that self-poured drinks of wine or spirit are likely to contain twice the assumed content of alcohol. Thus drinking which takes place in the home setting or out with licensed premises may be particularly hard to quantify.

Table 3. Examples from research of measures used to describe sessional alcohol intake

Country	Ref	Sessional Drinking definition	Term employed	Time period	Grams of alcohol for men	Grams of alcohol for women
New Zealand	Kypri et al. (2005) (Asked how many of drinking episodes resulted in intoxication)	Consumption of 6 or more drinks per occasion for men. 4 or more for women	'Binge Occasion'	7 day retrospective diary.	60g or more	40g or more
Spain	Valencia-Martin et al. (2007) (This group also calculated prevalence of frequent (3 or more episodes) or sporadic (1 or 2) episodes of binge drinking.)	Intake of 8 or more standard units of alcohol in men and 6 or more in women	Binge drinking	Drinking session in the preceding 30 days	80g or more	60g or more
Spain	Alvarez et al. (2006) (Also asked if respondents had at least one episode of drunkenness in last year.)	5 or more drinks on a single occasion	Episodes of 5 or more drinks	Preceding year	50 g or more	50 g or more
Canada	Murray et al. (2002)	Frequency of consumption of 8 or more drinks per occasion (no gender difference)	Binge drinking	12 months	104 g	104 g
Netherlands	Van den Wildenberg et al. (2007)	6 or more drinks on 1 occasion) (No gender distinction)	Binge drinking	2 weeks	60 g	60 g
Finland	Kauhanen et al. (1997)	Over six bottles of beer. (men only)	Binging	week	72 g	n/a
Sweden	Hansagi et al. (1995)	Half a bottle of spirit or 2 bottles of wine at one session.	Binge drinking	How often?	112/144 g assuming 40% ABV spirit; 12% ABV wine	112/144 g assuming 40% ABV spirit; 12% ABV wine
Sweden	Selin (2003)	One bottle of wine or a corresponding quantity of other alcoholic beverages on one occasion. (no gender distinction)	Binge drinking	week	Assuming 12% ABV = 72 g	Assuming 12% ABV = 72 g

Table 3. (Continued)

Country	Ref	Sessional Drinking definition	Term employed	Time period	Grams of alcohol for men	Grams of alcohol for women
Denmark	Yuan et al. (2004)	8 or more drinks for females.	Binge drinking	During pregnancy up to 36 weeks.	n/a	96
Norway	Alvik et al. (2005)	5 or more standard drinks, (women)	Binge drinking	During pregnancy	n/a	60-65 g or more
Norway	Alvik et al. (2006)	At least 5-7 standard drinks first antenatal visit, 8 or more at 30 weeks of pregnancy and 12 or more at 6 months after term (women).	Binge drinking	During pregnancy	n/a	60-84 g; 96 g or more; 144 g or more.
Germany	Alte et al.(2004)	Five or more drinks (no gender distinction)	Binge drinking	month	More than 60 g	More than 60 g
Germany	Dietrich, A et al. (2004)	Number of days with 5 or more drinks. (No gender distinction)	Binge drinking	month	More than 60 g	More than 60 g
Russia	Kristjanson et al. (2007)	5 or more drinks (women)		An occasion in the past 30 days.	n/a	70 g
Russia	Malyutina et al. (2002)	Consumption of 160g/day or more of pure ethanol usually lasting for a week and over'. (For males)		n/a	160	n/a
France	Com-Ruelle et al. (2006)	Frequency of drinking 6 or more glasses on one occasion such that they are drunk.			60 g	60 g

A further source of inaccuracy is highlighted by McAlaney and McMahon (2006). They suggest that the reported differences in the prevalence of binge drinking in different samples of the UK population may simply be explained by different interpretation of the 'same' binge drinking definition. The 8/6 measure referred to above was used in one national UK study to identify those drinking greater than this amount and by another to quantify drinkers drinking at this level *or* above. As might be expected the latter study reported higher values.

Surveys attempting to monitor levels of binge drinking should also consider the time point in the year when sampling occurs. Two US studies suggested that levels may be highest in the summer months, (Fitzgerald and Mulford, 1984; Cho et al., 2001) while Carpenter (2003) also from analysing US data reported similar findings but additionally applied them to January.

What is the pharmacological evidence to support the modifications made to the definition of binge drinking as proposed by Wechsler et al. (1994)?

As noted above the NIAAA council (2004) approved a definition of binge drinking which equated it to the result of drinking 5/4 US drinks drunk over a period of around two hours.

The BAC selected can be justified on the basis that Schuckit (2000) has linked a BAC of 0.08 to 0.15g/100ml to the symptoms of 'ataxia, decreased mentation, poor judgement and labile mood' (p69) Several countries have a BAC of 0.08g/100ml as the legal limit for driving (US, UK, Canada and New Zealand). The implication, it could be argued, is that this level of impairment increases 'risk' to an unacceptable level for a drinker and their associates i.e., the definition of binge drinking is appropriate.

The NIAAA council recognise that the definition cannot be correct for certain individuals with potentially altered alcohol metabolism e.g., the older person or those on medications. However, the definition has also been criticised for its failure to consider additional general factors known to influence the final BAC achieved, e.g., individual variations in alcohol tolerance, body weight, fat levels, food intake etc. This fact can be underscored by comparing the volume of distribution for a dose of alcohol for an 14 year old adolescent male and a 25 year old male. Using the algorithms of Watson et al. (1981), it is possible to calculate that the volume of distribution of the adolescent is 77% of that of the adult. The BAC resulting from a similar dose of alcohol will be proportionately different.

Several investigators have use field studies to investigate the BAC found in young adult drinkers drinking in a BD manner Three studies used actual BAC measurements (Lange and Voas, 2001; Thombs et al., 2003 and Wright,2006) while Kypri et al. (2005) estimated BAC from knowing a subject's gender, weight, alcohol metabolism rate and length of drinking period. In each study the quantity of drinks consumed predicted a greater proportion of 'binge drinkers' than the BAC values. Two of these studies were performed before the NIAAA published their definition of binge drinking which contains the additional caveat that the 4/5 drinks must be consumed in a 2 hour period. The 2 hour time interval in the definition is interesting. It is much shorter than the length of time many would spend socialising. The NIAAA definition would imply that if the drinker has spread this intake i.e., consumed their drinks slowly then their BAC would not have reached the critical value and they would not be classified as binge drinkers. In practice, however most research studies and surveys do not apply this condition and usually categorise BD simply on the basis of amount of alcohol consumed.

A comment made by Lange and Voas (2001) is interesting. They suggest that 'the use of this term [binge drinking] to describe drinking events that do not produce illegal BACs or significant impairment may affect the credibility of responsible drinking campaigns' (p315). Thus many who know that they have drunk 4/5 US drinks may also be aware that they have not experienced significant impairment. However there is an important counter argument; it is also crucial to stress that in the 'binge drinker' who spreads their consumption of alcohol, the liver will still have to process 70g/56g of alcohol. Spreading consumption may lower behavioural repercussions but our understanding of the long term health effects of frequently challenging the liver in this way at a relatively early stage in life, is still rather poor.

Additional criticisms of the 5/4 Measure

Dimeff et al., (1995) have suggested that the term is dangerous for it labels responsible drinkers with a pathological term while the, Higher Education Center in the US has criticised the 5/4 measure as being too insensitive to detect changes in student drinking in response to new programs and policies which were nevertheless suggested by other measures e.g., BAC levels (US Department of Education, 2000).

Some have criticised the 5/4 definition of Wechsler because it effectively categorises all binge drinkers within one group (Gruenewald et al. 2003). The range of consumption within the group may be very poorly described and heavily drinking individuals may be undetected but also given some degree of acceptability. White et al. (2006) found that among male binge drinkers around half consumed twice the binge threshold 10+ (US) drinks (= 140 g of alcohol).

Gill and O'May (2007) found that the definition of binge drinking offered by female student drinkers ranged from 24 g to 448g of alcohol while a range of actual consumption equal to 56g to 192g was reported for consumption on the heaviest day in the previous week (Gill et al.,2007) .

ALTERNATIVE TERMINOLOGY FOR BINGE DRINKING

Inevitably there has been a concentration on the harmful and damaging repercussions of BD and the consequent need to quantify and measure it. However the US Department of Education (2000) suggest that definitions of heavy sessional intake of alcohol involving wording which relays the impact on people's lives might be more beneficial. Thus in the equation *750ml of alcohol (12%v/v) = 72 g of alcohol = intoxication = risk of harming self or important others*, it might be better to concentrate the wording of messages on the last two variables. Similarly the International Center for Alcohol Policies (ICAP, 2005) would prefer a definition which enunciated the 'implications for risk of health and social harm' (p 6-2). In this regard the terminology suggested by Murgraff et al. (1999) (Risky Single Occasion Drinking) has much to commend it.

It is also important to recognise the views of the drinker. For example Miller et al. (2005) in their analysis of previous UK survey data split respondents into 'spreaders' and 'bingers' on the basis of the number of times drinkers consumed alcohol each week. They recorded the negative and positive experiences reported by drinkers. Interestingly the highest level of positive experiences were reported by the binge drinkers at high levels of consumption – the consumption of 232 g of alcohol in one or two drinking sessions.

There is also evidence among the younger age groups that they identify very poorly with the quantitative BD definitions listed earlier. Guise and Gill (2007) found that for a group of female university students the quantity of drinks was perceived as being less important than the effects produced. Gill and O'May (2007) reported that first year university students favoured a more qualitative definition of BD, one that described a behavioural end point e.g., 'being drunk', 'sick' 'hammered'. The UK health education definition was seen as clinical, quantitative, favoured by researchers but not really relevant to the drinker (O'May and Gill (unpublished findings)). The favouring of a more qualitative definition has been reported by others (WTAG, 2004). Another potential criticism of the mathematical rule to identify binge drinking is that it does not consider the social aspects of drinking. Drinking colleagues may act either positively or negatively in terms of making harm more likely. Furthermore several reports have identified some degree of self-management of sessional drinking; the initial drinks are taken to achieve a certain level of intoxication, later drinks to maintain it (Moore et al., 2007; Hammersley and Ditton, 2005).

An interesting perspective on the societal cost of 'binge drinking' to the UK, its impact on the night time economy and the government response to it, is presented by Hayward and Hobbs (2007). They suggest that 'the government continues an agenda of market led liberalization of the retailing of alcohol' (p450) and that 'Currently it is the logic of the market that informs government policy on alcohol, and it is in this chaotic environment the binge drinker has emerged from a plethora of definitions to capture the nation's headlines. Bingeing is central to the spectacle of the 'Night Time Economy' and 'is marketed as integral to the liminal quest' (p451).

CONCLUDING REMARKS

Binge drinking is a term which can be justifiably criticised on several grounds. Its continued use is probably attributed in part to its popularity within the media. There is evidence of particular risks being associated with a heavy single occasion drinking pattern. However, there is a clear need within the research community to adopt standardised descriptive methods when quantitative tools are employed. Additionally, a further goal should be the greater understanding of the associated health impact in the short and longer term, particularly for certain groups e.g., the young underage drinker and females. From this knowledge a more widely accepted definition of heavy single occasion use, and one that has greater resonance with these critical groups, may emerge. A qualitative behavioural definition may have some merit.

REFERENCES

Alcohol Advisory Council of NZ (2005) Low risk drinking. http://www. alcohol.org.nz/ LowRiskDrinking.aspx accessed 12/12/07.

Alcohol Concern (2003) Factsheet 20: Binge Drinking. London, UK: Alcohol Concern.

Alte, D., Luedemann, J., Rose, H. J., and John, U. (2004) Laboratory Markers Carbohydrate-Deficient Transferrin, gamma-Glutamyltransferase, and Mean

Corpuscular Volume Are Not Useful as Screening Tools for High-Risk Drinking in the General Population: Results From the Study of Health in Pomerania (SHIP), *Alcohol Clin Exp Res*, 28, 931-940.

Alvarez, F. J., Fierro I. and del Rio, M. C. (2006) Alcohol- related Social Consequences in Castille and Leon, Spain. *Alcohol Clin Exp Res,* 30, 656-664.

Alvik, A., Haldorsen, T., and Lindemann, R. (2005) Consistency of Reported Alcohol Use by Pregnant Women: Anonymous Versus Confidential Questionnaires With Item Nonresponse Differences, *Alcohol Clin Exp Res,* 29, 1444-1449.

Alvik, A., Haldorsen, T., Groholt, B., and Lindemann, R. (2006) Alcohol Consumption Before and During Pregnancy Comparing Concurrent and Retrospective Reports, *Alcohol Clin Exp Res*, 30, 510-515.

Anderson, P. and Baumberg, B. (2006) Alcohol in Europe. London. :Institute of Alcohol Studies, UK.

Alte, D., Luedemann, J., Rose, H. J., and John, U. (2004) Laboratory Markers Carbohydrate-Deficient Transferrin, gamma-Glutamyltransferase, and Mean Corpuscular Volume Are Not Useful as Screening Tools for High-Risk Drinking in the General Population: Results From the Study of Health in Pomerania (SHIP), *Alcohol Clin Exp Res,* . 28, 931-940.

Beirness, D. J., Foss, R. D. and Vogel-Sprott, M. (2004) Drinking on campus: self reports and breath tests. *J. Stud Alcohol* 65, 600-604

Bonomo, Y. A., Bowes, G., Coffey, C., Carlin, J. B. and Patton, G. C. (2004) Teenage drinking and the onset of alcohol dependence: a cohort study over seven years. *Addiction* 99, 1520-1528.

Brick, J. (2006) Standardization of Alcohol Calculations in Research. *Alcohol Clin Exp Res* 30, 1276-1287.

Brown, C. N. and Gunn, A. D. G. (1977) Alcohol consumption in a student community. *The Practitioner* **219,** 238-242.

Cahalan, D., Cisin, IH and Crossley, H. M. (1969) American Drinking Practices; A National Study of Drinking Behavior and Attitudes. Rutgers Center of Alcohol Studies, Monograph No. 6, New Brunswick, NJ, US.

Carpenter, C (2003) Seasonal Variation in Self-Reports of Recent Alcohol Consumption: Racial and Ethnic Differences. *J Stud Alcohol* 64, 415-418.

Cho, Y. I., Johnson, T. P. and Fendrich, M. (2001) Monthly Variations in Self-reports of alcohol consumption. *J Stud Alcohol* 62, 268-272.

Com-Ruelle, L., Dourgnon, P., Jusot, F., Latil, E. and Lengagne, P. (2005) Identification et mesure des problemes d'alcool en France: une comparaison de deux enquetes en population generale. Institute de Recherche et Documenattion en Economie de la Sante, Paris.

Cranford, J. A., McCabe, S. E. and Boyd, C. J. (2006) A New Measure of Binge Drinking: Prevalence and Correlates in a Probability Sample of Undergraduates. *Alcohol Clin Exp Res* 30, 1896-1905.

Department of Health (1995) Sensible Drinking. The Report of an Inter-departmental Working Group. Department of Health London, UK.

Dimeff, L. A., Kilmer, J., Baer, J. S. and Marlatt, G. A. (1995) (Letter) Binge drinking in college. *JAMA* 273 (24) 1903-4.

Eurobarometer (2003) Special Eurobarometer 186. Health, Food and Alcohol and Safety. European Opinion Research Group EEIG, European Commission.

Eurobarometer (2007) Special Eurobarometer 272. Attitudes towards Alcohol, TNS Opinion and Social, European Commission.

Fitzgerald, J. L. and Mulford, H. A. (1984) Seasonal changes in alcohol consumption and related problems in Iowa, 1979-1980. *J Stud Alcohol* 45, 363-368.

Gill, J. (2002) Reported levels of alcohol consumption and binge drinking within the UK undergraduate student population over the last 25 years. *Alcohol & Alcoholism* 37, 109-120.

Gill, J. and Donaghy, M. (2004) Variation in the alcohol content of a sample of wine and spirit poured by a sample of the Scottish Population, *Health Education Research* 19, 485-491.

Gill, J and O'May, F. (2007) How 'sensible' is the UK Sensible drinking message? Factors which impact on levels of alcohol consumption among newly matriculated female university students. *J Public Health* 29(1) 13-16.

Gill, J., Donaghy, M., Guise, J. and Warner P (2007) Descriptors and accounts of female undergraduate drinking in Scotland. *Health Education Research* 22, 27-36.

Goudriann, A. E., Grekin, E. R. and Sher, K. J. (2007) Decision Making and Binge Drinking: A Longitudinal Study. *Alcohol Clin Exp Res* 31, 928-938.

Gruenewald, P. J., Johnson, F. W., Light, J. M. and Saltz, R. F. (2003) Drinking to extremes: theoretical and empirical analyses of peak drinking levels among college students. *J Stud Alcohol* 64, 817-824.

Guise, J and Gill, J (2007) "Binge drinking? It's good, it's harmless fun": A discourse analysis of accounts of female undergraduate drinking in Scotland. *Health Education Research* 22, 895-906.

Hammersley, R and Ditton, J. (2005) Binge or bout? *Drug Education Prevention and Policy* 12, 493-500.

Hansagi, H., Romelsjö, A., Gerhardsson de Verdier, M., Andréasson, S. and Leifman, A. (1995) Alcohol Consumption and Stroke Mortality 20-Year Follow-up of 15 077 Men and Women. *Stroke* 26, 1768-1773.

Hayward, K. and Hobbs, D. (2007) Beyond the binge in 'booze Britain': market-led liminalization and the spectacle of binge drinking. *The British Journal of Sociology* 58, 437-456.

HEC (1985) *That's the Limit.* Health Education Council, London, UK.

ICAP (1998) *What is a "Standard Drink"?* International Center for Alcohol Policies ICAP Reports No. 5. ICAP, Washington, DC., US.

ICAP (2005) Binge drinking. International Center for Alcohol Policies ICAP Reports Module 6. ICAP, Washington, DC., US.

Jefferis, B. J., Power, C. and Manor, O. (2005) Adolescent drinking level and adult binge drinking in a national birth cohort. *Addiction* 100, 543-549.

Kauhanen, J., Kaplan, A. Goldgerg, D. E. and Salonen, JT. (1997) Beer drinking and mortality: results from the Kuopio ischaemic heart disease risk factor study, a prospective population based study. *British Medical Journal* 315, 846-851.

Kristjanson, A. F., Wilsnack, S. C., Zvartau, E., Tsoy, M., and Novikov, B. (2007) Alcohol Use in Pregnant and Nonpregnant Russian Women *Alcohol Clin Exp Res.* 31, 299-307.

Kypri, K., Langley, J. and Stephenson, S. (2005) Episode-centred analysis of drinking to intoxication in university students. *Alcohol & Alcoholism*, 40, 447-452.

Lange, J. E. and Voas, R. B. (2001) Defining binge drinking quantities through resulting blood alcohol concentrations. *Psychology of Addictive Behaviors* 15, 310-316.

Malyutina, S., Bobak, M., Kurilovitch, S., Gafarov, V., Simonova, G., Nikitin, Y. and Marmot, M. (2002) "Relation between heavy and binge drinking and all-cause and cardiovascular mortality in Novosibirsk, Russia: a prospective cohort study", *The Lancet*, 360, 1448-1454.

McAlaney, J. and McMahon, J. (2006) Establishing rates of binge drinking in the UK: anomalies in the data. *Alcohol & Alcoholism* 41, 355-357.

McCarty, C. A., Ebel, B. E., Garrison, M. M., DiGiuseppe, D. L., Christakis, D. A. and Rivara, F. P. (2004) Continuity of Binge and Harmful Drinking from Late Adolescence to Early Adulthood. *Pediatrics* 114, 714-719.

Measham, F. (1996) The "Big bang" approach to sessional drinking. Changing patterns of alcohol consumption amongst young people in North west England. *Addiction Research* 4, 283-289.

Midanik, L. T., Tam, T. W., Greenfield, T. K. and Caetano, R. (1996) Risk functions for alcohol-related problems in a 1988 U. S. national sample. *Addiction* 91:1427-1437.

Miller, P, Plant, M. and Plant, M (2005) Spreading out or concentrating weekly consumption: alcohol problems and other consequences within a UK population sample. *Alcohol & Alcoholism* 40, 461-468.

Moore, L., Smith, C. and Catford, J. (1994) Binge drinking: prevalence, patterns and policy. *Health Education Research 9, 497-505.*

Moore, S, Shepherd, J, Perham, N and Cusens, B (2007) The prevalence of alcohol intoxication in the night-time economy *Alcohol & Alcoholism* 42, 629-634.

Murgraff, V., Parrott, A. and Bennett, P. (1999) Risky single-occasion drinking amongst young people – definition, correlates, policy and intervention: a broad overview of research findings. *Alcohol & Alcoholism* **34**, 3-14.

Murray, R. P., Connett, J. E., Tyas, S. L., Bond, R., Ekuma, O., Silversides, C. K., and Barnes, G. E. (2002) Alcohol Volume, Drinking Pattern, and Cardiovascular Disease Morbidity and Mortality: Is There a U-shaped Function? *American Journal of Epidemiology*, 155, 242-248.

Naimi, T., Brewer, R., Mokdad, A., Denny, C., Serdula, M. and Marks, J. (2003) Letter. *JAMA* 289, 1635-1636.

National Health and Medical Research Council [NHMRC] (2001) Australian Alcohol Guidelines: health Risks and Benefits. Commonwealth Department of Health and Aged Care, Australian Government. Canberra, Australia.

National Health and Medical Research Council [NHMRC] (2007) Australian Alcohol Guidelines for low-risk drinking. Draft for public consultation. October 2007. Australian Government. Canberra, Australia.

National Institute on Alcohol Abuse and Alcoholism (2004) NIAAA council approves definition of binge drinking. NIAAA Newsletter, No. 3, Winter. US Department of Health and Human services, National Institute of Health, US.

Nezlek, J. B., Pilkington, C. J. and Bilbro, K. G. (1993) Moderation in excess: binge drinking and social interaction among college students. *J Stud Alcohol* 55, 342-351.

O'Malley, P. M., Bachman, J. G. and Johnston, L. D. (1984) Period, age and cohort effects on substance use among American youth, 1976-1982. *Am J Public Health* 74, 682-688.

Parliamentary Office of Science and Technology. (2005) Postnote, Number 244. Binge Drinking and Public Health, London, UK.

Perkins, H. W. (2002) Surveying the Damage: A Review of research on Consequences of Alcohol Misuse in College Populations. *J. Stud. Alcohol,* Supplement No. 14:91-100.

Rickards, L., Fox, K., Fletcher, L. and Goddard, E. (2004) Living in Britain: Results from the 2002 General Household Survey. National Statistics, London.

Schuckit, M. A. (1998) Editorial response. *Journal of Studies on Alcohol* **59**, 123-4.

Schuckit, M. A. (2000) Drug and Alcohol Abuse: a Clinical Guide to Diagnosis and Treatment. Kluwer Academic/Plenum Publishers, New York.

Schulenberg, J., O'Malley, P., Backman, J. G., Wadsworth, K. N. and Johnston, L. D. (1996) Getting drunk and growing up: trajectories of frequent binge drinking during the transition to young adulthood. *J Stud Alcohol* 56, 35-38.

Selin, K. H. (2003) Test-Retest Reliability of the Alcohol Use Disorder Identification Test in a General Population Sample. *Alcohol Clin Exp Res.* 27, 1428-1435.

Statistics Canada (2004) Health reports. How healthy are Canadians? 2004 Annual report. Canadian Institute for Health Information. Ottawa, Ontario, Canada.

Thombs, D. L., Olds, R. S. and Snyder, B. M. (2003) Field assessment of BAC data to study late-night college drinking. *J. Stud Alcohol* 64, 322-330.

Townshend, J. M. and Duka, T (2002) Patterns of alcohol drinking in a population of young social drinkers: a comparison of questionnaire and diary measures. *Alcohol & Alcoholism* 37, 187-192.

US Department of Education (2000) Higher Education Center for Alcohol and Other drug Abuse and Violence Protection. Note to the Field: On "Binge Drinking". Available at http://www. higheredcenter. org/press-releases/001020. html. Accessed 14/12/07

Valencia-Martin, J. L., Galan, I and Rodriguez-Artalejo, F (2007) Binge drinking in Madrid, Spain. *Alcohol Clin Exp Res* 31, 1723-30.

van den Wildenberg, E., Wiers, R. W., Dessers, J., Janssen, R. G. J. H., Lambrichs, E. H., Smeets, H. J. M., & van Breukelen, G. J. P. (2007) "A Functional Polymorphism of the mu-Opioid Receptor Gene (OPRM1) Influences Cue-Induced Craving for Alcohol in Male Heavy Drinkers", *Alcohol Clin Exp Res.* 31, 1-10.

Watson, P. E., Watson, I. D. and Batt, R. D. (1981) Prediction of blood alcohol concentrations in human subjects: updating the Widmark equation. *J Stud Alcohol* 42: 547-556.

Wechsler, H. and Austin, S. B. (1998) Binge Drinking: The Five/Four Measure. *J. Stud Alc* 59, 122-123.

Wechsler, H. and Nelson, T. F. (2006) Relationship Between Level of Consumption and Harms in Assessing Drink Cut-Points for Alcohol Research: Commentary on "Many College Freshman Drink at Levels Far Beyond the Binge Threshold" by White et al. *Alcohol: Clin Exp Res* 30, 922-927

Wechsler, H., Davenport, A., Dowdell, G., Moeykens, B and Castillo, S. (1994) Health and Behavioral Consequences of Binge Drinking in College: A national survey of students at 140 campuses. *JAMA* 272, 1672-1677.

Wechsler, H., Moeykens, B Davenport, A., Castillo, S. and Hansen, J. (1995) The Adverse impact of Heavy Episodic Drinkers on Other College students. *J. Stud Alcohol* 56, 628-634.

Wechsler, H., Lee, J. E., Kuo, M., Seibring, M., Nelson, T. F. and Lee, H (2002) Trends in college binge drinking during a period of increased prevention efforts. Findings from 4 Harvard School of Public Health College alcohol study surveys: 1993-2002. *J. Am Coll Health* 50, 203-217.

White, A. M., Kraus, C. L. and Swartwelder, H. S. (2006) Many College Freshman Drink at Levels Far Beyond the Binge Threshold. *Alcohol Clin Exp Res* 30, 1006-1010.

WHO Global status Report on Alcohol (2004) World Health Organization. Department of Mental Health and Substance Abuse, Geneva, Switzerland.

Wright, N. R. (2006) A day at the cricket: the breath alcohol consequences of a type of very English binge drinking. *Addiction Research and Theory* 14, 133-137.

WTAG Binge Drinking Research (2004) Report of research and consultation conducted by MCM Research Ltd for Wine Intelligence. Oxford UK.

Yuan, W., Sorensen, H. T., Basso, O., and Olsen, J. (2004) Prenatal Maternal Alcohol Consumption and Hospitalization With Asthma in Childhood: A Population-Based Follow-Up Study, *Alcohol: Clin Exp Res.* 28, 765-768.

In: Binge Drinking Research Progress
Editor: Kevin I. DiGuarde

Chapter 8

PERSONAL WAYS OF CONSTRUING OTHERS: AN APPLICATION OF PERSONAL CONSTRUCT THEORY METHODOLOGY IN DRUG ABUSE AND ALCOHOLISM

Bruce D. Kirkcaldy[1]*, Stephanie M. Potter[2]
and James A. Athanasou[3]

[1]International Centre for the Study of Occupational and Mental Health, Germany
[2]Business Consultancy, Ottawa, Canada
[3]University of Technology, Sydney, Australia

ABSTRACT

The study involving four case studies is a clinical exploration of the styles (among chemical dependent clients) of significant others using personal construct methodology. In this sense attempts were made to analyse the pattern of social networks which may characterise male and female alcohol or drug addicts, and identify the underlying personal characteristics they use in their description of family and non-family members. For this purpose, a series of multivariate techniques were implemented, including cluster analyses and linear discriminant analyses, as well as principal component analyses. The implication of the findings are discussed within the framework of providing an insight into the value of social relationships and social skill training among adolescents as a prophylactic method towards drug prevention.

INTRODUCTION

This study examines the role of a specific formulation of social capital, in the form of social networks, in understanding the problem of alcohol and drug abuse. While social networks serve as a conduit for the flow of resources such as social support, they are also essential in shaping the behaviours of those at their centre.

The link between social support in particular and the well-being of individuals has been a central theme of social scientists since Durkheim articulated the position that

---

* Reprint requests: Dr Bruce D. Kirkcaldy, International Centre for the Study of Occupational and Mental Health, Haydnstr. 61, D-40593 Düsseldorf, Germany

social isolation reduces a person's ability to cope with a variety of every day problems, as well as with more serious disturbances (Durkheim 1897). Social support networks have been identified as a key attribute, or determinant, of population health, which also include the following: income and social status, education, employment and working conditions, physical environment, biology and genetic endowment, personal health practices and coping skills, healthy child development, and health services (Single 1999). When examining individual behaviour, then, it only makes sense to acknowledge that individuals are embedded in social relations at the micro level – what Granovetter (1990) refers to as relational embeddedness – and that resources flow through these personal contacts, or social networks. In trying to understand individual and group behaviours, it is important to understand the web of relations in which these individuals or groups are embedded.

In this paper we present case studies from four persons in a drug and alcohol abuse therapy context. These illuminate the terms in which these individuals viewed significant others in their lives. They give an insight into aspects of their life and the terms in which they describe salient relationships. The key research questions were (a) what meanings do individuals involved (currently or formerly) in drug and alcohol abuse give to their relationships; and (b) are there any similarities in personal perceptions. In this study, repertory grid analysis was used to explore the perceptual similarities and differences. The personal construct grid represents a means of reaching idiosyncratic parameters, enabling single case studies of personal factors.

As far back as 1955, George Kelly pointed out the importance of describing individual perspectives and he indicated that commonly named experiences (such as stress) may not involve any shared meanings. The advantage of an idiographic approach is that each person acts as their own control. The regularity in individual responding is being analysed in what amounts to an interpretive and quantitative case study.

THE IMPORTANCE OF SOCIAL NETWORKS

Social network analysis is an approach that makes explicit the interplay between social structural factors and individual action. At the individual level, the structure of an individual's network (called an egocentric network) has been shown to greatly affect the types of resources that can be accessed through it. An egocentric network is comprised of all of a person's social contacts with immediate and extended family members, friends, neighbours, co-workers and acquaintances (Wellman, Carrington and Hall, 1988). The individuals with which *ego* – the individual at the centre of the network – is connected are called *alters*, and the actual relationships are called *ties*. One way of classifying an individual's network ties is to distinguish between kin versus non-kin ties, the premise being that kinship ties are based on relations of obligation as well as emotional attachment, and so are likely to provide access to larger amounts and a greater variety of social support (Wellman and Wortley 1990). Because in modern society families are often geographically or emotionally distant, and functions are replaced by other intimate contacts actively cultivated by the individual (Wellman 1979; Wellman et al. 1988), researchers therefore also differentiate between ties according to their *strength*. This allows for the possibility that friends and kin (typically immediate kin) can be social intimates and are called 'strong ties', while extended kin, co-workers, neighbours and other acquaintances generally play peripheral or specialized roles in an individual's network, and are typically called 'weak ties' (Granovetter 1973).

Significantly, the strength of a tie has implications for the type of social support that can be expected to flow along it. Strong ties generally occur among social similars, and therefore connect people of similar economic, cultural and social status. Such contacts provide people with access to information that is likely to be shared by all of the strongly connected network members (Burt 1992; Granovetter 1973; Lin 1982). By contrast, weaker contacts connect social dissimilars: the more heterogeneous a person's network (that is, the more diverse the network members), the more likely is the individual to have access to information which they would not ordinarily possess. As such, stronger, more intimate ties are said to provide large amounts of social support, while weaker ties are said to provide access to scarce resources, such as information on job openings (Granovetter 1973; 1985).

Thus, a network's structure can be described based on the relative occurrence of these tie-level characteristics. Characteristics that have been found to be important to understanding the flow of resources through the network are its size, density, composition, and predominance of weak or strong ties. Larger networks provide people with access to more individuals, and so potentially to more support; most importantly, larger networks are more likely to have a higher proportion of 'weak ties' that serve as bridges to scarce information, particularly in the context of occupational mobility (e.g. Granovetter 1973). Networks with a predominance of strong kinship ties have also been found to be associated with high levels of all kinds of social support (Wellman and Wortley 1990). Very dense networks (a high degree of interconnectivity among network members) are said to be associated with kinship, smaller size, and larger amounts of social support (Wellman 1979), while low density is more typical of loosely structured, larger non-kin dominated networks which do not necessarily preclude the provision of social support, as argued by Wellman (1979), and Wellman and Potter (1999), but which may depending on the proportion of weak versus strong ties.

The structure and content of social networks also vary according to ego's social roles, position in the life course (age), and gender. Among younger individuals, the principle of homophily tends to hold, so that younger people tend to associate with those of similar age, marital and parental status (Fischer 1982; Wellman and Wortley 1990). Women usually have more kin-based network members, as they tend to be the "kin-keepers" in the family, organizing family events and staying in touch with distant relatives – tasks which are also associated with working in the home, though these do tend to persist even for women working outside of the home. Women with children tend to be connected to their neighbours with children, through their children's friendships, day cares and schools. By contrast, men tend to have more network ties to co-workers, and smaller networks overall than women (Wellman and Wellman 1992).

EMPIRICAL STUDIES

The standard approach to investigating the correlates of substance abuse includes a detailed investigation of *respondents'* demographic and socio-economic characteristics. For example, a recent Canadian study by Single (1999) reported that "[0]verall levels of drinking and rates of heavy drinking are also associated with social isolation and low employment status. Those who have never been married report 24% higher consumption levels than married Canadians. Single persons are more likely to report drinking five or more drinks on an occasion on a weekly basis (10.5% vs. 4.3%) and to exceed the low risk drinking guidelines (23.6% vs. 16.0%). Thus, the portrait of the Canadian who tends to consume alcohol at high levels and in a high-risk pattern is that of a young, unattached male. High rates of drinking and high-risk drinking are also more common among the unemployed, lower status workers, Aboriginal Canadians and street youth. While Canadians of higher income and education are more likely to drink and have rates of drinking similar to low-income persons, they appear to be more moderate in their drinking, with fewer heavy-drinking occasions.

For some time, research concerning substance abuse has also examined the social structural - or contextual - component of users' behaviour. Particularly in the area of deviance, many studies measure the degree to which users are 'socially integrated' and adhere to social values. Explanations of users' behaviour typically take a 'social ability' or 'social disability' approach: in the former, addicts are said to be socialized into deviance, and that their social networks are very similar to those of non-addicts; in the latter, addicts are said to be poorly socialized, and their social networks are characterized as being smaller, less supportive, and less durable than those of non-addicts (For an excellent review, see Wortley 1996).

For example, Single (1999) has found that one distinct characteristic of illicit drug users is that they tend to have a lower degree of social integration; that is, they tend to be more socially isolated and have less investment in social values. From this perspective, the social networks of these drug users would be characterized as less resourceful and supportive than non-drug users' social networks.

By contrast, research by Black, Ricardo andand Stanton (1997) takes a 'social ability' approach to examining the behaviours of addicts. Their study looked at social and psychological factors associated with AIDS risk behaviours among low-income, urban, African American adolescents. The authors used questionnaires to explore the social and psychological factors associated with sexual intercourse and substance use among a relatively large sample of low-income, urban, African-American adolescents (11-14 yrs). Since older youths reported more sexual intercourse, attempts were made to control for the potentially confounding effects of age. Sexually active youths reported *more conflict with parents* and sexual intercourse among friends. Moreover, those children who were involved with illegal substances reported that more friends used illegal substances. There were no differences in delinquency, sensation seeking, intelligence, or locus of control associated with risk practices. There was no evidence that engagement in early sexuality was in any way linked with other risk practices, thus lending no credence to the tenet that within this culture, early sexual intercourse is part of a general theory of problem behaviour.

Indeed, the role of peers in affecting individuals' use of drugs and alcohol has been seen as an important explanatory element in both the social ability and disability models. Ziervogel, C. F.; Morojele, N. K., van der Riet, J., Parry, C. D. H., and Robertson, B. A. (1997) conducted a qualitative survey of alcohol binge drinking and non-binge drinking 10th-grade male high school students from three communities in South Africa. They used a revised Theory of Planned Behaviour as the theoretical framework for the semi-structured discussions and subsequent data analysis. Overall, the findings were complex, but clear differences did emerge between binge drinkers and non-binge drinkers, and between participants from the 3 different communities. Binge drinkers perceived positive outcomes from binge drinking, were embedded within a *peer group culture* of binge drinking, and found few obstacles to obtaining alcohol. The non-binge drinkers were more concerned with longer-term life goals, and were motivated to comply with family pressures not to drink excessively.

Similarly, Goleman's lucid account of binge-drinking, brings to the forefront the importance of social (interpersonal) factors, specifically *peer pressures*, in affecting respondents' desire to conform with the social proximal group (1996). He states:

> "Students at the local campus call it drinking to black - bingeing on beer to the point of passing out. One of the techniques [is to] attach a funnel to a garden hose, so that a can of beer can be downed in about ten seconds...One survey found that two-fifths of male college students down seven or more drinks at a time, while 11 percent call themselves heavy drinkers. Another term, of course, might be alcoholics."

Attention to the effects of social networks on rehabilitating individuals with addictions has increased considerably in the last decade: particularly with the appearance of HIV/AIDS, researchers and practitioners began to examine the role of addicts' social networks in spreading, but also in reducing, infection (e.g. Galanter 1997; Keller 1997; Latkin 1999; Miller 1998). In his comparison study of the networks of substance abusers and non-abusers, Wortley (1996) paid particular attention to the role of individuals' social networks in supporting or reinforcing addictive behaviours. Overall, Wortley's findings challenge conventional beliefs that substance abusers have smaller networks that provide less social support, and that substance abusers' relationships tend to be fleeting and unstable. By contrast, the social networks of substance abusers and a control group were not that different. Where differences did exists – in terms of amount of higher amounts of conflict, and in lower levels of admiration of network members by substance abusers – Wortley nevertheless maintained that these were not as significant as other researchers had found in the past (Wortley 1996). Indeed,

> "[t]he high level of social support and companionship provided by the networks of substance abusers map provide the with the resources and sense of belonging (even if it is a sense of belonging to the lost and disenfranchised) that can shelter individuals from outside influences and keep them in the world of drug use and addiction (Wortley 1995:31)".

Wortley concludes by saying his research suggests that treatment programs are doomed to failure if they do not take into account the important role that addicts' social networks play in helping them maintain their levels of substance abuse

This exploratory study using personal construct theory (PCP) methodology is an attempt to gain an insight into the social network of drug and alcohol dependents. As outlined, listing significant others, and generating the individual's constructs for describing social relationships (Kirkcaldy and Pope, 1992; Kirkcaldy, Siefen and Pope, 1993) will allow us to identify how drug and alcohol dependants perceive their relationships, in particular to their immediate families, and whether commonalties exist among drug dependants in the social perceptions. Overall, in addition to providing a description of the utility of the grid as an individualised method of assessment of substance abusers' constructions of their social networks, the grid procedure is useful in focusing on psychotherapy and evaluating its outcome.

METHOD

Participants

Four persons (2 male, 2 female) undergoing psychotherapy participated in this study. No claim is made for the representativeness of their conditions. The case studies comprised four therapy cases of past and current drug and alcohol abuse.

Procedure

As elements in the grid, each participant was asked to provide the names of significant people in their life. They were given totally free choice of elements. The self and ideal self were also included as elements. Constructs were elicited from triads of these elements, each participant being asked to identify a way in which two of the elements in each triad were similar and thereby different from the third. Participants were also invited to provide further bipolar constructs without the constraints of triadic elicitation. The process was completed when....Participants were then asked to rate all of their elements on a 10-point scale on each of their constructs.

Each person rated the elements on a 10 point scale (10=highest similarity rating) for each of the constructs. Participants were asked to assign a rank or rating to each of the elements in turn in terms of how they related to the construct poles.

The process of construct elicitation and rating continued until a number of permutations or triads were completed. Once participants grasped the notion of providing bipolar constructs it was possible to move to the context form in which the participants were free to offer further constructs without the constraints of triadic elicitation. The process was complete when the participant could not offer any new ways of differentiating between the elements or the researcher believed that he or she had a reasonable sample of constructs.

Analysis

A completed raw grid is a matrix with each element assigned a rating on each construct. Perusal of the types of constructs within a person's grid or across a number of grids will identify particular themes (Denicolo andPope, 1997; Shaw, 1980). The data matrix in grid format was analysed using a hierarchical cluster analysis based on squared Euclidean distances, and separate dendrograms were produced for elements and constructs. The results are displayed in a form where the original data as well as the analyses are represented in the results for each person (see Kirkcaldy, Athanasou andTrimpop, in press). It indicates the degree of relationship within the grid of ratings for each person's elements and constructs. The extracted grid is termed a 'modegrid'.

RESULTS AND DISCUSSION

The results are reported separately for each person. This is in keeping with the idiographic nature of this report.

Mr A – Alcohol Dependency During Adulthood

Mr A. is a 52-year-old married, self-employed businessman wihtout children. He entered therapy complaining of tinnitus, depression and suicidal thoughts. The alcohol problem was generally "underplayed" and emerged during subsequent sessions as a central feature of treatment. He had suffered by the premature death of his father, who died when Mr A. was 10 years old. His mother re-married a medical consultant, and had two sons from him, one of whom is seriously ill with a life-threatening illness. He remarks about his closeness to his brother, but it also became apparent that pronounced inward hostility is experienced regarding his siblings. He felt that he was "left to cope on his own" at at early age.

a Modegrid

	Dominant vs. submissive	Low initiative vs. innovative	Philanthropic vs. scornful of others	Obsessive vs. inactive	Success priented vs. fatalistic	Need recognition vs. understatement	Loving vs. underdeveloped	Ambitious vs. lazy	Family-conscious vs. asocial	Fighter vs. coward
Brother	9	3	1	5	1	3	3	9	7	7
Self	1	5	5	5	8	8	9	3	3	3
Brother	9	5	1	5	1	3	3	5	10	9
Mother	1	6	9	6	8	9	10	3	3	3
Therapist	1	8	5	8	8	8	9	3	7	7
Uncle1	2	6	5	5	8	5	3	10	10	10
Stepfather	1	5	6	7	8	8	5	9	9	9
Boss	1	1	10	8	10	10	10	9	9	9
Uncle2	2	8	9	8	6	8	9	9	9	10
Wife	1	6	9	8	9	8	9	10	9	10
Doctor	1	10	5	10	8	9	10	9	9	9
Girlfriend	1	9	9	8	9	8	9	10	9	10

Mr A identified 12 elements such as family members, therapist, employer and doctor (see Figure 1); and n10 bipolar constructs on which the elements varied. The bipolar constructs or dimensions of meaning such as submissive versus dominant or innovative versus low inititative are also listed. While at first sight the table and accompanying figures may appear a little unusual and complex, they represent an intensive investigation of an individual. They offer a succinct summary of the data and the results should become clearer after some familiarity with the presentation.

b. Dendrogram of constructs   **c. Dendrogram of elements**

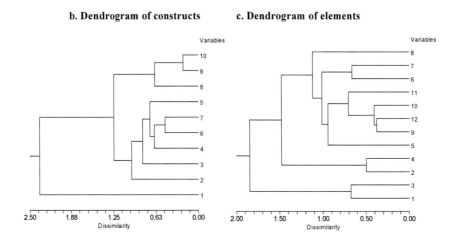

Figure 1. Repertory grid for MR A

The rows in the table present the elements or significant others in this person's life. The constructs or meanings attributed to the significant others are indicated in the columns. The numbers in the grid are the similarity ratings from 1-10. Below the table are listed the two cluster analyses of the results, firstly for constructs and then next to this is the cluster analysis for elements.

Shading in the modegrid represents the degree of ratings; ratings of 8-10 are darkest (12.5% shading), ratings of 4-7 are lighter (5% shading), and ratings of 1-3 are unshaded. To facilitate the interpretation of the modegrid, the constructs and elements have been listed so as to maximise the grouping together of similar shaded areas. The darkest shaded areas tend to fall towards the bottom right-hand corner of the table and the unshaded areas are grouped so that they ocupy most of the top left-hand corner of the table (see Kirkcaldy, Athanasou andTrimpop, in press, for an earlier example).

The mother, stepfather and uncle were closely related to self. The brothers shared similar features (commonality) but were most distant from Mr A's self. In effect the two brothers formed a distinct cluster and contrasted with the others. Interestingly, the scales which differentiated the two clusters were dominant ($F(1,10)=9.35$, $p<0.02$), low initiative ($F=633.75$, $p<0.001$), obsessive ($F=29.09$, $p<0.001$), success oriented ($F=90.00$, $p<0.001$), crave for recognition ($F=15.40$, $p<0.005$), ambitious ($F=58.40$, $p<.001$) and fighter ($F=50.00$, $p<0.001$). A cluster analysis of the personal constructs reveleaed these scales to coalesce into a major cluster.

The grid of Mr A underlined the elements of girlfriend, wife and uncle2. Mother and self were closely related as were both brothers. Constructs that correlated most closely were underdeveloped, understated, inactive and fatalistic. The picture that emanates from this person is an emphasis on clear groupings of persons in terms of a key set of negative characteristics. The modegrid is characterised by a concentration of high ratings in the lower left hand corner of the grid and many lower ratings throughout the remainder of the grid.

Mr D – Former Alcohol Dependency

A 50-year-old musician suffering from "diabetes, alcoholism, asthma, a buggered-up knee and shoulder... with excellent verbal skills and everyone relaxes around that. It's catalytic and this is marvellous in his work. His tongue can be vile, viscous or very funny. The brain is sharp but underused, or is it? Perhaps the sharpness in what it is...emotionally, far too sensitive. It's hard to say things without him feeling threatened. Frustrated by not knowing how to do functional things, yet a possessor of several talents to a very high level. Life was always fear, fear of rejection, being laughed at - and yet his reputation is of being so funny and so relaxed. If only they knew." (personal citation in autobiographical account).

Mr D produced a large table of elements and constructs. There were large groupings of low ratings of significant others on the constructs and this is portrayed by the very few areas of darkest shading. The first major grouping was his parents followed by a cluster of elements that were related to two teachers and a student. The most closely related constructs for him were related to the experience of music and sounds.

a Modegrid

	Love each other vs nothing	Awareness vs rigid expressionless	Being a father vs knowing nobody	Music listening vs not learning to hear	Music as a language	Music as languag vs allowing sounds to wash over you	Great love sof my life vs nothingnesss	Noses up in the air vspassion and freedom	Control vs acceptance	Existing vs passion	Opportunity vs nothingness	Discovery vs restriciton	Geography boundarie svs rest of the world
Mother	1	1	1	1	1	1	4	9	1	10	1	1	5
Father	1	1	1	1	1	1	4	9	1	10	1	1	5
Stepfather	3	1	2	1	1	1	2	6	4	10	1	1	10
Stepmother	4	1	2	1	1	1	2	8	10	10	1	1	10
Ex-wife	3	3	6	1	2	2	3	8	10	8	3	6	10
Reverend	3	7	4	5	4	4	4	7	6	6	5	5	10
Girlfriend	6	8	5	5	6	5	6	6	4	5	6	6	7
Teacher3	4	8	3	7	7	7	6	2	8	7	9	8	2
Teacher2	3	5	6	7	7	7	5	5	5	5	6	8	9
Son	8	6	8	8	6	5	9	4	4	3	6	8	6
Teacher1	4	5	7	7	7	8	6	4	3	4	8	9	9
Self	6	6	7	8	8	8	5	3	8	3	9	9	2
Females	6	4	6	4	6	6	9	7	9	4	8	5	9
Student	5	7	7	8	8	9	5	4	4	4	9	8	8
Ideal	9	9	8	9	9	10	9	2	2	2	10	10	1

b. Dendrogram of constructs   c. Dendrogram of elements

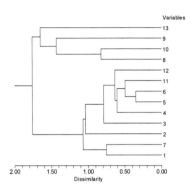   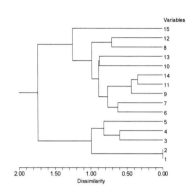

Figure 2. Repertory grid for MR D

Two major person clusters emerged, firstly the group; self, teachers (I,II, and III), student colleague, girlfriend, son, and female singer friend. He was adopted as a baby and never got to know his "real parents". He felt isolated and misunderstood by his adoptive parents, who although obviously well-meaning were not particularly loving and sympathetic. A second group is stepmother, stepfather, biological mother, reverend (first employer) and ex-wife. Significant differences merged on almost all the construct scales, with the first group (including self) being less "existing (and more passionate) (Mself 4.11, M-other 8.8; F(1,12)=25.56, p<0.001), higher on "opening out" (Mself 7.89, M-other 2.20; F=39.39, p<0.001), "music listening" (Mself 7.22 M-other 1.80; F=37.36, p<0.001), "being a father" (Mself 6.33 M-other 3.00; F=11.91, p<0.01), enablement to discovery (Mself 7.89, M-other 2.80; F=22.86, p<0.001), nutritional awareness (as opposed to rigid, expressionless) (Mself 6.44 M-other 2.60; F11.54, p<0.01), "love each other" (Mself 5.67 M-other 2.80; F=9.11, p<0.05), introduced knowledge (Mself 7.00 M-other 1.80; F=31.80, p<0.001), "listening ear" (Mself 7.11 M-other 1.80; F=69.35, p<0.001), "great love of my life" (Mself 6.67 M-other 3.00; F=17.29, p<0.001), and less "noses up in their air " (hence, more passion and freedom) (Mself 4.11 M-other 7.60; F=16.72, p<0.01). Certainly we witness here yet again, an example of a client who was exposed to tensions originating from "torn" relationships in early life between biological parents and his adoptive parents.

Mrs J – Current Alcohol Dependency

Mrs. J. is a 35-year-old graphic designer, divorced with one 8 year old son. She entered therapy with panic attack disorders, depression and suicidal thoughts. In addition she complained of bodily tension, chronic headaches, stomach and well as back pains. She was the second youngest of four daughters, whose father had died when she was pregnant. The father had had his first of three heart attacks when he was 35 years old. He appears to have been an alcoholic (and self-professed workaholic, self-employed). She felt closely bound to her father, in contrast to her mother (and ex-husband) who she has a strong antipathy towards.

Mrs J. produced a large table with more elements than constructs. The pattern of ratings was scattered with only a small concentration of high ratings in the lower right hand of the table. Friends and ideal self were matched and three concentrations of constructs clustered together: (a) cold and maternal; (b) stupid and superficial; and (c) controlled and goal conscious. These constructs acted as filters for her perception of others.

Mrs. J. diagram has been corrected with constructs ordered

Cluster analyses revealed two pronounced sets of significant others. The first includes self, son, father, sisters (1 and 2), friend (1), girlfriend (a) and friend 82). Close examination of distance to self revealed the closest was her father and two friends followed by the son, and most distant were the ex-husband, ex-friend, sister (3) and mother. The rejection experienced by her mother and ex-husband represent central losses in her life. The strong affiliation to her father and his premature death added to the pain she experienced in her significant relationships. The last four elements formed the second distinct cluster of persons. The two person clusters differed significantly on both the first cluster set incorporating the scales, "maternal" ($F(1,11)=12.46$, $p<0.005$), "sensitive" ($F=46.99$, $p<0.001$), "reliable" ($F=13.87$, $p<0.003$), and "warmth" ($F=5.62$, $p<0.04$), as well as the second cluster set, "careless" ($F=34.17$, $p<0.001$), "clumsy" ($F=7.38$, $p<0.02$) and "motherly" ($F=4.93$, $p<0.05$).

a Modegrid

	Clumsy vs. controlled	Free vs. unfree	Careless-unconcered vs. goald conscious	Motherly vs. to release	Playful vs. serious	Warmth vs. cold	Humorous vs. stupid	Reliable vs. unreliable	Hatred vs. maternal	Contemplative vs. superficial
Ex-friend	5	5	8	8	4	1	3	3	1	6
Sister1	2	1	4	6	5	3	9	2	7	8
Self	1	2	1	1	2	7	10	10	10	10
Mother	8	1	8	10	1	9	2	4	7	6
Sister3	5	5	8	6	10	3	2	2	8	7
Father	1	1	1	3	7	5	10	10	10	10
Ex-husband	10	8	10	7	5	1	1	10	1	5
Friend2	1	6	1	5	2	10	10	10	10	10
Son	8	1	4	3	8	7	9	10	7	10
Girlfriend	4	10	5	4	8	8	7	5	10	7
Friend1	1	6	4	5	7	10	7	10	10	10
Ideal	1	8	3	5	5	10	8	10	10	10
Sister2	6	1	5	10	10	8	5	10	10	6

b. Dendrogram of constructs

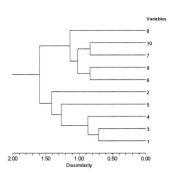

c. Dendrogram of elements

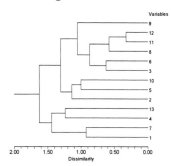

Figure 3. Repertory grid for MRS J

a Modegrid

	Introverted vs relaxed	Alliance oppsoing grandparent vs complementary	Sensuous vs serious	Creatively playful vs rigid	Nurturing vs hostile	Relaxed vs disciplined	Domineering vs submissive	Transitonal vs permanent	Trusting vs rejection	Unpredictbale vs calm
Grandmother	1	1	2	3	5	2	10	6	8	3
Husband1	8	5	2	3	5	1	5	2	10	7
Husband2	8	5	2	3	5	1	5	2	10	7
Midwife	1	1	5	9	10	5	3	10	10	5
Self	8	5	2	5	8	3	5	1	10	5
Aunt	4	1	5	8	10	5	5	7	10	3
Mother	5	8	5	2	1	9	2	6	2	9
Mums friend	2	5	7	4	5	9	1	10	1	5
Sport teacher	1	1	5	1	1	5	10	10	5	10
Son	8	1	8	8	1	4	5	4	10	6
Stepfather	1	10	7	2	5	9	7	6	2	9
Ideal	5	5	5	8	10	5	5	3	10	3
Daughter	5	1	7	9	9	6	10	4	10	7
Ex-friend	1	10	9	8	1	10	7	10	3	10

b. Dendrogram of constructs   c. Dendrogram of elements

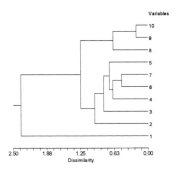

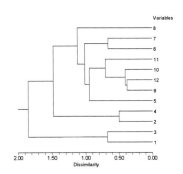

Figure 4. Repertory grid for MRS S

Mrs S – Adolescent Drug Abuse

The client is a 43-year-old married mother of two children. She attended the practice because of symptoms of tinnitus and panic attacks as well as hypochondriacal behaviour. She reported her relationship to her mother had been tense. After her birth her mother had left her in the clinic for adoption. After 3 months - as a baby- she was transferred to a woman's house who took care of her, staying there for over 2 and a half years. The woman was to become her Godmother. Her relationship to her mother remained ambivalent. She never got to know her father and after 32 years managed to secure contact with him by telephone (but they never met). Both parents had died at the time of her entering therapy.

Mrs S also presented a patchwork of high and low ratings in the modegrid. Husband1, husband 2 and self were closely clustered, whereas ideal self and an aunt were grouped together. Constructs such as sensuous and relaxed and transitional were linked, whereas most other constructs were relatively independent.

The cluster analysis revealed that there were two main clusters which distinguished two separate groups of significant others in the life of Frau S. The first is defined by six people; midwife, biological mother, stepfather, mother's boyfriend, ex-friend, and sports teacher. These are described as significantly different from the second cluster on the dimensions **relaxed** (Mself 3.71 and M-other 7.83; $F(1,119)=13.62$, p<0.01), **transitionary** ((Mself 3.86 and M-other 8.67; $F(1,119)=17.06$, p<0.002), **trusting** ((Mself 9.71 and M-other 2.17; $F(1,119)=110.86$, p<0.001), **introverted** (Mself 5.57 and M-other 1.83; $F(1,119)=9.10$, p<0.02), and **incalculable** (Mself 4.86 and M-other 8.00; $F(1,119)=7.19$, p<0.05). In other words, individuals who are perceived as close in proximity to the client's self (aunty, grandmother, husband, daughter, son and ideal-self) are more likely to be considered as **more disciplined and harsh, relationships are more transitional in nature, marked rejection, relaxed and unpredictable**. Using the F-ratios as a measure of the order of magnitude of the difference between the two clusters generated, it is "rejection" /parental and teachers) which seem to distinguish the two groups. Listing the proximity of the elements (significant others) to the self we see that the husband, aunt, daughter and son are all very close. The importance of the relationship to the aunt is reflected in the client's summary of her relevance in the treatment of drug-abuse early in her career.

CONCLUSIONS

The findings from this study emphasise definite idiosyncratic perceptions of the significant others in these people's lives. Significant others varied, but all four participants shared a common core of parental figures, siblings, relatives, spouses, and friends except for the two males, who added external figures such as teachers or employers. For the cases presented above, these relationships represent significant sources of stress in their early childhood, and then adult, lives. This fact points to the dual nature of social networks – as sources of support, but also of conflict and stress.

This fact is supported by a study by Kirkcaldy and Furnham (1995), where they found evidence for the indirect effect of coping mechanisms – that is the value of social support as a buffering agent on the stress-health linkage. On the other hand, social support did have a *direct effect* on health outcome variables, but in the opposite direction to what was predicted. They proposed a double-edged nature of social support, suggesting that social support is often reciprocal. In other words, the more support you receive from others implies the more you are expected to give, so that high seeking of support produces a heavier burden on the individual. Hence, "social support represents a mixed blessing, serving as a buffer against potential stressors but themselves a source of stress". Furthermore, one of the major problems that such quantitative measures of social support have, is that they are generally unidimensional and of low reliability. Such questionnaire measures assess the quantity of social support, but provide scarce information, if any, about the *quality* of support (Etzion, 1984). Furthermore, Warr (1987) stresses the need to distinguish between instrumental sources of support, involving advice and information, and emotional sources of support (associated with empathy and understanding).

Hence, there are not only advantages in social networks, but distinct disadvantages, and indeed some assert that there are pathogenic characteristics of social systems, with dysfunctional social dynamics being involved in the aetiology of certain psychological ailments. For instance, there is evidence that the family network of psychiatric patients are different from non-clinical groups e.g., schizophrenics have been shown to exhibit few, relatively isolated social contacts (generally family members) with little opportunity to practise social skills with others. There is marked emotional distancing and the relationships are often of negligible social support. Moreover, they are frequently asymmetrical and have an aversive nature with pronounced dependency (Röhrle anddandand Stark, 1985). Whitaker and Garbarion (1983) have made attempts to taxonomise the configurations of other clinical groups such as depressives, drug dependants, and alcoholics.

The chemical dependent perceives social relationships through a unique set of hierarchically organised systems of personal constructs "transparent template patterns". Social anxiety is experienced in instances where the "significant other" is outside the range of convenience of a construct. Psychological therapy attempts to reactivate the motion of construing by offering alternative pathways for reconstruction and elaboration of the construct system (Winter, 1992). Winter (1985) had demonstrated that repertory grid methodology offers a very flexible and individualised method of evaluating therapeutic outcome, which has been implemented in a wide range of therapies.

The differences between the grids reflects the particular orientations to life felt by the individuals concerned. Their backgrounds were not uniform and there are significant variations in the perception and construction of the meanings associated with significant others. The repertory grid permits this idiographic analysis because the grids operate at the level of personal meaning rather than the pre-structured questionnaire. The grids are illuminating for therapeutic management. Effective communication and understanding requires a shared system of meaning, and the grid method permits a point of entry for using the individual's own language. This study in effect supports the work by Kelly (1955), who underlined the importance of understandings one's own navigational system or chart – that is, the personal constructs generated by an individual, which in turn have a powerful influence on the subjective perception of our relationships and personal meaning. By gaining an insight in these "psychological lenses" we can experiment with alternative ways of construing reality, which permits one to be freed from the "chains of biography". Scheibe (1979) expressed this element of construct theory as releasing one's prejudices and recent categories.

Let us try and find some implications for clinical psychotherapy. Repertory grid literature offers many single case studies, which reveal the sensitivity of the method to aspects in the therapeutic process.

Overall, there were some differences and commonality between the clients. Mrs J., and Mr D., have continued therapy and have been able to "give up" their drug/alcohol problem for several years, and continue to attend individual therapy. Mrs J., and Mr A. appear to have retained their habits and prematurely terminated their therapies after several months. Both were characterised by marked failures in their social relationships (marriage), marked introverted personality styles (withdrawn, introverted and an apparent lack of social skills) and a chronic desire for approval and recognition. Their drug usage habits were commonly in isolation, living a "concealed" social problem. It is also possible that these two individuals have consciously isolated themselves from their social network members, who do not support them in their addictions. In contrast, Mrs S., and Mr D., who also have marital disharmony (Mr D. is divorced) display more socially appropriate behaviour and their previous habits of drug abuse were characterised by quite strong social components (acceptance of the group, etc).

On the other hand, all four clients, whether male or female, ex-dependents or continued chemical dependents, exhibited a history of personal inadequacies, parental rejection or parental loss at an early age. They all reported pronounced tensions in their childhood family backgrounds. Certainly, underlining the social network aspect of treatment may offer a buffer against the potentially adverse impact of daily stressors. Drinking and drug usage seem the central, inappropriate stress-coping mechanisms which, whilst relieving short-term anxieties, reinforce the self-destructive cognitions which form an integral part of their self-perceptions.

In this study, providing optimal psychological interventions for drug and alcohol dependants appears to profit from implementing social network structural analysis. By using the grid analysis method, we have increased access into the idiosyncratic method of construing social situations, particularly self-concept and a client's relationship to significant others. It was possible to use such available networks as a means for stabilising therapeutic changes.

During the early stages of therapy we used the PCP-grid methodology to provide feedback to the client in the form of graphical representations of significant others and the constellation of constructs elicited which offered discussion material for subsequent sessions. Furthermore, we were frequently able to invite significant others to the session (e.g. wife, mother, or daughter), and gain familiarity with early child-rearing practises or marital relationship interactions. Alternatively, try and use the extended network (friends and colleagues) to initiate changes in social behaviour. More importantly, using this method we can teach the client alternative ways of construing and testing alternative roles to adopt in novel social situations.

It is also possible to make use of alternative social resource systems to compensate for deficient social support systems, e.g., suggesting alternative community social groups such as Alcohol Anonymous (AA), Recreational groups, Occupational-related anti-stress management programmes, or Self-Help groups for emotional disorders, etc. The success of groups such as AA illustrates the impact of social networks on an individual's behaviour: by surrounding themselves with others with similar histories and problems, as well as current goals and behaviours, the individual in treatment reinforces their own decisions to change their addiction behaviours. In the case of the individuals presented in this study, it is possible that isolation from their personal networks of intimate family would also have a positive impact on their behaviour, given the amounts of conflict and stress associated with many of these so-called "intimate relationships" (e.g. birth mother; divorced parents; step-parents; etc.)

There are various measures which can be selected from the grid analyses which allows us to make estimates of degree of *self-esteem* (distance between self and ideal-self elements); *identification with the father* (distance between self and father elements); *identification with the mother* (distance between mother and self-element); *cross-sex parental identification* (low sexual identification score); *evaluation of parents* (proximity between ideal self and parental elements). For example, a large distance between mother and father elements suggest operation of splitting mechanism in construing of parents, and a large number of elements distanced from the self would indicate isolation and dissimilarity from others, etc. (Caine, T.M., Wijesinghe, O.B.A., and Winter, D.A.,1981). Certainly, the multivariate cluster analyses offer a graphical résumé of the social network structure of clients, and these can be subsequently matched with other clinical groups or population norms. In addition, we can *generate categories of constructs* (in this study the two major taxonomic groups would be the class of *emotional* constructs e.g., scornful, obsessive, loving, asocial, rigid expressionless, introverted, etc., and another would be the *object/need-related* terms such as success-oriented, craving for recognition, fighter, discovery, reliable, etc.)

ACKNOWLEDGMENT

Thanks go to Professor David Winter, freind and colleague, who kindly read an earlier darft of this article and provided some suggestions for improvement.

REFERENCES

Black, M. M.; Ricardo, I. B.; Stanton, B. (1997) Social and psychological factors associated with AIDS risk behaviors among low-income, urban, African American adolescents. *Journal of Research on Adolescence*. Vol 7(2) 173-195

Burt, R. (1992). *Structural Holes: the Social Structure of Competition*. Cambridge, Mass.: Harvard University Press.

Caine, T.M., Wijesinghe, O.B.A., and Winter, D.A. (1981) *Personal Style of Neurosis. Implications for Small Group Psychotherapy and Behavioural Therapy.* Routledge and Kegan Paul, London, Boston and Henley.

Goleman, D. (1995) *Emotional Intelligence. Why it can matter more than IQ.* Bloomsbury, London.

Denicolo,P., and Pope, M. (1997). Sharing constructivist ideas. In Denicolo, P. and Pope, M (Eds.), *Sharing Understanding and Practice,* Famborough: EPCA Publications, pp 1-10.

Durkheim, Émile, 1897[1951]. *Suicide*. Glencoe, IL.: Free Press.

Etzion, D. (1984) Moderating effect of social support and the buffering hypothesis. *Psychological Bulletin*, **98**, 310-357.

Fischer, C. S., (1982). *To Dwell Among Friends: Personal Networks in Town and City.* Chicago: University of Chicago Press.

Galanter, M. (1997). "Network therapy for addiction: assessment of the clinical outcome of training". *American Journal of Drug and Alcohol Abuse* v23(August) : 355-67.

Granovetter, M.(1990). "The Old and the New Economic Sociology: A History and an Agenda", in *Beyond the Marketplace*, R. Friedland and A.F. Robertson (eds.). New York: Aldine de Gruyter.

Granovetter, M.(1985). "Economic Action and Social Structure: The Problem of Embeddedness", *American Journal of Sociology* **91**:481-510.

Granovetter, M. (1973). "The Strength of Weak Ties." *American Journal of Sociology,* **78**(May): 1360-1380.

Keller, D., 1997. "Validation of a scale for network therapy: a technique for systematic use of peer and family support in addiction treatment", *American Journal of Drug and Alcohol Abuse* v23(February): 115-27.

Kelly, G. A. (1955). *The psychology of personal constructs*. NY: Norton.

Kirkcaldy, B.D., Athanasou, J., and Trimpop, R. (2000) The idiosyncratic construction of stress: examples from medical work settings. *Stress Medicine* (in press)

Kirkcaldy, B. D. and Furnham, A., (1995), Coping, seeking social support and stress among German police management. *European Review of Applied Psychology*, **45**, 32, 121-126.

Kirkcaldy, B. D., Siefen, G., and Pope, M., (1993), Sociogrid analysis of a child and adolescent psychiatric clinic. *Social Psychiatry and Psychiatric Epidemiology*, **28**, 296-303.

Kirkcaldy, B. D. and Pope, M., (1992), A Structural Analysis of a Psychooncology Unit. *European Work and Organisational Psychologist,* **1**, 33-51.

Latkin, Carl, 1999. "Drug network characteristics as predictors of cessation of drug use among adult injection drug users", *American Journal of Drug and Alcohol Abuse* v25(3): 463-73.

Lin, Nan, 1982. *Social Structure and Network Analysis*. Beverly Hills: Sage Publications.

Miller, Maureen, 1998. "Social network characteristics as mediators in the relationship between sexual abuse and HIV risk", *Social Science and Medicine* v.47(6): 765-77.

Röhrle, B., and Stark, W. (1985) Soziale Netzwerke und Stützsysteme - Perpektiven für die klinisch-psychologische und gemeindepsychologische Praxis. DGVT, Tübingen.

Scheibe, K.E. (1979) *Mirrors, masks, lies and secrets. The limits of human predictability.* New York, Praeger Publ.

Shaw, M.L.G. (1980). *On becoming a personal scientist*. London: Academic Press

Single, E. (1999). *"Substance Abuse and Population Health"*, Workshop on Addiction and Population Health, Edmonton, Alberta, Canada

Wellman, B.(1992). "Which Types of Ties and Networks Provide What Kinds of Social Support?", *Advances in Group Processes* **9**: 207-235.

(1979). "The Community Question: The Intimate Networks of East Yorkers." *American Journal of Sociology* **84**: 1201-31.

Warr, P. (1987) Work, Unemployment and Mental health. Oxford, Clarendon Press.

Wellman, Barry and N. Scot Wortley, 1990. "Different Strokes From Different Folks: Community Ties and Social Support", *American Journal of Sociology* **96**(November): 558-588.

Wellman, Barry, Peter Carrington and Alan Hall, 1988. "Networks as Personal Communities." Pp. 130-184 in *Social Structures: A Network Approach*, edited by Barry Wellman and S.D. Berkowitz. Cambridge: Cambridge University Press.

Wellman, Barry and Stephanie Potter, 1999. "The Elements of Personal Communities", in Barry Wellman (ed.) *Networks in the Global Village,* Boulder CO.: Westview Press.

Wellman, Beverly and Barry Wellman, 1992. "Domestic Affairs and Network Relations", *Journal of Social and Personal Relationships*, Vol. 9: 385-409.

Whitaker, J.K., and Garbarino, J. (1983) *Social support networks: Informal helping in the human services*. New York, Aldine Publ.

Winter, D.A. (1992) *Personal Construct Psychology in Clinical Practice: Theory, Research and Applications*. London, Routledge.

Wortley, N. Scot, 1996. *Social Networks, Social Support, and Substance Abuse: Testing Conflicting Theories of Deviance*. Ph.D. dissertation, Department of Sociology, University of Toronto.

Ziervogel, C. F.; Morojele, N. K.; van der Riet, J.; Parry, C. D. H.; and Robertson, B. A. (1997) A qualitative investigation of alcohol drinking among male high school students from thee communities in the Cape Peninsula, South Africa.

In: Binge Drinking Research Progress
Editor: Kevin I. DiGuarde

ISBN 978-1-60692-065
© 2009 Nova Science Publishers, Inc.

Chapter 9

LINK OF ALCOHOLIC TENDENCY TO MOTIVATION

Jon L. Karlsson
Institute of Genetics, Reykjavik, Iceland

ABSTRACT

Ethyl alcohol is a simple chemical substance produced by yeast as it ferments a readily available naturally occurring sugar compound. It is a psychoactive drug widely consumed and promoted for recreational or relaxational purposes. Like other such agents it is often abused, some individuals being prone to develop a dependency or addiction after chronic drinking. With long term use alcoholics may suffer serious complications, such as liver disease or brain disorders. The hereditary nature of alcoholism tendency has been fully established through investigations of twins and foster reared individuals. Pedigree studies as well as precise determinations of comparative risks in close relatives of alcoholic patients have been found to be consistent with a dominant form of inheritance, showing incomplete penetrance that is lower in females than in males. Personality information on families of alcoholics reveals attitudes of self assurance, verbal fluency, and preference for certain types of occupations. They appear to seek fields requiring socialization and communication skills. Leadership tendencies and desire for power are predominant. Performance is sought in the political arena or entertainment industries as well as in business. High activity level and motivation for prominence are characteristic of families prone to alcohol use. The high frequency of the alcoholism gene is presumably maintained by these favorable traits.

INTRODUCTION

Ethanol is a simple chemical substance whose structure contains a two carbon chain and an oxygen atom, surrounded by six units of hydrogen. It is a liquid which mixes easily with water in any proportion. The boiling point of pure alcohol is 78 degrees Celsius or 173 degrees Fahrenheit, making it easy to concentrate the chemical by distillation. Ethyl alcohol has been known to mankind since antiquity. It arises by fermentation when yeast is allowed to grow in fluids containing sugar. Accidental spoilage of stored food can easily result in accumulation of alcohol. Its effects on the brain were thus bound to be discovered, particularly in areas of the world with warm climates. Production of alcoholic beverages on a larger scale, even for commercial purposes, dates back thousands of years. Distilled spirits followed later. Grapes, grains, or even wood could be used as the starting raw material for fermentation. In the industrial world, alcoholic drinks are legally sanctioned and often classified as food readily available as beer, wine, or liquor.

MENTAL EFFECTS OF ALCOHOL

Recreational use of alcohol appears to have been its main purpose throughout history. Relaxation and tension release were no doubt additional factors promoting consumption. Most societies favored temperate use, and heavy drinking has generally been frowned upon. Soldiers were often given alcoholic beverages to reduce their inhibitions. Another major function assigned to alcohol was in connection with religious ceremonies. Mystical beliefs or association with gods and devils were easily tied to the mental effects of a brain influencing substance. Often this also involved dances and attempts to cure diseases. Ethanol must be viewed as a mind altering drug, a psychoactive material basically in the same class as other chemicals used for recreational activities or escape from life's pressures. All such substances have a habit forming potential, and abuse often leads to addiction. Only some individuals are prone to chronic abuse, becoming dependent on increasing quantities of intake. When the alcohol addicted person tries to discontinue drinking, withdrawal symptoms ensue, as happens with other habit forming chemicals. These are characterized by nausea, weakness, unsteadiness, and disorientation. Later come tremors, vomiting, incontinence, convulsions, and hallucinations, referred to as delirium tremens. Craving for alcohol by the addict is not different from the compulsive need for continued intake by those dependent on other substances.

Dependency on alcohol usually advances in stages, taking several to many years. First comes tolerance, ability to consume increasing amounts, commonly occurring in social situations. Gradual augmentation of intake leads to memory lapses, the individual finding it difficult to recall his actions after drinking episodes. This may be followed by loss of control, inability to cease drinking once consumption has started. Finally come binges of prolonged intoxication or even settlement in downtrodden areas with other alcoholics who are classified as bums. During this process gradual behavioral changes are likely to be seen. Irritability, uncontrolled anger, grandiosity, difficulties at work, and marital problems may slowly increase. Personality changes occur, and mental confusion may become prominent. Periods of stress can aggravate the drinking tendency.

Since alcohol consumption is legally protected in Western societies and considered a normal or sometimes desirable activity, overuse and dependency often go unnoticed even in the presence of fairly heavy daily intake. The drunk and his family are liable to try to cover up the abuse, denying that there is a problem. As tolerance increases, more drug is needed to obtain the same effect. Then memory lapses are experienced, loss of control, impaired judgment, and failure at work. The alcoholic may exhibit a self destructive tendency, leading to family breakup, vehicular accidents, and even crime. Some end up as skid row drunks. Suicide is not uncommon.

Many physical problems arise as health of a severely addicted person declines. Liver disease is frequent, culminating in cirrhosis. There may be heart impairment and neuropathies. Brain deterioration, with advancing memory deficiencies may eventually result in need for institutional care. Alcoholic hallucinosis may lead to frantic episodes of terror. Korsakoff's psychosis is a late complication which is occasionally seen.

EVIDENCE FOR BIOLOGICAL FACTORS

Scientists have long regarded alcoholic inclination as a familial disorder, probably conditioned by hereditary factors. This opinion has been based on the observation of numerous pedigrees, some gathered systematically and extending over several generations. No doubt there are also strong environmental influences, including exposure to the use of alcohol when it is freely available. For example, it is well documented in Eskimo populations that craving for alcohol becomes a problem once introduction of it into the community has occurred, although drinking has not been possible in the past for obvious reasons.

There is much debate about the relationship between addiction tendency for other habit forming chemicals and alcohol. In Western countries illegal drug use is likely to be confined largely to young people while alcoholism afflicts more those who are older. Many drug addicts shift to alcohol as they age. Still there is some evidence that relatives of drug users are more prone to abuse illegal drugs than alcohol. Whether there is a biological tendency for addiction in a broad sense remains to be clarified.

Many investigators interested in alcoholism have devoted their efforts to biochemical studies. Intoxication is to a degree related to blood concentrations of ethanol, and for legal purposes a certain level has been selected to define whether an individual is to be considered functionally impaired. Still, tolerance is known to develop, so that persons who habitually consume alcohol require a larger dose to obtain the original effect seen in inexperienced drinkers. The physiological basis of tolerance has not been explained.

The first metabolic product of ethyl alcohol is acetaldehyde. This transformation occurs primarily in the liver under the action of the enzyme alcohol dehydrogenase. Various hypotheses have been explored in attempts to explain the possible function of acetaldehyde in intoxication and in the secondary effects of ethanol, but its role in the total effect is still obscure.

Acetaldehyde is rapidly metabolized and therefore does not accumulate. Once that stage is passed the substance becomes an energy source without further pharmacological or toxic influence. Alcohol itself has sedative effects and is poisonous in large doses, sometimes lethal. The agent antabuse has been used to treat alcoholics since it interferes with the metabolism of ethanol, causing unpleasant side effects which prevent further intake, but its use requires cooperation of the patient in taking the medication. Membership in the organization Alcoholics Anonymous has helped many addicts, in part by providing socialization and activity to prevent boredom.

Alcoholism is seen primarily in males, many reports indicating that women show only one tenth as much risk. Estimates indicate that over two percent of Western populations suffer from severe dependency on alcohol. Investigations of twins and of foster reared individuals have contributed important evidence concerning the basic etiology.

For many years it was claimed that alcoholic tendency had no genetic links. However the information, revolving mainly around foster reared individuals, was very limited in scope and most of the subjects relatively young. In particular a study by Roe and Burks was widely quoted to have ruled out any genetic influence. But a review of the data showed such conclusions to be entirely unwarranted because the material covered only a few individuals eligible for the investigation, contained inadequate information, and involved no long-term follow up. No solid conclusions should have been based on such meager evidence. Reports on comparisons of monozygotic and dizygotic twins had shown much higher concordance in the former, but these findings were disregarded.

A quarter century ago more definitive research was conducted by investigators in several countries. One study was done in Denmark [1], evaluating individuals who had been raised in foster homes. The findings showed clearly that sons of alcoholics had a definite increase in risk, and the rate was equally high even when they were reared by adoptive parents without any contact with the biological relatives. A second study was conducted in the United States, comparing half siblings in families where the mother had been married more than once [2]. Again it turned out that sons of alcoholic fathers remained at risk when reared by a nonalcoholic stepfather. Sons of nonalcoholic fathers showed no increase in risk when they were raised by an alcoholic male. These studies were so definitive that the previous opinions were quickly discarded and it became accepted that genetic factors were indeed paramount. The results were in harmony with the older twin studies which had shown double the expected concordance in monozygotic twins. No genetic relationship exists between the risk of psychosis and alcoholism. Relatives of individuals suffering from one of these conditions show no increase in risk of the other.

GENETIC MECHANISM

With these findings in hand attempts were renewed to unravel the genetic mechanism. An investigation done in Iceland indicated that involved families sometimes showed segregation into high and low risk branches, seeming to rule out polygenic inheritance. Studies by Swedish investigators helped to delineate the basic family patterns. Thus the risks were high and about equal in fathers, brothers, and sons of index cases, tapering off in more distant relations. Data from Iceland have revealed the same kind of distribution and provided greater precision [3]. Risks in first degree male relatives are now considered to be in the order of 30 percent and in second degree relatives just over half that figure.

The preponderance of male alcoholics has raised the possibility of sex linkage, but a detailed Swedish study has ruled out that mechanism [4]. Transmission often occurs from father to son, although the disorder can also travel through an unaffected daughter to the grandsons. The question of recessive inheritance has been explored and pretty well excluded. Multiple factor mechanisms have been popular despite little support for such systems; the necessary gene frequencies are prohibitive.

Modified dominance thus emerges as the most plausible mechanism. The family data are quite consistent with such a hypothesis although it becomes necessary to accept that penetrance can be exceptionally high in certain groups of relatives. While the total information is more limited than in the case of disorders such as schizophrenia, a Swedish study shows the risk to be double in siblings with an affected parent as compared to siblings with nonalcoholic parents. Monozygotic cotwins also must be postulated to exhibit high penetrance.

The question has been raised whether to be overtly alcoholic women perhaps require a heavier genetic loading than men. This would explain their relatively low risk. But available data do not show a higher risk in brothers of alcoholic women than in brothers of male index cases. Presumably females are somehow protected, their penetrance rate being quite low.

If the alcoholism prone individual has the genotype Aa as compared to AA for other males, the frequency of the altered gene in Western nations can be computed as approximately 0.06 with overall penetrance in males being 50 percent. Alcoholic inclination is then still another hereditary condition transmitted in a dominant fashion. In view of the high frequency of the proposed gene it appears that a balanced genetic polymorphism must be operative. This expression is employed by geneticists to describe occurrence of mutant genes at frequencies higher than expected from mutation pressure counteracted by natural selection. There has been considerable interest in the apparent beneficial influence of the gene on personality traits, which could explain its persistence at an elevated level.

PERSONALITY EFFECTS

Studies by MacAndrew [5] of certain aspects of the Minnesota Multiphasic Personality Inventory (MMPI) test indicated that alcoholics and prealcoholics tended to respond to questions in specific ways. Thus they were described as unconventional, bold, uninhibited, expansive, sociable, or energetic. They saw themselves as rebellious, carefree, prone to gamble. Further indications of personality effects were encountered in Iceland, where hospital treated alcoholic patients and their relatives were found to prefer certain types of occupations [6]. The relatives seemed to be motivated to seek positions of leadership, often being members of the parliament, licensed lawyers, or clergymen. These fields require high energy levels and skills in communication.

There were also some indications that relatives of alcoholics had in the past been high performers in the Icelandic secondary schools, when these institutions served mainly to train future professionals. But after the emphasis shifted from the classics, including literature in Greek and Latin, to science and mathematics, the academic advantage linked to alcoholism seems to have disappeared. Although it cannot be demonstrated in present day populations that the alcoholism gene may have a beneficial effect on learning, there still is an influence on certain favorable personality traits.

Most people are aware of the alcohol or drug use tendency among entertainers, athletes, and other performers. The elevated energy level required in these fields may favor those who carry an alcoholism gene. The public has also heard about alcohol use among legislators and social leaders. While it is well recognized that antisocial or criminal behavior is often associated with alcohol abuse, a definite link to favorable personality traits similarly appears to be adequately documented.

The basic personality influences of the proposed alcoholism gene are obviously of great interest, although there is much variation in the net result, ranging from beneficial effects to destructive behavior. Limited attention was paid in the past to the possibility of favorable personality effects linked to alcoholism. But newer studies of academic and social achievement leave little doubt that many individuals who carry the proposed gene are people of success and productivity. Here the high activity level seems to have a positive influence and provide the energy necessary for leadership and drive.

The connection of alcoholic tendency to antisocial acts has been more thoroughly documented. Even in childhood future alcoholics have been found to engage in destructive activities, such as fire setting or stealing. More overt criminal behavior comes later. It is indeed well established that a strong association exists between tendencies toward alcohol consumption and illegal activity. Although some law breaking may result from overactive behavior, lack of concern for others or failure in moral values is also postulated to be a factor.

The hyperactive child syndrome has been claimed to be biologically linked to alcoholic tendency [7]. This disorder is seen mainly in boys and is characterized by impulsive actions, inability to concentrate on learning, distractibility, and disruptive behavior. It starts early in life and persists into adulthood. Many young males are treated with medications of the amphetamine type in attempts to make their activities acceptable in the classroom. Although in the past the possibility of minimal brain damage was considered, there is no evidence in support of that kind of etiology for hyperactive behavior. Family studies have revealed an increased risk of the same problem in close relatives, and systematic explorations show a pattern consistent with a partly dominant transmission. Even twin studies have established an elevated concordance in monozygotic pairs.

A large longitudinal study of a population of hyperactive youngsters indicated that aberrant behavior indeed persisted into maturity [8]. And as adults the subjects often suffered from alcoholic problems. Elevated rates of alcoholism were found in their fathers, and sociopathy was also prominent. Other investigations have similarly suggested that a link exists between hyperactive behavior and alcoholism. Perhaps this syndrome is another expression of the proposed genetic factor.

Efforts to find the chromosomal location of the alcoholism gene have suggested a relationship to brain characteristics involved in pleasure and arousal, but the findings are not definitive. These qualities may increase the penetrance rate in individuals burdened with the basic factor. Identification of the major gene has not as yet been achieved.

The augmented energy levels that appear to be exhibited by alcoholism-prone individuals and their relatives seem to be often expressed in motivations to gain power and recognition. They tend to be self assured and confident, feeling that they possess superior judgment. Verbal fluency and socialization tendency are strong factors in their personality traits. It is tempting to speculate about the role that these characteristics may have played in the molding of early modern humans. For example, the Indo-European people that had settled in northern Russia during late interglacial periods must have experienced severe hardships when the climate again cooled, perhaps comparable to more recent conditions suffered by Eskimos and other northern natives. The stringent circumstances may then have led to a build-up of heterozygous states dependent on genes now found to be related to alcoholism, myopia, and psychosis. When these populations were forced to migrate south, the resultant balanced polymorphisms linked to improved intelligence may have enabled them to exploit the opportunities found in Mesopotamia to build an advanced culture.

REFERENCES

[1]   Schulsinger F: Biological psychopathology. *Annual Review of Psychology* 31:583-606, 1980.

[2]   Schuckit MA, Goodwin DA, and Winokur G: A study of alcoholism in half-siblings. *American Journal of Psychiatry* 128:1132-1136, 1972.

[3]   Karlsson JL: Mental characteristics of families with alcoholism in Iceland. *Hereditas* 102:185-188, 1985.

[4]   Kaij L and Dock ML: Grandsons of alcoholics. *Archives of General Psychiatry* 32:1379-1381, 1975.

[5]   MacAndrew C: The differentiation of male alcoholic outpatients from nonalcoholic psychiatric outpatients by means of the MMPI. *Quarterly Journal of Studies on Alcohol* 26:238-246, 1965.

[6] Karlsson JL: *Genetics of Human Mentality*. Praeger, New York, 1991.

[7] Cantwell D: *The Hyperactive Child.* Spectrum Publications, New York, 1975.

[8] Robins LM: *Deviant Children Grown Up.* Williams and Wilkins, Baltimore, 1966

INDEX

E

H

N

O

P

Q

Y

Z